THE ELT CURRICULUM

Applied Language Studies
Edited by David Crystal and Keith Johnson

This new series aims to deal with key topics within the main branches of applied language studies — initially in the fields of foreign language teaching and learning, child language acquisition and clinical or remedial language studies. The series will provide students with a research perspective in a particular topic, at the same time containing an original slant which will make each volume a genuine contribution to the development of ideas in the subject.

Series List

THE ELT CURRICULUM

Design, Innovation and Management

Ronald V. White

BLACKWELL
Oxford UK & Cambridge USA

First published 1988
Reprinted 1989, 1991, 1993 (twice), 1995 (twice)

Blackwell Publishers Ltd.
108 Cowley Road
Oxford OX4 1JF, UK

Blackwell Publishers Inc.
238 Main Street
Cambridge Massachusetts 02142
USA

British Library Cataloguing in Publication Data

White, Ronald, V.
   The ELT curriculum: design, innovation and management
   1. English Language—Study and teaching—
   Foreign students.   2. Curriculum planning
   I. Title
   428 2′4′071   PE1066
   ISBN 0–631–15152–4 pbk

Library of Congress Cataloging in Publication Data

White, Ronald V.
   The ELT curriculum: design, innovation and management/Ronald V. White
   p. cm.
   Bibliography, p.
   Includes index.
   ISBN 0–631–15152–4 (pbk.)
   1. English language—Study and teaching—Foreign speakers.
   I. Title.
   PE1128.A2W517   1988
   428′.007—dc 19   87–29365
                       CIP

Typeset in 10 on 12 pt Ehrhardt
by Columns of Reading
Printed in Great Britain by Athenæum Press Ltd, Gateshead, Tyne & Wear

This book is printed on acid-free paper

Contents

Note to the Reader

This book is arranged in four parts, of which each contains a number of chapters. Each chapter has a number of sections and the final two include a summary of the chapter and suggested follow-up reading.

In the Appendix, there are follow-up activities for each chapter. These activities are intended to be done by groups, and they should involve discussion. Some of the activities can also be done individually; they are linked to the content of each chapter, and provide some 'hands on' or practical development of the points covered in the chapters themselves.

You may find it useful to skim the follow-up activities *before* you read each chapter.

Acknowledgements

Authors always take a great risk: they receive praise if their work is good – and criticism if it isn't. Whatever the reception of this publication, I should like to distribute some praise of my own. Firstly, to the students who have attended the courses which provided the basis for this book. Secondly, to my colleagues, for their helpful suggestions. Thirdly, to Keith Johnson, series editor, for his critical comments and encouragement. Fourthly, to Sue Vice, for her keen editorial eye which identified many a solecism before it reached print. Finally, but most significantly, to my wife, Nora, for the kind of support and understanding which only she can provide.

The blame for what follows is entirely mine.

The author and the publishers are grateful to the following for permission to reproduce material which originally appeared elsewhere: The Council for Educational Technology for the United Kingdom, for two figures from R. Havelock (1971) 'The utilization of educational research and development', *British Journal of Educational Technology*, 1, 2/2: 84–97. The British Council for figures from *Dunford House Seminar 1979: ELT Course Design*; *ELT Documents 116, Language Teaching Projects for the Third World*; *ELT Documents 118, General English Syllabus Design*, copyright © The British Council. B. T. Batsford Ltd for a figure from R. T. Bell (1981) *An Introduction to Applied Linguistics: Approaches and Methods in Language Teaching*. Unesco for a figure from A. M. Huberman (1973) *Understanding Change in Education: An Introduction* copyright © Unesco 1973. Cambridge University Press for figures, one from J. Yalden (1983) *The Communicative Syllabus: Evolution, Design and Implementation*; and one from J. C. Richards and T. Rodgers (1986) *Approach and Methods in Language Teaching*. Simon and Schuster for a figure from C. Candlin and D. Murphy (eds) (1987) *Lancaster Practical Papers in ELT*, vol. 7.

Ron White
Reading

1 Approach, Design, Procedure

Introduction

I have written this book in the way that I have because I have become increasingly aware that the issues which face anyone concerned with developing and introducing a new language syllabus are not only – or even primarily – questions of content. Although in the 1970s there was much concern with the content of syllabuses as a result of the notional/functional 'revolution', most of the problems which actually face anyone attempting to introduce a new syllabus did not change. These problems tend not to have anything to do with either the theoretical basis of the syllabus or curriculum changes themselves, nor the content of the changes. Rather, they are issues which have to do with ideas about education, and with people and organizations. They are, in short, educational and managerial issues.

Thus, it seems to me that to talk of syllabus design in isolation from broader educational issues is to deny access to an important body of theory, research and practice, none coming under the umbrella of applied linguistics, which has formed the primary academic reference for language pedagogy. I am not alone in this. Stern (1983) devotes a whole section of his book, *Fundamental Concepts of Language Teaching*, to a consideration of educational issues, beginning with a discussion of curriculum theory. Thus, we can say that curriculum studies have very definitely taken their place among the concerns of language teaching.

Yet other issues arise when new principles and practices are advocated. These issues have been documented for innovation in other fields of education, but language teaching seems to have remained curiously aloof from this body of knowledge. The management and implementation of innovation is, of all things, crucial to the design and take-up of new syllabuses – in language teaching as in any other part of education. And so it seems to me that we may benefit from studying some of the problems and practices of innovation management.

This, in short, provides the background to my thinking. Naturally, there are other issues and questions which will be revealed during the course of this book. Among them is the influence of the recent research on second language acquisition (SLA). Although we are a long way from having an established body of empirical data on which to base proposals for language curriculum

design, traditional views on selection and grading, not to mention methodology, will have to take on board the findings of SLA research. Indeed, I
believe that we are now entering an era in language teaching when important
new developments are likely to occur as a result of the insights provided by
SLA research and innovations in language curriculum are likely to be quite
considerable. Let us hope that we shall be prepared to meet them.

In the meantime, I should like to begin by considering some of the
terminology in the title and which I have already been using. We will start by
considering the three terms at the heading of this chapter.

Method: Approach, Design, Procedure

In their 1982 paper of this title, Jack Richards and Ted Rodgers, adopting a
similar three part analysis proposed by Anthony (1963), set up a useful
framework for the systematic description and comparison of methods and I
propose to adopt their scheme and terminology in what is to follow. They
define method in terms of three levels: *approach*, *design* and *procedure*. By
approach, they mean a theory of language and of language learning, by *design*
they mean the definition of linguistic content and a specification for the

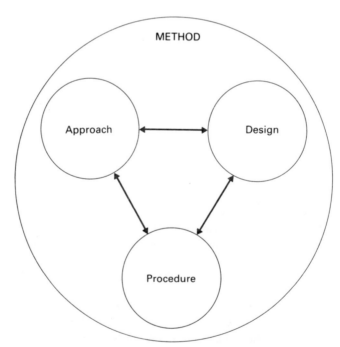

Figure 1.1 Approach, design, procedure
(from Richards and Rodgers 1982)

selection and organization of content and a description of the role of teacher, learner and teaching materials, while by *procedure* they mean the description of techniques and practices in the instructional system. The relationship between these three elements is indicated in figure 1.1.

In this book I shall be primarily concerned with level two: *design*. However, as will become clear in our historical review, design is influenced by *approach*, while practice is also subject to theories of language and learning. Thus, any discussion of syllabus design will tend to refer to the other levels in the Richards and Rodgers scheme. Furthermore, as we move into the arena of curriculum studies, we shall see that language teaching is part of a network of elements which go well beyond the scheme suggested by Richards and Rodgers. None the less, their scheme provides a useful starting point.

Syllabus

In his investigation into the ways teachers planned their courses, Taylor (1970:32) found considerable variation in the size and style of the syllabuses which were sampled: 'Some were no more than one or two pages in length, others over one hundred pages. Some were well laid out and carefully bound. Others were cramped and barely legible.' In spite of such diversity in the actual form of the document, there appears to be a consensus as to what a syllabus is, and this has been summarized by Brumfit (1984a).

1 A syllabus is the specification of the work of a particular department in a school or college, organised in subsections defining the work of a particular group or class;
2 It is often linked to time, and will specify a starting point and ultimate goal;
3 It will specify some kind of sequence based on

   a) sequencing intrinsic to a theory of language learning or to the structure of specified material relatable to language acquisition;
   b) sequencing constrained by administrative needs, e.g. materials;

4 It is a document of administrative convenience and will only be partly justified on theoretical grounds and so is negotiable and adjustable;
5 It can only specify what is taught; it cannot organize what is learnt;
6 It is a public document and an expression of accountability.

Brumfit's summary raises other points, such as questions of the theoretical basis of a syllabus and issues of negotiability, which will be discussed in more detail later. Also, in this account of syllabus, the focus is on selection and organization of content whereas, as we shall see, there are other approaches to syllabus which shift attention to methodology.

Curriculum

The question of methodology brings us to the next term: *curriculum*. Some confusion exists over the distinction between syllabus and curriculum, since the terms are used differently on either side of the Atlantic. In a distinction that is commonly drawn in Britain, 'syllabus' refers to the content or subject matter of an individual subject, whereas 'curriculum' refers to the totality of content to be taught and aims to be realized within one school or educational system. In the USA, 'curriculum' tends to be synonymous with 'syllabus' in the British sense.

The hierarchical distinction usual in Britain places syllabus in a subordinate position to curriculum, and this is a relationship which I will continue to follow. However, curriculum should not simply be seen as a kind of super syllabus, since there is a qualitative difference between the two, though characterizing this difference is not easy since definitions of curriculum vary. On the one hand, curriculum may be viewed as 'the programme of activities . . . the course to be run by pupils in being educated (Hirst 1969 in Hooper 1971:234).' On the other, curriculum may be defined as 'all the learning which is planned and guided by the school, whether it is carried on in groups or individually, inside or outside the school (Kerr 1968:16).' Hirst refers to the *programme* of activities, while Kerr refers to the *activities themselves*. One school of thought regards the curriculum as *a plan*, whereas the other views it as *activities*. Sockett (1976:22) succinctly characterizes this distinction as 'the difference between a plan of a house or a journey and the house or the journey.' Taking the house metaphor a stage further, we could see the curriculum as being one or all of three things. Firstly, it could be like a plan of a house yet to be constructed. In this sense, the curriculum is future directed towards an objective yet to be realized and it is, in essence, synonymous with syllabus as discussed in the previous section.

Secondly, curriculum could be seen to be like a plan of how to build the house. Again the orientation is to the future, but in this case the concern is with the systems that are needed in order successfully to build the house. The specification for such systems and their effective operation will draw upon resources and personnel not immediately involved in the construction process itself, while the successful operation of the systems will also require the skills of the manager as well as those of the craftsmen.

Thirdly, the curriculum could be seen to be like the view of the house after it has been completed and is a dwelling for its inhabitants. The conception of the house possessed by the people living in it will be determined by the use they make of the dwelling: does it match their living requirements; how do they use the spaces and facilities within the structure; what modifications might they want to make to it to make it conform more usefully to their requirements?

In the discussion which follows, I shall repeatedly return to these three views of the curriculum-as-house, which, though they emphasize different aspects of curriculum, are by no means mutually exclusive. The first view (*curriculum/house = plan*) shows a concern with *objectives and content*, which are two of four elements in the traditional model of the curriculum to be discussed further in chapter 3.

The second view (*curriculum/house = construction system*) adds methods to the model. The methods are the means by which the ends – the objectives – are to be achieved and this forms the basis of a process view of the curriculum, to be considered in more detail in chapter 3.

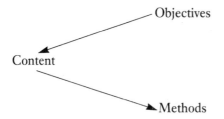

The third perspective (*curriculum/house = dwelling*) adds a fourth and final element: *evaluation*. In other words, do outcomes match objectives? This brings us to the situational model of curriculum, also to be reviewed in chapter 3.

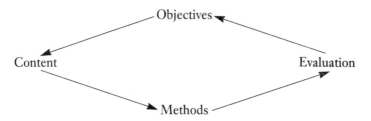

Evaluation, as feedback (or monitoring), will also form a component of the construction-systems model, since quality control will be an important element of any production system. It is through monitoring and feedback that planned and actual outcomes can be compared and appropriate remedial action taken to repair failures or deficits. Thus, feedback will have a *formative* effect on action. The role and types of evaluation will be reviewed in chapter 9.

The future orientation of the first two perspectives may be contrasted with the 'here and now' viewpoint of the third approach, as I have characterized it. The distinction reflects what I see as a difference in attitudes towards curriculum, although they should be regarded as being complementary rather than being in conflict. Problems can arise, of course, if, by focusing on the future, attributes of the present are ignored or sacrificed. Furthermore, if one may take the house metaphor a step further, it is rarely the case that curriculum developers are able, unlike property developers, to begin with a clean site. Most curriculum development and curriculum proposals occur within existing systems.

Thus, the third perspective may represent a more realistic approach, since it takes account of existing systems before initiating proposals for change. The systematic changes and the installation of new elements will, of course, require planning and the effective use of systems in order to realize new objectives, so that each of the first two approaches will make important contributions to an overall process of curriculum development.

The characterization of different approaches to curriculum which I have outlined above provides a basis for the more detailed discussion of curriculum models to be given in chapter 3. Also, as will be clear when we come to considering the process of language curriculum design, there is a role for all three curriculum models.

2 Two Traditions

Introduction

Ever since human groups speaking different languages made contact with each other, there has been a need to *learn* other languages while, since the development of urban civilizations, with their specialization of functions within a society, there has been a need to make provision for the *teaching* of other languages. The formalization involved in teaching raises questions about purpose, organization and methodology (Cook 1983). A review of the history of language teaching (e.g. Kelly 1969), or of the teaching of English (Howatt 1984) or of modern language teaching (Hawkins 1981) demonstrates how views on such issues have evolved, changed, disappeared and reemerged over the centuries.

In his survey, Kelly suggests that three different views of language have prevailed over the centuries: the *social* view that language is a form of social behaviour; the *artistic* or literary view that language is a vehicle for creativity; and the *scholarly* view, which often confuses the description and analysis of language with teaching the language. At each period of history, Kelly believes that one of these views has become predominant, generating its own approach to method. In terms of syllabus design, each view will be manifest in both content and organization.

The Modern Language/English Language Traditions

At the risk of establishing a dangerous dichotomy, I would like to suggest that there are two traditions at work in language teaching, one founded on the distinction between modern language teaching (MLT), e.g. French, German, etc. and English language teaching (ELT), while the other is geographically based on the division between Europe and North America. Let us begin by looking briefly at the ML/EL divide.

The reader of Howatt's history of ELT and of Hawkins's account of MLT will be struck by the parallels, contrasts and overlap which characterize these two different traditions. Before the nineteenth century, the provision of widespread access to education – let alone to learning a modern language – was an alien concept, and the majority of the population were illiterate, still less lettered in a foreign tongue. Those few who did need to learn a modern language would do so by whatever means were available (which meant either with a tutor for the rich, or by untutored exposure for the less affluent), and it was not until the nineteenth century, with the opening up of educational opportunities, that modern languages came to occupy a place in the school curriculum. In doing so, the division between the ELT and MLT traditions became institutionalized.

What is striking in both Hawkins's and Howatt's accounts of the nineteenth century is that modern languages were regarded as a 'soft' option, and to avoid being dismissed as being beyond serious consideration, MLT drew upon the model of Latin teaching which, during this period, was taught through the grammar-translation method. Briefly, grammar-translation involves the learning and application of rules for the translation of one language into another. Vocabulary is learned as isolated items and words are combined according to rule. Knowledge of the rule is regarded as being more important than application and the focus is on teaching about the language. There is no oral or pronunciation work, since it is the written language which is taught, and 'mental discipline' is stressed rather than any ability actually to use the language.

Because of the influence of the universities, which then as now controlled the public examination boards, language teaching conformed to the kind of academicism which the universities considered appropriate, and which is embodied in the classical-humanist ideology, one of the three value systems underlying the curriculum, to be discussed in chapter 3. Essentially, within this tradition, language is a body of esteemed information to be learnt, with an emphasis on intellectual rigor.

The effect of treating living languages in much the same way as the dead classical languages may, as Howatt rather ruefully observes, have led to the British tradition of 'being bad at languages'. What is more important from the point of view of the evolution of the two traditions is that MLT and ELT took quite separate paths. The modern languages became fixed within the grammar school system, which was heavily influenced by the academicism of the universities. Furthermore, the universities, in Hawkins's view, refused to take the *teaching* of modern languages seriously, with the consequence that no real attention was given either to research into language teaching or into the training of language teachers. Thus, it is difficult not to resist the conclusion that the institutionalization of MLT within an essentially conservative state grammar school system catering for only the most academically gifted pupils stultified the development of MLT for generations.

The Rise of English as a World Language

The separation of the two traditions can also be attributed to other influences, the most important of which is the emergence of English as an international language. Whereas in medieval times English was the language of an island nation and French was the language of a continental one, in the twentieth century English has become the language of the world thanks to the linguistic legacy of the British Empire, the emergence of the USA as an English-speaking superpower and the fortuitous association of English with the industrial and technological developments of the nineteenth and twentieth centuries. Simultaneously, the status of the modern languages has declined together with motives for learning them among the linguistically dominant English-speaking world.

In MLT in Britain, changes in aims, content and methodology were absent for decades, largely as a consequence of the back-wash effect of the A level examination system under the control of the essentially conservative university sector. Changes were, however, inevitable given the massive rise in the number of children taking a modern language, following the change to comprehensive, non-selective schools and the dismantling of the grammar school system. From only 25 per cent of 11-year-olds taking a modern language in the early 1960s, the percentage rose to 85 in 1977. This unprecedented rise coincided with a period of widespread confusion during the changeover to a comprehensive secondary school system.

It is scarcely surprising that modern language teachers were unprepared for the change, nor that the results were criticized by Her Majesty's inspectors in a report published in 1977. The HMIs noted that the unfortunate modern language teachers had been 'caught up in the process of major educational reform with the introduction of comprehensive secondary schools' following a period during the 1960s when they had been 'asked to review the aims of their teaching and to study new approaches, new methods and new techniques.'

English language teaching, by contrast, was largely unfettered by such considerations and it was not until the 1960s that ELT, in the guise of teaching English to immigrants, became an issue within the state-maintained educational system in Britain. Meanwhile, ELT had gone abroad and it is not without significance that the most influential British figures in the evolution of ELT as a profession (notably Palmer, West, Hornby) spent important periods of their careers outside their home country. When, with the founding of the first pre-service teacher training course in the UK at London University in 1946, a quite different ELT tradition had already evolved.

Further factors have promoted different traditions within ELT. I have already noted the status of English as a world language. In a time of recession among MLT, ELT entered upon a boom period with all that this implies in terms of financial resources and professional innovation and morale. Furthermore, throughout the world English is a compulsory subject in the secondary school curriculum – even, in some cases, continuing during tertiary level. The instrumental function of English as a key to knowledge, recognized 60 years ago by Michael West in India, ensures that demand for English will continue both in the compulsory school system and in the worlds of business, commerce and industry. Thus, whereas in Britain, secondary school pupils are able to drop a foreign language after two years' study, in continental Europe the study of a foreign language (which for the majority means English) continues throughout the secondary school stage.

Fortunately, for both MLT and ELT, the separate traditions have shown many signs of coming together. Among the reasons for this, two are obvious. Firstly, since the shift to non-selective comprehensive secondary schooling, MLT has had to face many of the issues which ELT has also had to confront, most notably the provision of language teaching across a wide ability range and the problems associated with mass provision of a foreign language. Secondly, since the 1950s, both MLT and ELT have been subject to the same influences from theory and research in applied linguistics. Thus, many of the theoretical and practical controversies that preoccupy ELT specialists now exercise the concerns of their colleagues in MLT so, although professionally and socially there are still two traditions, intellectually and practically they have come to occupy common ground. The most conspicuous manifestation of this sharing of influences can be seen in the effects of Wilkins's and the Council of Europe's work on notional–functional syllabuses which have resulted in major changes in the design of teaching programmes and examinations.

One direct result of this common influence can be seen in MLT in the Graded Objectives Movement which 'means the definition of a series of short-term goals, each building upon the one before, so that the learner advances in knowledge and skill' (Page 1983:292). Likewise, the importance now given to the spoken language in both ELT and MLT examinations demonstrates the recognition now accorded by both traditions to the ability to communicate orally in a foreign language. In short, both traditions acknowledge the social view of language as social behaviour (Kelly 1969).

The ELT Tradition and The Reform Movement

The origins of a separate ELT tradition during this century can be traced to a group of teachers who came together at the end of the nineteenth century under the banner of the Reform Movement. This movement advocated an approach to language teaching which challenged the tradition already established by MLT – a challenge largely ignored by MLT but which founded the basis for the British ELT tradition.

The Reform Movement was founded in continental Europe by an international group of academics concerned with the state of language teaching: 'The Movement was a remarkable display of international and disciplinary co-operation in which the specialist phoneticians took as much interest in the classroom as the teachers did in the new science of phonetics' (Howatt 1984:169). Of the four principal phoneticians in the movement, three – Vietor in Germany, Passy in France and Jespersen in Denmark – had begun their careers as teachers, and this accounts for the concern which the

Movement had with teaching. The fourth phonetician, Henry Sweet, was an academic, but in spite of his academic background he was much concerned with pedagogial issues, which Klinghard, a Realgymnasium teacher from Silesia, applied and evaluated, thus helping to give the group credibility in the eyes of practising teachers and, coincidentally, providing an early example of the importance of trialability in curriculum innovation – a point to be noted in chapter 9 in the discussion of managing successful curriculum innovation.

What were the principles of the Reform Movement, and why were they so innovatory? The first principle, the primacy of speech, was clearly opposed to existing practice, which focused on the written language. The second principle, which emphasized the centrality of connected text as the heart of the teaching–learning process, was also out of step with current practice, which tended to work with isolated, unconnected and decontextualized sentences. The third principle, advocating absolute priority of an oral methodology in the classroom, also flew in the face of contemporary concern with the written language in the grammar–translation method.

The emphasis on speech is scarcely surprising in view of the fact that so many of the Reform Movement were phoneticians, and their stress on the importance of phonetics and correct pronunciation did lead to a controversial emphasis on the use of phonetic notation and an unrealistically long period of training in its use. However, the importance they gave to connected text was not controversial, while their oral method introduced techniques such as text-based question and answer work, and retelling of the story, which actually required the learner to use the language and which are still part of the repertoire of techniques available to the language teacher.

As the text was a key element in the method, selection and grading were important, foreshadowing the principles to be greatly developed by Palmer, and thus laying the foundation for language grading, to be discussed at greater length in chapter 4. Text grading was based on a functional typology, beginning with descriptive, proceeding to narrative, and ending with dialogues which, in contrast with much current practice, were not introduced at the beginning but at the end. Good teaching texts, it was suggested, should be direct, clear, simple and familiar. They could also, Sweet suggested, 'be dull and commonplace, but not too much so.' Vocabulary was to be controlled, based on around 3,000 common words.

In formulating their proposals for reform, Sweet and his colleagues combined two disciplines which have become the basis for much subsequent work in applied linguistics and which are included under Richards and Rodgers' 'approach', namely linguistics and psychology.

Harold Palmer: The Scientific Study of Languages

The applied linguistics upon which British ELT was founded was developed further in the work of Harold E. Palmer whose major publications, such as

The Scientific Study and Teaching of Languages (1917), *The Principles of Language Study* (1921) and *A Grammar of Spoken English* (1924), 'provided a statement of intellectual principle on which the English language teaching profession was to build for the next half century' (Howatt 1984:232).

The descriptive apparatus developed by Palmer was influenced by Bloomfield's *An Introduction to the Study of Language* (1914), a seminal work in the evolution of American structuralist linguistics. Although terminologically quaint, Palmer's system paid considerable attention to sentence patterns and syntactic (or 'ergonic') relationships, presented in an ergonic chart, which 'teaches us (1) to classify the units of a given language according to their functions in the sentence and (2) to build up original (unknown) units from the smaller known units of which they are composed' (Howatt 1984:237). The principles of working from simple to more complex, from known to unknown, and of a 'rational order of progression' form the basis of most subsequent attempts within the British tradition of ELT to grade linguistic material and so have considerable implications for language syllabus design, as discussed in chapter 4. Similarly, Palmer's methodological principles, of which habit formation was the core, acted as a strong influence on ELT methodology for the next two generations, though it is important to realize that the bulk of the psychological research into habit-formation had not yet been published and so it is anachronistic to think of Palmer as a behaviourist. Indeed, his methodology was largely uninformed by psychological principles as such. Yet, his distinction between the 'spontaneous' and trained or 'studial' capacities of the classroom learner prefigures a dichotomy recently revived by Krashen (1982), whose contrast between 'acquisition' and 'learning' is a basic tenet for his Input Hypothesis. What both Palmer and Krashen are doing is to draw a distinction between the capacity of a learner to pick up a language in an informal and untutored fashion compared with the ability to learn through formal classroom study.

Michael West: Surrender Value

Palmer's interest in controlled vocabulary coincided with that of Michael West, whose name is closely associated with two important developments: the *New Method Readers*, and *General Service List of English Words*. West began his career in Bengal, where he became concerned with wastage within the Bengal education system. He believed that the current approach to teaching English had 'low surrender value' because pupils derived little benefit from the amount of teaching they received during an incompleted course of instruction which, at that time, attempted to teach Bengali children a command of *spoken* English, for which they would have little use – a view echoed on a wider scale in a recent paper by Abbott (1987).

West carried out what we would now call a needs analysis (to be further discussed in chapter 6), and the results of his survey were published in a report in 1926, in which he advocated developing practical information *reading* in English, which would enable Bengalis to have access to the technological knowledge needed for economic development of their country. He proposed two main ways of improving reading texts for children; first, simplifying the vocabulary by replacing old-fashioned literary words with more common modern equivalents; and second, by applying the principles of readability and lexical distribution by presenting fewer words more often. In one of the first attempts to evaluate the efficacy of a new method, West experimented with new and old materials, demonstrating the superiority of his proposed innovations, although it must be said that his experiment lacked the rigour and precision which would nowadays be required of such an investigation.

Hornby: The Situational Approach

The culmination of the British tradition established by Sweet and Palmer is the work of Hornby, who is probably best known for his *Advanced Learner's Dictionary of Current English*, first published in 1954. He united the tradition of oral method advocated by Palmer and the concern of Sweet and Jespersen with connected text. Hornby termed his method the *Situational Approach*, as each new pattern or lexical item should be introduced to the class in advance of the work with the text, and the presentation be linked to classroom situations in which the meaning of the new item would be established. In spite of its name, his approach was not situational in the more commonly used sense of contextualizing language in 'real life' situations found outside the classroom.

Hornby's *Guide to Patterns and Usage in English*, also first published in 1954, is based on a graded and sequenced language syllabus together with procedures for introducing each new item. Although his approach is rather austere, the syllabus which formed the basis of his *Guide* has been very influential and there are many structurally based courses published since his *Guide* appeared in which features of this syllabus may be discerned.

The Two Traditions: the USA and Europe

We have now dealt with the first major tradition based on the distinction between MLT and ELT and it is time to turn to a geographically – and even culturally – based tradition founded on the difference between British and American ELT. Aspects of the differences between the US and UK traditions are embodied in the emergence of 'theory' as a key term within the American tradition, as compared with 'principles' within the British one.

The academic basis to American language teaching is exemplified in audio-lingualism, which became the prevailing American orthodoxy in the generation following World War II. The foundations of audio-lingualism may be traced to the work of Bloomfield, the doyen of American linguistics, whose *Introduction to the Study of Language* and *Language* established the tenets of structural linguistics, which set out to describe languages by segmenting and classifying utterances into their phonological and grammatical constituents. The job of the linguist in the field was to reveal the structure of a language by employing a set of discovery procedures and a native-speaking informant. By applying such procedures, the linguist would be able to identify and describe the phonemes, morphemes and syntactic structures of the language. Among the techniques used is that of identifying words which contrast in only one sound. Where such minimal sound differences coincide with differences in meaning a phonemic contrast is revealed, and by systematically applying this discovery technique, the phonemes – or minimal units in the sound system of the language – are established. Examples in English are the phonemic contrasts in such so-called minimal pairs as *pit* and *pet*, *pat* and *pot*.

Such linguistic field procedures were described by Bloomfield in a pamphlet called *An Outline Guide for the Practical Study of Foreign Languages*, published in 1942. As Howatt observes, this guide to elementary linguistic fieldwork became rather unexpectedly a basic source for the Army Specialized Training Program (ASTP), which arose in response to the need for large numbers of foreign language speaking army personnel with the US's entry into World War II. Adapting the field work techniques from the *Outline Guide*, the ASTP used linguists and native-speaking informants who together analysed the target languages, devised teaching materials and acted as classroom teachers. The linguist instructors introduced the new material, giving explanations where necessary, and the native speakers were left to drill the patterns by a simple method of imitation and repetition. Known as the 'mim-mem' method (mimicry and memorization), 'this is the obvious forerunner of the audiolingual approach and the early language laboratory techniques' (Howatt 1984:266).

The development of this methodology was taken a step further by Charles Fries, whose Michigan Oral Method was founded on an applied linguistics base. Drawing on scientific descriptions of the source and target languages, the applied linguist

> has to select and grade the structures taken from the original description to suit the relevant pedagogical purposes, and prepare a contrastive description of source and target languages in order to pinpoint areas of potential difficulty. Secondly, he has to write teaching materials which will illustrate the patterns of the new language and provide special practice on difficult points. The materials are then passed on to the teacher for use in class. (Howatt 1984:267)

This approach tended to emphasize the role of the teacher as user of materials written by trained 'experts' and thus established what some might see as a disabling tradition of the teacher as consumer and the materials producer as expert, each inhabiting rather different worlds and with communication between them being in one direction – from the 'expert' to the 'practitioner'.

From the point of view of syllabus design, the priority given to speech and the principle of contrastive analysis of the native and target languages are fundamental, as is the selection and grading of patterns or structures. Methodologically, the emphasis on language learning as the formation and performance of habits led to the use of pattern practice of the structure drill which, as Brooks (1960:146) says, 'makes no pretense of being communication . . . It is . . . exercise in structural dexterity undertaken solely for the sake of practice, in order that performance may become habitual and automatic.' In fact, there was more to audio-lingualism than structure drilling, although this was an important procedure. Control, guidance, the avoidance of error and practising correct forms of the language, while being features of audio-lingualism, were by no means confined to this particular method. We have already noted how Sweet, Palmer, West and Hornby all made similar proposals so that such principles were already well understood within British ELT and are reflected in the language curricula developed within this tradition, as may be seen in Hornby's *Guide to Patterns and Usage in English.*

In spite of such similarities, there remain some important differences between the British and American traditions. Audio-lingualism was founded by structural linguists whose concern was with the form rather than the use of the language, whereas British linguistics, which evolved under the influence of J. R. Firth, became concerned with the relationship between language and context of situation. So, at a time when the American approach to language teaching gave absolute priority to the training of speech habits, in Britain interest was growing in situational approaches in which a social model of language use was applied to the design of language curricula. This British interest was later to find common cause in the concept of communicative competence, as we shall see.

A New Paradigm: Transformational–Generative (TG) Linguistics

In one of the great ironies of academic history, Skinner's definitive behaviourist explanation of language learning, *Verbal Behaviour*, was published in 1957, the same year Chomsky's *Syntactic Structures* launched an entirely new theory whereby both language and language learning could be explained. The shortcomings of a behaviourist explanation of language learning were to be mercilessly criticized two years later in Chomsky's much-cited (though doubtless seldom read) (1959) review of Skinner's *Verbal Behaviour*, while the concept of linguistic competence proposed by Chomsky was to provide a basis for future development in linguistic theory and research.

To Chomsky, a view of language as a collection of structures was too limited. Instead of concentrating on taxonomic classifications of structures, Chomsky (1965) proposed in *Aspects of the Theory of Syntax* that linguistics should develop the rules which would account for these structures. These rules constitute linguistic competence, which is the unconscious knowledge of the 'ideal speaker-listener' operating in 'a completely homogeneous speech community'. Thus competence is an idealization and is to be distinguished from 'performance', which is 'the actual use of language in concrete situations.' As performance is the imperfect realization of competence, it was regarded as being of little interest to the theoretical and descriptive linguist.

Chomsky's view of language as a mental phenomenon posited that humans' capacity for language was unique and innate. His approach to describing this mental phenomenon is very different from that of the structural linguist, whose use of discovery procedures and data obtained from a native-speaking informant were repudiated by Chomsky and TG linguists. Instead, they attempted to produce a logical model whose rules would enable the production of grammatical sentences. It is important to realize that this is a *model* of competence and therefore does not necessarily replicate what actually occurs in the mental processes of a language user, even though psycholinguistic research carried out under the influence of TG in the 1960s attempted to demonstrate the psychological reality of TG rules. Subsequently, much research into both L1 (first language) and L2 (second language) acquisition has been carried out within the theoretical framework established by Chomsky, and the origins of Second Language Acquisition (SLA) research can be traced to the First Language Acquisition (FLA) research which was stimulated by TG theories of language acquisition. The implications of some of the findings of SLA research for syllabus design will be reviewed in Chapter 4.

Contextual Factors and Communicative Competence

While the TG view of language competence set a new direction for linguistic research, the lack of attention to contextual factors omitted what, for the sociolinguist, is a crucial aspect of competence, namely the ability of a speaker to *use* language appropriately according to setting, social relationships and communicative purpose. The concept of communicative competence, first put forward by Hymes in a lecture in 1966, and subsequently published in Gumperz and Hymes (1972), greatly extends the notion of competence to include such factors together with the speaker's tacit awareness of such constraints on language use. In short, Hymes (1966) turned attention from the ideal speaker–hearer in a homogeneous speech community, to '*differential competence* within a *heterogeneous speech community*', pointing out that 'there are rules of use without which the rules of grammar would be useless.'

Although Hymes makes the point that 'rules of use are not a late grafting', but are acquired from the first years of language acquisition his account of communicative competence focuses on language in use rather than on language in acquisition. As a means of analysing and explaining language use, Hymes's theory of communicative competence proved to be an important theoretical influence on the evolution of communicative language teaching (CLT) during the 1970s. Indeed, the formative influences on CLT were sociolinguistic rather than psycholinguistic, and include not only the theoretical impetus provided by Hymes, but the influence of speech-act theory, through the work of Austin (1962) and Searle (1969), and discourse analysis (e.g. Sinclair and Coulthard 1975). In fact, it is only very recently that language teaching has turned to language acquisition studies as a source of guidance and inspiration. Meanwhile, we shall review some of the developments in ELT which were taking place in Britain and the rest of Europe during the 1960s and 1970s.

From Structuralism to Communication

In the 1960s it was taken for granted that a structural syllabus, based on widely accepted principles of selection and grading as outlined by Palmer and Hornby, would form the basis of language teaching materials, and in Britain two such courses published during this decade became international best sellers: L. G. Alexander's *New Concept English* (1967) and G. Broughton's *Success With English* (1968). These courses also employed teaching procedures which combined features of the situational method and audio-visual techniques, while many of the controlled and guided practice activities showed similarities to those found in American audio-lingualism. In MLT, a similar combination of features may be found in the materials produced by the Nuffield Project during the late 1960s and early 1970s.

The 1970s were characterized by a concern with meaning, and this was to form the basis of the Council of Europe's 'Threshold Level' or 'T-Level' project, initiated in 1971. Whereas the structural approach to language had emphasized differences among languages as revealed in contrastive analysis, the 'notional–functional' approach, as it came to be called, emphasized that all languages expressed the same meanings, but with differing structural realizations. Thus, it became possible to develop a meaning-based syllabus which could be specified for any language, and the Council of Europe working group set itself the task of specifying the content for a 'common core' which all learners would acquire before specializing in language related to specific purposes. The influence of this work for syllabus design will be taken up again in chapter 6.

Needs Analysis and Notional Syllabuses

There were two important outcomes of this project, which have had a widespread and lasting influence on the design of language teaching syllabuses. The first was the development of a systematic approach to needs analysis, expounded in *A Model for the Definition of Language Needs of Adults Learning a Modern Language* by René Richterich (1972) and *Identifying the needs of adults learning a foreign language* by Richterich and Chancerel (1977/80). The significance of needs analysis for syllabus design will be taken up in chapter 6.

The second outcome was to make meaning (specifically functional meaning) rather than structure the basis of the language syllabus. The specification of a meaning-based syllabus poses difficulties addressed by D. A. Wilkins in *Notional Syllabuses* (1976). He specifies three types of notional category: (1) semantico-grammatical, such as past, future, location, etc., (2) modality, such as possibility, necessity, obligation, etc., and (3) communicative function, such as asking questions, expressing agreement and disagreement, inviting, accepting, declining, etc. The lists of categories which appear in *Notional Syllabuses* are not, however, a syllabus within the terms defined earlier, since such lists do not provide any indication of grading and sequencing which, as we have seen, are important in a syllabus intended as a guide to teaching, while the problems of combining structural and notional–functional elements in a teaching syllabus have remained a continuing difficulty, as will be discussed in chapter 6.

The influence of the Threshold Level's new approach was soon to be seen in published materials. By the mid-1970s new textbooks incorporating a functional dimension, such as the *Strategies* series (Abbs, Ayton and Freebairn 1975) began to appear, while, instead of having such chapter or unit headings as 'articles before a vowel sound' or 'Present Perfect Simple Tense', such textbooks now included titles like 'Ask for, Give and Refuse Permission' and 'Expressing personal opinions'. The power and influence of this new set of categories for ELT syllabus design have been enormous, to the extent that it has become conventional for syllabus designers to take them as given.

LASP

Another development of the 1970s was the growth of language teaching for specific purposes (LASP), which spawned a number of acronyms, of which ESP, EOP and EAP are now part of the ELT lexicon: English for Specific Purposes, English for Occupational Purposes and English for Academic Purposes. In these we can see the response of the profession to new demands made upon both the English language and ELT teachers with the intimate association between English, technological change and national development. We also see in the development of LASP another example of the dichotomy between training and education, the former being concerned with the teaching of predetermined skills, the latter attempting to teach an understanding of the underlying rationale or principles; although in his discussion of this issue, Widdowson (1983:19) rejects such a characterization, seeing the distinction more in the difference between *conformity* as the goal of training on the one hand, and *creativity* as the aim of education on the other.

ESP has been characterized by a concern with content rather than method, as is shown by the development of techniques to analyse the product (i.e. analysis of target texts: see, for instance, Ewer and Latorre 1967) and to determine learners' needs (i.e. needs analysis: see, for instance, Munby 1978, to be discussed in chapter 6). However, such analyses have been criticized on the grounds that 'They do not tell us what the language user does with the knowledge that has been so neatly itemized, nor, by the same token, how the language learner acquires this knowledge' (Widdowson 1983:87). However, recent work in ESP has shown equal concern with how the learner might most effectively learn, and Hutchinson and Waters (1987) have outlined a learning-centred approach to ESP which also provides a sound model for general course design. Furthermore, there are signs of a development of ESP programmes in which professional or occupational training and language training are combined (McCallen (1989)), drawing upon techniques developed in such areas as management training. Indeed, it may well be that ESP will become increasingly important.

The Link with Curriculum

Before concluding this historical review, we need to look briefly at the background to the other term in the title: *Curriculum*. Curriculum studies, as a branch of education, originated in the work of Taba and Tyler, American educationists, whose respective publications *Curriculum Development: Theory and Practice* (1962) and *Basic Principles of Curriculum and Instruction* (1949) attempted to address the fundamental question of this field of study: What ought to be taught in an educational institution?

Curriculum theory encompasses philosophy and value systems; the main components of the curriculum: purposes, content, methodology and evaluation; and the processes whereby curricula are developed, implemented and evaluated. And because curriculum studies are so all-encompassing, it is a characteristic of curriculum development that it involves a wide range of issues and people. It is the breadth and depth of curriculum development which distinguishes it from syllabus design, whose concerns and ramifications are restricted to questions of content.

The Isolation of LT from Curriculum Studies

Language teaching – MLT and especially ELT – has been for the most part isolated from curriculum studies. A number of reasons have been suggested. As we have seen, ELT developed out of an applied linguistics tradition and the academic reference group to whom practitioners have referred is the applied linguist rather than the educationist. MLT, as already noted, drew its inspiration from the language scholar, and any concern with methodology, which has always been of primary interest to the educationist, was much less prominent.

ELT has also only recently emerged as a profession, with its own traditions, values, preoccupations and identity. Whereas modern language teachers could found an association in 1892, the setting up of equivalent ELT organizations did not take place until over 60 years later, with the founding of TESOL in the USA (1966) and IATEFL in Britain (1967). Furthermore, the first issue of *English Language Teaching* (now *ELT Journal*) did not appear until 1946. Yet another important influence on the development of ELT as a profession – the British Council – is also of recent origin, having celebrated its fiftieth anniversary in 1985. The fact that the British Council conducts most of its work abroad draws attention to the geographical dispersal of ELT and its practitioners, with the consequent absence of a firm home base for the development of professional unity, in comparison with the UK-based ML teaching profession which has evolved within one national education system.

A further reason for the isolation of ELT, in particular, from education in general – and thus from curriculum studies – is the fact that the actual practice of ELT tended to take place in two contexts which were themselves isolated from mainstream metropolitan education, namely the private language school and the colonial education system. The private language school stands outside the state education system and thus is not constrained by the values, assumptions and aims of that system. Indeed, it might be argued that in some contexts the private language school system evolved because of the failures of the state system to provide an adequate language education for its clients. Furthermore, private language schools are fee-paying and tend to be subject to market forces, from which state systems are (traditionally, at least) largely protected. Thus, a different set of purposes and a different ethos prevail.

The development of ELT in the British Empire also isolated ELT from developments at home. The role of English language teaching within a colonial education policy was not generally disputed within the metropolitan arena; nor were the aims of education open to such debate. However, with the development of an Anglophone Commonwealth, consisting of independent nations, and the new needs which education (and ELT) had to meet, a reappraisal of ELT has been inevitable. Such a reappraisal has coincided with the unprecedented spread of English teaching in developing countries around the world, reaching a wider range and greater number of pupils than in any previous era. The age of mass education has coincided with the emergence of English as a key to technological knowledge and thus to economic development, recalling West's recognition of the instrumental function of the English language in Bengal over 60 years ago.

The Growth of an Educational Orientation

We have already noted that until the 1970s the concerns of language teaching were with procedure rather than design. The change of emphasis to design, characteristic of the 1970s, inevitably led to a reappraisal of the role and purpose of language teaching, which in turn has led to questions which go beyond considerations of content or technique. This development has been accompanied by the realization, through aid projects and consultancies, that the wholesale export of metropolitan materials and methods may not be appropriate because other education systems exist within quite different cultural, economic and political contexts than those which apply in western Europe or north America. ELT experts, as participants in curriculum development projects in such countries, have found that solutions to the new educational issues which they have to face will not be found within applied linguistics theory and research. ELT has begun to look to education as a source of new theories and procedures, particularly in matters of developing and implementing innovations in content and methodology.

Meanwhile, MLT, which in Britain and north America has been within the state sector, has found itself in the middle of the reappraisals of aims and methods which have characterized educational systems in the 40 years since World War II. Just as prevailing values and assumptions within the system have influenced other parts of the curriculum, so, too, MLT has come within the scope of curriculum studies, under whose aegis such reappraisals have taken place. Thus, in a period which put stress on efficiency, behavioural objectives became a vogue, and language curriculum developers attempted to express language teaching aims in such terms (cf. Richterich 1973). The subsequent swing to humanist values has witnessed an emphasis on the social and interpersonal nature of language.

Although it would not be true to say that language teaching has become a branch of curriculum studies, the influence of the latter on the former is seen in such work as A. M. Shaw's (1975) Ph.D. thesis, *Approaches to a Communicative Syllabus in Foreign Language Curriculum Development*, while more recent discussions of ELT, such as *Language Teaching Projects for the Third World* (British Council 1983), have placed the concerns of managing innovations in ELT syllabus, materials and methods quite firmly within the arena of curriculum studies. Meanwhile, the approach to communicative language teaching advocated by Candlin, Breen and others at the University of Lancaster has consciously drawn upon curriculum theory, as we shall see in subsequent discussions of the process curriculum model (chapter 3) and process syllabuses (chapter 7). Curriculum studies have now provided a field of discourse in which many of the concerns of language teaching, as they have evolved, can be and are being discussed and for this reason the language syllabus designer is obliged to be informed by and, indeed, to participate in this area.

Conclusion

Language teaching is a branch of education. During the development of a distinctive and independent profession, ELT evolved from an applied linguistics base established by the late nineteenth century Reform Movement and Palmer, West and Hornby, within the British tradition, and by Bloomfield, Fries and Lado within the American. While the American tradition focused on grammatical structure as the basis for the content of the language syllabus, the British school developed an interest in contextualized language use, which was combined with a longstanding concern with language structure. The development of new theories of language learning, under the impact of Chomskyan linguistics, gave rise to theories of the learner's own innate language learning capacities and to revised views on both L1 and L2 acquisition, leading to the evolution of SLA theory and research, whose influence on language syllabus design is only just beginning to be felt.

The purely linguistic nature of competence, as defined by Chomsky, was extended by Hymes (1966) to embrace the capacities underlying the communicative use of language, and the interests of British and American schools of thought have come together in their concern with learning language for the fluent expression of the language user's intentions in a variety of contexts. A reappraisal of the principles upon which content and methodology are selected has been accompanied by a consideration of the role of language teaching within education, and by the realization that curriculum studies may provide a body of theory and practice which can inform decision-making in language teaching curriculum development and innovation.

Suggested Reading

General

The most extensive review of language teaching appears in Kelly (1969), *25 Centuries of Language Teaching*, while a condensed overview may be found in Part Two of Stern (1983), *Fundamental Concepts of Language Teaching*. Undoubtedly the best history of ELT has been written by Howatt (1984), *A History of English Language Teaching*. There is no comparable book on the history of MLT, but Hawkins (1981), *Modern Languages in the Curriculum*, covers much the same ground as Howatt, though he writes from the viewpoint of the UK educational context. Another account from the MLT viewpoint is provided by Clark (1987), *Curriculum Renewal in School Foreign Language Learning*, framed within Skilbeck's curriculum ideologies, to be discussed in chapter 3. Finally, a comprehensive review of developments in ELT from the viewpoint of the early 1980s has been provided by Roberts (1982).

The role of ELT

Bowers (1986) discusses the international role of English and ELT, while Judd (1981 and 1984) addresses policy and political questions in his two papers. Cook (1983) asks 'What should language teaching be about?' and Abbott (1987) stakes an educational claim for ELT.

Audio-lingualism

Rivers (1964), *The Psychologist and the Foreign Language Teacher*, reviews audio-lingualism, its tenets and its psychological basis, while an account of audio-lingualism from one of the founding fathers is given by Fries (1945). A standard account of audiolingualism teaching methodology appears in Brooks (1960). Within recent British ELT tradition, Widdowson has been a major contributor to the evolution of theory and practice, and two publications of his date from the period dealt with in this chapter: Widdowson, (1978), *Teaching Language as Communication* and (1979) *Explorations in Applied Linguistics*.

Threshold Level

Another major influence on the design of language teaching programmes has been Wilkins and his colleagues on the Council of Europe 'Threshold' level scheme. Wilkins (1976), *Notional Syllabuses*, is a comprehensible account of meaning-based syllabuses. An earlier proposal appears in Wilkins (1972), *Linguistics in Language Teaching*.

Graded Objectives in Modern Language Teaching (GOMLT)

Page reviews the GOMLT movement in a state of the art article in *Language Teaching* (1983). As an example of teacher- and school-based curriculum renewal in language teaching, the GOMLT Movement has implications which go beyond questions of syllabus content.

LASP

The field of Languages for Specific Purposes is reviewed by Robinson (1980), *English for Specific Purposes*, while a series of case studies of ESP is provided by Mackay and Mountford (eds) 1978, with the same title. For a clear and carefully thought out discussion of ESP, which also has much of value for general course design, see Hutchinson, T. and Waters, A. (1987) *English for Specific Purposes*. Cambridge: Cambridge University Press.

Discourse Analysis

Discourse analysis, conversational analysis and speech-act theory have been important influences on language teaching during the past decade and a half, and there is an extensive literature in these areas. For a well judged and readable survey of the field, read Stubbs (1983), *Discourse Analysis*.

3 Language Curriculum: Values and Options

Introduction

Since one of the purposes of this book is to place language syllabus design within the wider context of curriculum, it is important to review some of the major value systems or ideologies which underlie approaches to curriculum, as well as the curriculum models associated with these ideologies. Such a review will serve to show where some ideas – such as behavioural objectives and proposals for process syllabuses – have come from, while also providing some perspective on the place of such ideas within the field of curriculum studies and, thus, on their status within ELT.

It is also important to be aware that different models of curriculum represent the expression of different value systems and, consequently, of quite divergent views on education. Indeed, it is hardly surprising that views on these issues will be value-laden, given the fact that curriculum studies attempt to answer quite fundamental questions about the nature and purpose of education. Even though the concerns of the language teacher and syllabus designer might seem remote from such considerations, I hope it will become clear that any decisions about developing a language teaching programme must reflect the assumptions and beliefs of those engaged in such an enterprise, and that it is important to illuminate such planning by working out where one stands in relation to the numerous options available. I shall begin this review of curriculum options by considering the important issue of the major value systems which underlie them.

Value Systems

Views on the nature and purpose of education include those which emphasize the transmission of an esteemed cultural heritage; which stress the growth and self-realization of the individual; and those which regard education as an instrument of social change. Respectively, these three orientations or ideologies have been termed classical humanism, progressivism and reconstructionism. Classical humanism is associated with Matthew Arnold and T. S. Eliot, progressivism with J. J. Rousseau, J. H. Pestalozzi and Friedrich Froebel, and reconstructionism with John Dewey.

In language teaching, each of these ideologies is expressed in different proposals for aims, content and methodology. The grammar-translation method, as already noted in chapter 2, is an expression of classical humanism. Audio-lingualism and notional–functional syllabuses can be viewed as different realizations of reconstructionism. The proposals of Krashen and Terrell (1983), Breen and Candlin (1980) whose process syllabus will be reviewed in chapter 7, and Prabhu (1987) whose procedural syllabus will also be discussed in that chapter, are differing products of progressivism. As will be clear even from these examples, different ideologies give rise to very diverse views on both the purposes and methods of language teaching and the most effective ways of implementing curriculum innovation, the latter topic being the subject of chapters 8 and 9.

Reconstructionism is associated with a systems-behavioural approach (see Crawford-Lange 1982), in which the pedagogical procedures are based on Skinner's (1968) application to education of the principles of operant conditioning. The emphasis is on incremental and mastery learning, in which each step is based on the preceding one, and 'it is assumed that, given appropriate learning activities, all students can achieve mastery if they have enough time' (Crawford-Lange 1982:88). In language syllabus design, such views have been realized in the grading of structural syllabuses (to be discussed in further detail in chapter 4), and in the concept of graded objectives.

Progressivism, by contrast, coincides with what Crawford-Lange characterizes as 'problem-posing education', which 'extracts a concern for the real-life situation of the learners as well as a perception of the student as decision-maker' (Crawford-Lange:88). The two central pedagogical concepts of this approach are *praxis* and *dialogue*, the former consisting of reflection and action upon the world in order to transform it (Freire 1973 and 1976), the latter 'the educational context, the place where praxis occurs', the purpose of which is 'to stimulate new ideas, opinions and perceptions rather than simply to exchange them' (Crawford-Lange:89). As we shall see in chapter 7, both the concepts and the terminology have been drawn upon in proposals for process syllabuses in language teaching (see Breen and Candlin 1984).

Whereas progressivism is concerned with 'doing things for' or 'doing things with' the learner, reconstructionism involves 'doing things to' him or her (Davies 1976:32). Reconstructionism emphasizes the importance of planning, efficiency and rationality, and it involves 'the elevation of teachers and other members of a carefully selected and highly trained elite of educators who are designated the agents of cultural renewal' (Skilbeck 1976). Reconstructionism, to return to the house analogy of chapter 1, plans for an ideal future dwelling (i.e. society), though not necessarily taking account of the constraints which stand in the way of achieving such an ideal. Progressivism is more concerned with the processes of building the dwelling or of adapting it to the needs and requirements of the community living within it.

Having considered the ideological basis of these approaches to curriculum,

I shall now turn to an account of two curriculum models which reflect these different perspectives, beginning with the means–ends or Rational Planning model.

Means and Ends

As Stern (1984:501) observes, 'a means–ends view of teaching is unavoidable in language pedagogy', so it is hardly surprising that the means–ends or objectives model has provided a popular framework for language curricula. The rationale underlying the objectives model is associated with Taba and Tyler, and because it assumes a four-stage cyclic sequence, beginning with clear specification of goals, it is sometimes called the rational planning model 'on the grounds that it is rational to specify the ends of an activity before engaging in it' (Taylor and Richards 1979:64). A flow-chart representation of the Taba–Tyler curriculum model appears in figure 3.1.

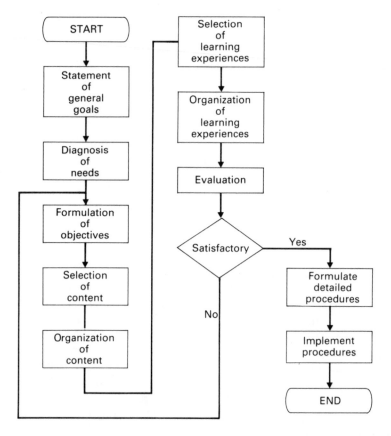

Figure 3.1 Flowchart representation of the Taba–Tyler curriculum development model

In this model, a distinction is made between goals, aims and objectives (Taba 1962). Goals are very general and broad. Aims are more specific, and are long-term – the target to be aimed at. These are what Bell (1981:50) refers to as 'key objectives'. Conventionally, objectives are the short- to medium-term goals, which in Bell's terms are 'critical' or 'specific' objectives. Both aims and objectives are generally regarded as important because, without general aims to provide direction, it is possible to become lost in the attempt to satisfy a range of short term objectives. Merritt (1971) in Hooper 1971:202 neatly summarizes the distinction between aims and objectives in the following terms: 'The satisfaction of hunger may be an aim. A plate of steak might be the correlated objective.' A similar distinction is drawn by Widdowson (1983:7) in his discussion of EGP (English for General Purposes) and ESP (English for Specific Purposes), in which he contrasts them in terms of the place of aims in each type of course.

ESP	specification of objectives: equivalent to aims	training: development of restricted competence
EGP	specification of objectives: leads to aims	education: development of general capacity

By 'objectives', Widdowson means 'the pedagogic intentions of a particular course of study to be achieved within the period of that course and in principle measurable by some assessment device at the end of the course.' By 'aims' he means 'the purposes to which learning will be put *after* the end of the course' (Widdowson 1983:6–7). Objectives, following Mager (1962), are conventionally stated in *behavioural* terms which are intended to be specific, unambiguous and measurable. Mager identifies three components:

1 *Behaviour* 'First, identify the terminal behaviour by name; you can specify the kind of behaviour that will be accepted as evidence that the learner has achieved the objective.'
2 *Conditions* 'Second, try to define the desired behaviour further by describing the important conditions under which the behaviour will be expected to occur.'
3 *Standards* 'Third, specify the criteria of acceptable performance by describing how well the learner must perform to be considered acceptable.'

The core of the behaviour statement is an *action verb*, such as *identify*, *define*, *justify*, *classify*, etc.

In the 1950s, a massive attempt was made to translate objectives into behavioural terms by Bloom, Englehart, Furst, Hill and Krathwohl (1956) in the *Taxonomy of Educational Objectives*. Objectives were classified under three domains: the *cognitive*, which is concerned with intellectual abilities and operations; the *affective*, which is the domain of attitudes, values and appreciation; and the *psychomotor*, the area of motor skills, important in technical contexts. Many of the objectives which the authors listed in the cognitive domain have since been adapted for the specification of comprehension skills in reading, as will be clear from the list of categories given below from the cognitive domain.

1   Knowledge of facts, conventions, procedures.
2   Comprehension, which subsumes understanding, translation (or reformulation), interpretation (inferencing, summarizing, generalizing) and extrapolation (estimating, predicting on the basis of the current situation).
3   Application, or the transfer of training and skills to new or novel applications.
4   Synthesis, or putting together elements and parts to form a whole, or drawing upon elements from many sources and putting them together into a structure or pattern not clearly there before.
5   Evaluation, or making judgements about the value, for some purpose, of ideas, solutions, methods and material by reference to internal evidence and external criteria.

In the affective domain, they also listed five categories:

1   Receiving or attending, e.g. attending carefully when others speak in direct conversation, on the telephone.
2   Responding, e.g. finding pleasure in reading for recreation.
3   Valuing, e.g. assuming responsibility for drawing reticent members of the group into a conversation.
4   Organizing, e.g. forming judgements of the responsibility of society for conserving human and material resources.
5   Characterization by a value or value-complex, e.g. readiness to revise judgements and to change behaviour in the light of evidence.

These affective objectives are especially noteworthy in the light of the subsequent development of humanistic approaches to language teaching, in which affectivity is recognized as both a means and an end of the teaching–learning process.

In language teaching, in contrast to general education, one notable attempt to adapt behavioural objectives has been made by Steiner (1975). Another important application, following the classical form of behavioural objectives specified by Mager, is to be found in the Council of Europe's 'Threshold Level' (see Van Ek in Trim, Richterich, Van Ek and Wilkins (1973)). A more recent development may also be found in the Graded Objectives in Modern Language Teaching (GOMLT) movement.

Following the classical prescription for behavioural objectives, Steiner proposes that a performance objective should state:

1 What the student will do (e.g. write an essay, answer five questions orally).
2 Under what conditions (e.g. in class without notes, in an individual conference with the teacher).
3 Within what time (e.g. 40 minutes, 5 minutes, no time limit).
4 To what level of mastery (e.g. must include 5 pertinent ideas each supported with specific documentation; must have good paragraph and essay construction; must contain no more than 5 errors of grammar, punctuation or spelling; 4 out of 5 oral answers must be correct in content; no more than 3 errors in pronunciation).

Such a specification provides a detailed guide to the learner, the teacher and the tester – the last two often being one and the same person. As a statement of desired teaching–learning outcomes, such objectives constitute a guide to criterion-referenced or mastery learning and testing. If the learners' behaviour matches the specification, they have achieved mastery of the objective concerned.

An example of a performance objective for a first-level language course might be:

In an individual conference with your teacher you will be assigned one of four topics (your family, the weather, your schedule, or the classroom.)

Your teacher will ask you 5 questions orally in the target language and you will answer these orally in the target language and in complete sentences.

Criteria: 4 of 5 must be correct in content (according to the information you provided the teacher). You should make no more than 3 errors in pronunciation.

Steiner outlines three main criteria for terminal course objectives. Firstly, terminal course objectives must provide clear *guidance* to the prospective users and 'as the specificity increases through the refinement process, greater clarity should appear.' Secondly, the terminal course objective should be *relevant* by being meaningful to the learner, 'related to the educational goal from which it is derived' and 'desirable in terms of the present and future expectations of the school and its related groups.' Finally, such an objective should be *feasible* 'if there is a good probability of its being achieved'. If objectives meet these criteria, the entire set of objectives should be reviewed by asking the following questions:

1 Does the set contain an appropriate representation of cognitive behaviours?
2 Does the set contain an adequate representation of affective behaviours?
3 Is the set of objectives broad enough to cover the subject adequately?
4 Are all of the objectives internally consistent?

To screen objectives, Steiner suggests matching each terminal course objective with a purpose.

Behavioural Objectives: Some Problems

In spite of the appeal of behavioural objectives, there have been a number of objections to them on philosophical, educational and practical grounds. For instance, Tumposky (1984), in an article tellingly entitled 'Behavioral Objectives, the cult of efficiency, and foreign language learning: are they compatible?', points out that the development of behavioural objectives was associated with the scientific management movement in education during the period between the two world wars. Bobbitt (1924), a curriculum specialist concerned with the need for efficiency, 'attempted to apply the techniques of business to the schools. In the name of efficiency, he gave paramount importance to the setting of acceptable performance standards and to their measurement.' The attention given to efficiency and predicted outcomes brings us to the heart of much criticism of behavioural objectives and illustrates how all aspects of education are value-laden. If education is viewed as a voyage of discovery, the pre-specification of outcomes inherent in behavioural objectives may be seen as conflicting with the essentially speculative nature of the educational process. Indeed, Stenhouse (1975:82) takes the view that 'education as induction into knowledge is successful to the extent that it makes the behavioural outcomes of the students unpredictable.' Sockett (1976:50), like Stenhouse, is philosophically opposed to the prescriptive character of the objectives model and he is suspicious of the dogmatism to which the rigid adherence to an objectives model can give rise. He points out that the demand for objectives to be measurable 'presupposes a dogmatic attachment to the one way of making scientific progress' and 'that different teaching practices are ruled out', while 'the teacher is seen as a technician or a manager.'

Indeed, as Tumposky observes, Bobbitt's views resembled those of the advocates of programmed learning in that both 'give the impression that their products are, or should be, "teacher-proof".' Such a view of the teacher as technician, working to a plan provided by an expert, is strikingly similar to that advocated by Fries; whose views are in line with a reconstructionist ideology, but in conflict with progressivism, which values consultation with and participation by teachers and learners in decisions affecting professional practice. Thus it is not difficult to see why behavioural objectives are treated with such circumspection, particularly when they become associated with the politics of education and questions of control, power and authority. Tumposky's critique is clearly motivated by more than questions about the *educational* value of behavioural objectives.

One of the strongest arguments which advocates of behavioural objectives put forward lies in the claim that they enable goals to be specified unambiguously. However, as Taylor and Richards (1979:70) point out, 'objectives cannot have exact, true and real meaning, because the meaning of words depends on the way they are used, and the way they are used does vary.' This is especially true in the teaching of language itself, and efforts to produce a list of agreed behavioural objectives for a language curriculum can founder on differences in 'values and interpretation underlying superficial agreement on objectives' (Taylor and Richards 1979). Another problem is the tendency to concentrate too much on low-level objectives which can be most readily specified, although it does not follow that 'trivial outcomes need be emphasised at the expense of those of greater importance' (Nicholls and Nicholls, 1978:34).

Davies (1976:72), while rehearsing the arguments against behavioural objectives, suggests that the strongest argument for them

> lies in the power of the methodology as a means of exposing underlying assumptions. Once objectives for a learning experience have been isolated and defined, it is possible to go beyond them to the very value structure that they apparently reflect. Objectives are the consequences of values, and it is these values – rather than the objectives themselves – that need to be revealed when previously they may have been concealed.

Indeed, Davies sees attempts to specify objectives as

> a very useful stimulus to clear thinking as well as a means of allowing teachers to communicate with each other in a relatively precise and unambiguous manner. They force you to come down to earth, and start thinking in specific terms rather than in terms of vague hopes and aspirations.

The last point should be kept in mind when we come to discuss the issues involved in the management of curriculum innovation because of the importance of an unambiguous understanding of both the current position and future intentions. To the extent that objectives can act as a means of focusing thought and discussion, they will serve a very useful purpose.

Although, as we have seen, behavioural objectives are open to criticisms on many grounds, 'even two of the foremost critics ... accept that behavioural objectives have a part to play, though necessarily a limited one' (Taylor and Richards 1979:71). One of these critics, Eisner (1972), distinguishes three types of objective that can be used in curriculum design: *instructional* objectives, which can be expressed in behavioural terms; *expressive* objectives, which are concerned with personal responses and are not susceptible to behavioural specification; and finally, what he calls *Type III* objectives, which specify problems, the solutions to which are left to pupil initiative and justification.

Another critic of behavioural objectives, Stenhouse (1975), suggests that education has four aims: *induction* into knowledge; *initiation* into social norms and values; *training*; and *instruction*. Though repudiating the role of objectives, he acknowledges that behavioural objectives may appropriately be used to specify the goals of training and instruction, but not of induction and initiation. To Stenhouse, 'knowledge is not something to regurgitate, but something to think with' (Taylor and Richards 1979:72) and he believes that education is concerned with speculation about ideas and not mastery of behaviour. Improvements in education, he believes, come from raising teachers' awareness and self-criticism rather than from specifying objectives with precision. Instead of objectives, Stenhouse proposes principles for the selection of content, the development of a teaching strategy, making decisions about sequence, and so on.

The distinction Stenhouse raises between training and education, between mastery and speculation, is at the heart of much argument about the aims of teaching. Tumposky's objections to behavioural objectives in language teaching mirror the values implicit in this distinction: training is concerned with the inculcation of fixed forms of behaviour, education with the development of unexpected outcomes. Clearly, there is an ideological divide between those who regard education as training the student in pre-specified behaviours and those who see it as liberating the student to deal effectively, autonomously and creatively with the novel and unplanned.

We may be unwise, however, to join Stenhouse and Tumposky in repudiating so completely the role of objectives, since it can be argued that 'in teaching we are not satisfied merely with fostering or seeking to effect learning, we quite properly look for evidence that learning is occurring . . . It is not necessary to suggest that "mastery" is our goal to insist that qualities of performance are of vital concern to us in education' (Skilbeck 1984:223). Skilbeck goes on to say that

> The implausibility of predicting detailed performances (when there can be unexpected outcomes) and the inherent freedom of the learner in an educative process are not reasons for supposing that we cannot or must not try to specify performance objectives. We can agree that student performances (a) cannot or should not be prespecified in detail and (b) are a part but not the whole of what we mean by education, but why should either of these considerations be inconsistent with stating objectives as the directions in which we are trying to guide student learnings?

In fact, as we are about to see, a process approach to curriculum which focuses on means as ends is not directionless, while the specification of aims is not necessarily inconsistent with a focus on the processes of learning or on the procedures involved in developing cognitive skills. Skilbeck's argument may serve as a reminder to the language curriculum designer that, although communicative competence involves being able to use language creatively and in unpredictable ways, this ability itself constitutes an aim which suggests a criterion against which to measure learner performance. Thus, in designing language curricula, there will certainly be a place for aims, the nature of which will depend on the level of behaviour concerned. However, we must not forget that such aims are, as Skilbeck observes, 'a part but not the whole' of what is meant by communicative competence.

The Process Approach

In chapter 1, I suggested that one approach to curriculum was analogous to working out the plan of a dwelling from the viewpoint of the inhabitants. In his survey of how teachers plan their courses, Taylor (1970) discovered that the steps followed by teachers were rather like this model of curriculum, and much less like the model proposed by rational planners. The contrast is summarized in the diagrams below.

Rational Planners

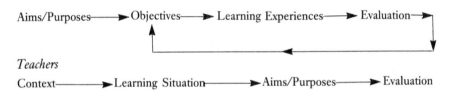

Teachers

As we have seen, in a rational planning model aims and objectives are defined first, and content, learning experiences and evaluation follow in linear sequence, although as Wiseman and Pidgeon (1970) and Davies (1976) point out, the entry point can, in fact, be at any stage in the model, which is recursive rather than strictly linear

Teachers, in actual practice, tend to begin with the context in which they are working (i.e. the dwelling), taking due regard of sequence, time and methods. In other words, practical concerns figure prominently in their approach to curriculum design. Next, they consider the pupils' interests and the selection of subject-matter. It is only after such practical factors have been considered that teachers attend to aims and purposes, which come third and not first in the sequence of planning stages. As Kelly (1977:34) says, taking his cue from Sockett (1976),

> It may be that they have thus come to realize, long before the curriculum theorists got onto it, that to state one's objectives in advance in terms of intended behavioural changes and to stick rigidly to such a plan or programme is to fail to take account of the complexities of the

curriculum and of the importance of the individual context in which every act of teaching occurs.

A process approach to curriculum turns out to be closer to the practice of the teachers in Taylor's survey than to the proposals of some curriculum theorists. What is also notable is that a process approach allows for the personal and professional autonomy of teachers and the exericse of their judgement on the spot. A process approach to curriculum is firmly based on the school and the classroom. Finally, a process-based curriculum is viewed in terms of procedures rather than in terms of content, behavioural outcomes or measurable products. It is, in short, concerned with the process rather than the product of learning. In this respect, it is more like the second view of curriculum which I proposed in chapter 1, namely curriculum/house = construction system.

This is not to say that a process curriculum is without aims or direction. Instead of tightly formulated short-term objectives, general principles are defined and it is these overall, looser aims which provide direction to the curriculum. Implicit in this is a view of education being concerned with intrinsically valuable content, the development of understanding rather than the acquisition of knowledge, and the promotion of individual autonomy and a capacity for continuing learning.

The psychological basis for the process curriculum may be found in the work of Piaget (1967) and Bruner (1960). Piaget's concern was to explore the growth of intelligence and to establish how a child is able to learn, and he advocated adapting teaching methods to the ways in which the child's thought processes develop. Educational applications of Piaget's work are found in active learning and the enquiry and discovery techniques common in primary school education. A second important principle is that active experience cannot be displaced by verbalizing about experience, while a third is the importance of social interaction in children's cognitive development.

Bruner, too, sees learning in terms of cognitive growth. It is through learning that children master their environment. Learning first to cope with the world through action, children proceed to images and pictures and eventually to symbolic means, usually through the use of language. Like Piaget, Bruner emphasizes the importance of experience for cognitive growth; the task of the teacher is to provide stimulation and to convert what is known into a form that can be mastered by children.

Bruner's own application of his theories to education were in MACOS (*Man – A Course of Study*), described in Bruner (1960). In this course 'the broad aims of the project centre around the processes of learning rather than the products, and include teaching children the skills of enquiry; helping them to develop methods of observation and research; encouraging them to reflect on their own experiences; and helping them to use original source material and to evaluate it critically' (Kelly 1977:80). The speculative nature of knowledge which is a feature of Bruner's approach is also found in the

Humanities Curriculum Project, associated with Lawrence Stenhouse who, rejecting an objectives model, claimed that a process model is more appropriate in areas of the curriculum which centre on knowledge and understanding as opposed to training.

In the Humanities Curriculum Project, the emphasis was on defining acceptable principles of procedure for dealing with such issues as protecting divergence of opinion within the group, with developing critical standards by which evidence can be appraised, and with extending the range of relevant views and perspectives accessible to the group (Stenhouse 1970). A series of themes was chosen: war, poverty, education, relations between the sexes. These formed the basis for discussions involving the pupils, with the teacher as neutral chairman. The novelty, for both pupils and teachers, was that there were no preordained outcomes, since the ideas and procedures were generated by the pupils themselves. What was important was that the group would develop ways of handling discussion and divergence of opinion and extending the range of relevant views. In other words, the emphasis was on the processes involved and not in reaching a predetermined goal.

Taylor and Richards note that Stenhouse's version of the process curriculum has yet to be subject to much evaluation, although certain difficulties have been revealed in application, notably the demands it makes on teacher competence. Furthermore, assessment is difficult given the absence of predetermined outcomes. Finally, although Stenhouse denies that it is a means–ends approach, Hirst (1975) argues that it is still concerned with ends, even if they are not specified in a behavioural manner.

From the viewpoint of language curriculum, the process model offers an important alternative to an objectives model at a time when applied linguistic theory and research is devoting more attention to the processes of language learning (Faerch and Kasper 1983); to the strategies and techniques used by language learners (Cohen 1984, Cohen and Hosenfeld 1981, Naiman et al. 1978, Wenden 1986); and to the effects on interaction and learning which result from varying forms of classroom organization and activities (Bygate 1987, Doughty and Pica 1986, Gass and Varonis 1985, Long 1975, Long and Porter 1985).

There is a significant coincidence of viewpoint between a process approach to education and the views of such applied linguistics as Widdowson (1983) and Brumfit (1984c) on the open-endedness and creativity of language. Language use cannot be predicted in advance and the prepackaging of language, implicit in an objectives model, is similarly rejected in a process curriculum. Likewise, the distinction between training and education, which Widdowson (1983) equates with the dichotomy between ESP and EGP, leads to a consideration of preparing learners for 'the purposes to which learning will be put *after* the end of the course' (Widdowson 1983:7) – in other words, to unexpected and unpredictable outcomes.

The influence of progressivism and of a process curriculum model is most conspicuous in the proposals of Breen and Candlin (1984), to be discussed in chapter 7. It is no coincidence that their proposals for language syllabuses should so closely resemble the model summarized above, both in ideology and terminology. And it is no coincidence that such a radical approach to the design of language programmes will upset a means–ends view of the language teaching process. In fact, what we have in this product–process dichotomy is a tension which must always exist in language teaching between the 'unavoidable' means–ends view noted by Stern and the unpredictability of language use, stressed by Widdowson; between the linear, graded organization of content, which is such a strong tradition in language teaching, and the non-linear, organic growth picture of language learning, which is emerging from second language acquisition (SLA) research.

The Situational Model

Having reviewed two curriculum models whose ideological basis has been traced to reconstructionism on the one hand and progressivism on the other, we now come to the third model, which stands apart from the other two by using the context in which curriculum planning is to take place as the starting point. In this respect, it might be best called a curriculum *renewal* model since, unlike reconstructionism or progressivism, it begins by acknowledging existing practices. It does not begin with the assumption that curriculum proposals are to be written on a blank slate – or even that what is already on the slate should be obliterated. In terms of the analogies suggested in chapter 1, the model we are about to discuss adopts the third perspective of curriculum/house = dwelling.

The situational model proposed by Skilbeck (1984a) has its basis in cultural analysis and begins with an analysis and appraisal of the school situation itself. Such an appraisal is, in any case, an important starting point, since one of Skilbeck's major concerns is with school-based curriculum development, which he defines as 'the planning, design, implementation and evaluation of a programme of students' learnings by the educational institution of which these students are members' (Skilbeck 1984:2). He goes on to say that an educational institution 'should be a living educational environment, defined and defining itself as a distinct entity and characterized by a definite pattern of relationships, aims, values, norms, procedures and roles.' Skilbeck points out that curriculum development will be something internal to the institution, not imposed from without, but at the same time 'the curriculum should not be parochially conceived' because the institution is part of a network of relationships which include stake-holders other than members of the school itself. Among these stake-holders are the students, and Skilbeck advocates participatory decision-making in the curriculum which will involve the students 'in determining the pattern of experiences they are to undergo'.

In advocating school-based curriculum development Skillbeck is well aware of the effects of controls which are extrinsic to the school and he notes that neither the independent initiatives of the school nor those larger external forces in the curriculum are by themselves sufficient for achieving the systemwide kinds of changes that are needed. Imposed change from without does not work, because it is not adequately thought out, or it is not understood, or resources are not available to carry it through, or because it is actively resisted. Within-institution change is, by its nature, situation specific, often piecemeal, incomplete, of mediocre quality and so on. Each process requires the other, in a well worked out philosophy and programme of developments. (Skilbeck 1984a:5)

Here, Skilbeck raises issues which we shall not meet again when we come to consider the management of curriculum innovation.

Skilbeck's summary of his situational model for school-based curriculum development is set out in the diagram below (from 1984a:231).

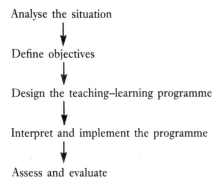

Analyse the situation

↓

Define objectives

↓

Design the teaching–learning programme

↓

Interpret and implement the programme

↓

Assess and evaluate

Skilbeck acknowledges that 'such a diagrammatic representation of the process of curriculum making must simplify and risk distortion by its very brevity and apparent orderliness.' He says, 'Let us be ready to take concurrently or even in reverse what may suggest themselves to the orderly-minded as items for step-by-step progression,' thus echoing the point made by Wiseman and Pidgeon (1970) on the overlapping of activities which will occur in any truly effective developmental programme.

The usefulness of such a sequence of actions, Skilbeck suggests, lies in three things:

First, we may use it to provide a resume, a kind of prospectus of tasks to be accomplished. Second, it can be the basis of agreed action and hence help in reducing arbitrary or authoritarian decisions, a matter of some importance when hierarchies may feel challenged by unstructured reviews and evaluations. Third, it will be useful if it encompasses, in simplified ways, crucial and productive kinds of action. . . . Fourth, what is proposed is useful if it helps in the presentation and communication to interested parties of what is planned and is happening in the curriculum. (Skilbeck 1984a: 232)

Skilbeck deals with each element in more detail, as follows (1984a: 234–6).

1   Analyse the Situation

The question to be asked here is, 'What are our curriculum problems and needs and how can we meet them?' In order to answer this question, Skilbeck proposes a set of key questions to ask and answer in a situational analysis. These are set out below.

Within the School

1   What is the existing curriculum including the school rules, rituals and value sets?
2   What is the students' experience of (performance in, perception of) the curriculum?
3   What is the curriculum context within the school (i.e. social climate, patterns of conduct, etc.)?
4   What are the strengths and capabilities of the staff?
5   What are the available resources for the curriculum?

Wider Environment

1   What kind of neighbourhood, community, society are we serving?
2   What are the key educational policies to which we should be responding (Local Education Authority, national)?
3   What kinds of resource/support can we draw upon (LEAs, teachers' centres, community, teacher education, research, etc.)?
4   What are some of the changes, proposals and developments in curriculum practice and ideas that could be useful for us here?

2   Define Objectives

Objectives are not a once-for-all matter which occurs at an initial stage of a planning model, and the question of objectives will already arise during the situational analysis. Skilbeck makes four points about objectives:

1   Objectives in a curriculum should be stated as desirable student learnings and as actions to be undertaken by teachers and those associated with them to affect, influence or bring about these learnings; they need to be clear, concise and to be capable of being understood by the learners themselves.
2   Objectives are directional and dynamic in that they must be reviewed,

modified and if necessary reformulated progressively as the teaching–learning process unfolds.

3   Objectives gain their legitimacy by being related systematically both to general aims and to the practicalities of teaching and learning, and by the manner of their construction and adoption in the school. . . . it is desirable to try to show that the objectives have a rational and legitimate basis.

4   There are several types of objectives: broad and general–specific; long and short-term; higher order cognitive – lower order informational; subject-specific – global; and so on. Working groups . . . .need to select and plot types of objectives.

5   The construction of curriculum objectives has to be participatory, involving students as well as teachers, parents and community as well as professionals.

3   Design the Teaching–Learning Programme

The general procedural principles advocated by Skilbeck refer to:

1   fundamental orientation of the curriculum, as for example areas of experience in a core curriculum, or academic specialization or leisure interests in the electives part of the curriculum;
2   the groupings and combinations of subject matter;
3   the groupings of students, for example mixed ability, or special interest groups;
4   the relationship of learning in the different subject areas to the overall objectives of the curriculum;
5   the scope, sequence and structure of teaching content;
6   space, resources, materials, equipment;
7   the proposed methods of teaching and learning;
8   staffing needs and allocations;
9   timetabling and scheduling.

Skilbeck lays stress on the school's autonomy in making curriculum decisions about defining objectives and interpreting and implementing programmes. It is worth noting, given the items enumerated above, that Skilbeck's proposals in many ways match those practices which are characteristic of the successful business enterprise (Goldsmith and Clutterbuck 1984), among which are clarity of and agreement on long term objectives and the basic philosophy of a company or organization.

4   Interpret and Implement the Programme

The interpretation and implementation stage is both crucial and problematic as it depends on 'achieving what was envisaged, coping with uncertainty, confusion, resistance perhaps or indifference, being flexible enough to adjust and modify according to circumstances'. (Skilbeck 1984a:237) Furthermore, 'Problems of communication, shared values and expectations, of differences of interpretation, of inadequate implementation, frequently arise.' Skilbeck suggests that school-based curriculum development, in which the people interpreting and implementing it also influenced its design, should be more effective because 'the curriculum is not an accidental extra; but is of the essence of the institution.' However, successful implementation cannot be taken for granted – and this takes us to Skilbeck's fifth step.

5   Assess and Evaluate

Skilbeck distinguishes between assessment and evaluation in the following terms: 'assessment in the curriculum is a process of determining and passing judgements on students' learning potential and performance; evaluation means assembling evidence on and making judgements about the curriculum including the processes of planning, designing and implementing it' (p. 238). From a curriculum viewpoint, continuous rather than summative assessment is indispensible, which means a change in evaluation aims and procedures (see Parlett and Hamilton 1972), with evaluation forming part of planning as a cyclical process. In fact, evaluation has come to occupy a central place in much recent discussion on curriculum development generally and language teaching specifically (e.g. Alderson 1985). As such, it is an issue to which we shall return in chapter 9.

The Situational Model and Language Curriculum Design

The situational framework can embrace both objectives and process models, depending on which aspects of the curriculum are being designed. Skilbeck, in fact, doesn't see the objectives and process models as being in conflict and, as is clear from the steps enumerated in his model, the definition and redefinition of aims is crucial. One appeal of this model is that it involves an understanding of the situation as it currently exists, which requires gathering information from which a definition of a problem may emerge. Another appeal of this model is that the development procedures which are advocated take account of the problems involved in implementing curriculum innovation so that, far from being divorced from the arena in which change will occur, the situational model takes this as its starting point. Or, to put it another way, we begin with the dwelling and the way it is used and perceived by its inhabitants.

The rationality of Skilbeck's framework encourages a moderately systematic approach to curriculum development, and it provides a useful scheme within which to plan language curricula and, indeed, in some ways it serves to systematize existing practice in language curriculum development. Furthermore, as language curriculum development has tended to be closely focused on questions of content and objectives, the breadth of Skilbeck's model may serve to open up the field in a way that should be enormously helpful. Finally, his emphasis on curriculum development as school-based matches the rise of local as opposed to national initiatives in language curricula, and thus it can inform and guide an existing trend. In short, it seems to me to offer both a practical as well as a rational basis for dealing with the complexities involved in language curriculum renewal, and it integrates well with the approach to the management of curriculum innovation to be outlined in chapters 8 and 9.

Conclusion

As we have seen, there is a wide range of options when it comes to curriculum planning and development. Any approach to curriculum is, as I have suggested, influenced by the value system and attitudes of those involved. No curriculum choice or decision is value-neutral.

These values are expressed in the different ideologies and models of curriculum which have been described in this chapter. Both reconstructionism and a means–ends model have the attraction of rationality and clarity. Both are essentially a plan of the building yet to be constructed. The association of behavioural objectives with this model is not entirely fortuitous, given the concern with pre-specifying outcomes. Accepting that a means–ends view is difficult to avoid in language teaching, the appeal of this model of teaching is obvious.

The process approach and progressivism, with their focus on exploration and growth, also have an appeal, given the fact that language learning involves growth and development. However, there is a conflict of interests (and values) between means–ends and process models. The process model tends to substitute only a very vague idea of what kind of house we might be building, and instead focuses on the procedures whereby the dwelling may be constructed.

The situational model, which attempts to provide a plan of the house from the occupants' and users' viewpoint, offers a third approach. The flexibility of this model is one of its attractions. It also provides a comprehensible introduction to the process of curriculum renewal, and it does not rule out the use of rational planning and an objectives models if this is appropriate. Aspects of the process model are not excluded, either, since concern with how learning takes place well as with content and outcomes is an important aspect of curriculum renewal within the situational model.

Suggested Reading

General

There is an extensive curriculum literature, including specialist journals. The review in this chapter is no more than an introduction, but it helps establish a broad context into which different aproaches to and proposals for language curriculum design may be placed.

Value Systems

Discussions of the value systems underlying the different curriculum approaches dealt with in this chapter appear in Davies (1976), *Objectives in Curriculum Design*, and Skilbeck (1976), 'Three educational ideologies', which is also used by Clark (1987).

For activities on value clarification, see Simon, Howe and Kirschenbaum (1978), *Values Clarification: a handbook of practical strategies for teachers and students*. An enlightening account of some of the influences on experiential learning, one of the cornerstones of progressivism, may be found in *Experiential Learning* by Kolb (1984).

Curriculum

Often cited, though now out of print, is Taba (1962), whose *Curriculum Development: Theory and Practice* established a foundation upon which much subsequent curriculum thinking and practice has been based. Tyler's *Basic Principles* (1949) is available in a 1973 reprint.

For general introductions to curriculum studies, see Barrow (1984), *Giving Teaching Back to Teachers*, Kelly (1977), *The Curriculum Theory and Practice*, Nicholls and Nicholls (1978), *Developing a Curriculum: a Practical Guide*, Sockett (1976) *Designing the Curriculum*, and Taylor and Richards (1979), *An Introduction to Curriculum Studies*.

A review of curriculum development within the UK context, which includes an historical survey by Stenhouse, is to be found in Galton and Moon (1983), *Changing Schools... Changing Curriculum*. Among the papers assembled in this collection are several on evaluation.

Behavioural Objectives

Barrow's title indicates the trend of his wide-ranging discussion, which includes a consideration of behavioural objectives, also dealt with by Kelly, as well as by Rowntree (1982) *Education Technology in Curriculum Development* in a very clear and extensive account. A classic statement on behavioural objectives appears in Gagne (1975), *Essentials of Learning for Instruction*. Meanwhile, Raths (1971) proposes teaching *without* specific objectives, Findley and Nathan (1980) consider them essential for ELT, and Tumposky (1984) casts serious doubt on them. There is a discussion on graded objectives by Rowell in British Council (1984).

In an encyclopaedic collection of papers on curriculum, edited by Golby, Greenwald and West (1975) for the Open University, there is McDonald Ross's much cited critique of objectives, together with discussions on objectives by Eisner and Davies, as well as Cronback on course improvement through evaluation.

The Process Curriculum

The late Lawrence Stenhouse is one of the most stimulating and influential figures in curriculum studies, and there is a substantial philosophical basis to his theories, while the significance he attaches to curriculum development and teacher professionalism has important implications for all teachers. See *An Introduction to Curriculum Research and Development* (1975). Rudduck and Hopkins have edited a posthumous collection of Stenhouse's writings, *Research as a Basis for Teaching* (1985).

The Situational Curriculum

Skilbeck's situational model and his proposals for school-based curriculum development are lucidly outlined in Skilbeck (1984a), *School-based Curriculum Development*, which also contains a clear and helpful survey of the main approaches to curriculum development.

Curriculum and ELT

Stern is one of the few writers in the field of language pedagogy to see a relationship between language teaching and curriculum studies, which he discusses in his *Fundamental Concepts of Language Teaching* (1983) Part 6, 'Concepts of language teaching'. Strevens also adopts a curriculum-based perspective in his *New Orientations in the Teaching of English* (1977) and in a paper on teacher training and the curriculum in British Council (1982). Another important contributor to the evolution of such thought in ELT is Brumfit. See his paper, 'Key issues in curriculum and syllabus design for ELT' in British Council (1984a). For further reading, see also Dubin and Olshtain (1986), Ullman (1982), Wilson (1976) and White (1983).

Psychology and Education

Entwhistle (1987), in *Understanding Classroom Learning*, opens with a helpful perspective on psychological theories which have influenced educational thought and practice, ranging from behavioural objectives to process curricula, while the rest of the book provides insights for anyone concerned with learning in classroom settings.

4 Language Syllabus Design: Two Types

Introduction

In chapter 3, three models of curriculum were described and a connection suggested between these models and ideology: a rational-planning model tends to be associated with reconstructionism while a process model is linked to progressivism. A similar set of distinctions and associations occur in the types of syllabus reviewed in this and the following two chapters, in which, as with the classification of curriculum models, two basic types will be proposed, each reflecting quite different orientations to language, learning and teaching.

Language Syllabuses: Types A and B

The two main approaches to curriculum and the underlying value systems discussed in chapter 3 are reflected in two approaches to language syllabuses, which I call Type A and Type B. I have summarized what I consider to be the salient characteristics of these two types, drawing upon the curriculum classifications suggested by Davies (1976).

Type A What is to be learnt?	*Type B* How is it to be learnt?
Interventionist	
External to the learner	Internal to the learner
Other directed	Inner directed or self fulfilling
Determined by authority	Negotiated between learners and teachers
Teacher as decision-maker	Learner and teacher as joint decision makers
Content = what the subject is to the expert	Content = what the subject is to the learner
Content = a gift to the learner from the teacher or knower	Content = what the learner brings and wants
Objectives defined in advance	Objectives described afterwards

Type A What is to be learnt? Subject emphasis	*Type B* How is it to be learnt? Process emphasis
Assessment by achievement or by mastery	Assessment in relationship to learners' criteria of success
Doing things to the learner	Doing things for or with the learner

Certain points emerge from this summary. An approach which emphasizes process, while giving attention to socially desirable behaviour and the formation of approved attitudes, may lose sight of culturally valuable content, while an approach which stresses the acquisition of approved content may be orientating learners towards conformity rather than divergence and independence. In one case, the approach tends towards intervention in the learning process through the pre-selection, specification and presentation of content, while in the other, the approach eschews such intervention by an authority, such as the teacher. In either case, the significance of different value systems will be obvious.

In relation to language teaching syllabuses, these two types can be summarized in terms of the distinction between an interventionist approach which gives priority to the pre-specification of linguistic or other content or skill objectives on the one hand, and a non-interventionist, experiential, 'natural growth' approach on the other, 'which aims to immerse the learners in real-life communication without any artificial preselection or arrangement of items' (Allen 1984:65).

Discussing this distinction, Prabhu (1987:89) notes that the syllabus as an 'illuminative construct' 'is concerned with the product of learning: it is a specification of what is to be learnt, in terms of a conceptual model which aims to provide an understanding (hence the term "illuminative") of the nature of the subject area concerned.'

He contrasts such content syllabuses with the syllabus as an 'operational construct', in which

> The syllabus is a form of support for the teaching activity that is planned in the classroom and a form of guidance in the construction of appropriate teaching materials. It is concerned, from this point of view, with what is to be done in the classroom, not necessarily with what is perceived to be taught or learnt thereby; its role is essentially to make it possible for one teacher to draw on the experience of another (p. 86).

The list of tasks which a teacher had found 'feasible and satifying' would constitute what he terms a 'procedural syllabus' 'with the intention of indicating that it was only a specification of what *might* be done in the classroom – that is to say, only an operational construct.'

Whereas, in Prabhu's terms, a 'content' syllabus 'may be said to be an illuminative construct which is also used as an operational construct ... a procedural syllabus is an operational construct which is deliberately different from illuminative constructs' and he contrasts the control of learning through understanding, which is the basis of a content syllabus, with the development of 'organic growth' through the provision of favourable conditions, which is the starting point for a procedural syllabus.

In the content syllabus, knowledge of the subject assumes an important role, and Ellis (1984) suggests that what I have termed a Type A syllabus contributes directly to *analytic* L2 knowledge, which is the kind of knowledge involved in knowing *about* the language – its parts, rules and organization. It is this kind of knowledge which, he suggests, is not available for 'unplanned discourse', that is, the kind of language use which occurs in spontaneous communication where there is no time or opportunity to prepare what will be said. In comparison, a Type B syllabus contributes to what Ellis has called 'primary processes', which automatize existing non-analytic knowledge. This type of knowledge is available for 'unplanned discourse'.

The approach found in Type A can, in fact, give rise to syllabuses which may appear to have little in common simply because of differences in *content*. A structural syllabus, for instance, will specify rather different content to that in a functional syllabus, which is defined in terms of categories of communicative language use, while a skills syllabus will list those skills which are characteristic of the proficient language user. Whether the focus is form, function or skills, the basis for such syllabuses remains essentially the same, however: it is on objectives to be achieved, content to be learned. Indeed, any such syllabus will be based on lists of items to be learnt, whether these are grammatical structures, categories of communication function, topics, themes or communicative and cognitive skills. Such lists may run to many items, as a glance at the Council of Europe's Threshold Level or Munby's (1979) list of 'Language Skills' will reveal.

By contrast, in a Type B syllabus, content is subordinate to learning process and pedagogical procedure. The concern of the syllabus designer is with 'How' rather than 'What' and the basis for such a syllabus will be

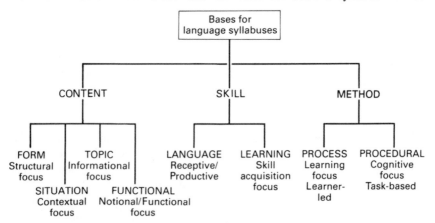

Figure 4.1 Bases for language syllabus design

psychological and pedagogical rather than linguistic, the view being either a learner-centred or a learning-centred one. Accordingly, in such a syllabus, the selection and grading of language content will be 'roughly tuned' in terms of selection and difficulty, and there is little or no attempt to intervene in the language learning process through the selection, ordering and presentation of content by the syllabus designer or teacher. Such syllabuses call for the same kind of radical break with tradition as Stenhouse's process curriculum, as we shall see.

We shall begin a review of different syllabus types (see figure 4.1) by looking at content syllabuses. There are a number of reasons why it is important to be familiar with such syllabuses. Firstly, they represent the conventions upon which the most widely used language course books have been based and, indeed, the most popular newly published materials continue to draw upon this tradition. The reluctance to break away from established tradition reflects, no doubt, widespread teacher and student preferences and expectations on the one hand and the caution and realism of publishers on the other. Secondly, it is unwise to dispense with an existing tradition without first becoming familiar with it. Thirdly, it is as yet too early to accept unhestitatingly the proposals of process syllabus designers in the absence of any substantial evaluation of the approach they advocate.

The Type A Tradition

The introduction of a functional–notional language syllabus in the 1970s provided a powerful and useful new set of categories for the syllabus designer. It was motivated by a reconstructionist concern with bringing about social changes through developing international understanding via functionally based language learning goals; however, this innovation was not, in one sense, as radical as it seemed at the time. Both structural and functional syllabuses were, in their time, motivated by similar considerations and both took *content* as their basis, even though the definitions and details are different in each case. Furthermore, the selection of content depends on the priorities of the syllabus designer so that a structurally based syllabus will tend to give more importance to the artful selection and organization of structures. A functionally based syllabus however, will take communicative functions as the leading element, with structural organization being largely determined by the order already established by the functional sequence. In practice, syllabus designers will try to balance structural control and functional requirements, and today a typical Type A syllabus will consist of a combination of both, as we shall see in the discussion of proportional and hybrid syllabuses in chapter 6.

Discussing the question of organizing language content, Allen (1984:66) says 'It seems that some form of grading, either implicit or explicit, is a universal requirement in language teaching.' Grading – or 'gradation' as Mackey prefers to call it – answers the questions: What goes with what? and,

What comes before what? (Mackey 1965:204). If language is a system, argues Mackey, then gradation matters a great deal: 'It means that we cannot start anywhere or with anything; for in a system one thing fits into another, one thing goes with another, and one thing depends on another.'

Halliday, McIntosh and Strevens (1964) distinguish between two different aspects of grading, to revert to the more widely used term. The division of a course into time segments they call *staging*. This is related to the number and frequency of lessons and the intensity of teaching. By *sequencing*, they mean deciding the order in which the items should be taught. Staging is important in deciding how much of any given item to teach during the time available, while sequencing is concerned with decisions about which elements may have to be taught before others are introduced. In spite of the wealth of examples of grading in syllabuses, 'there exist very few statements of principles for the guidance of others who wish to do likewise' (Halliday, McIntosh and Strevens 1964:210) and, 'In fact, for an intelligent approach to sequencing it is almost essential to have practical teaching experience with the pupils for whom a given course is intended, because here above all the teaching programme must be sensitive to the precise needs of the pupils, both in general terms and in close detail.' Although there is, as Halliday, McIntosh and Strevens have noted, a surprising lack of published guidance on syllabus grading, a number of criteria have been proposed and have become accepted through use, and these are listed below according to focus: structural, topic or functional.

Criteria for Selection and Grading

STRUCTURAL	TOPIC	FUNCTIONAL
frequency	interest and affectivity	need: immediate and long term
coverage	need	utility
availability	pedagogic merit	coverage/ generalizability
simplicity/complexity	relevance	interest
learnability/teachability	depth of treatment	complexity of form
combinability	practicality	
contrast	utility	
productiveness/ generalizability		
natural order of acquisition		

Selection and Grading

The selection and grading of vocabulary provides a good starting point for looking at the criteria to be used, since these have been subject to much study and discussion over the years. I have already noted, for instance, Michael West's concern with vocabulary selection, and many of the principles he advocated remain in use.

The first of these is *frequency*, the total number of occurrences of an item in a given corpus of language. Frequency counts are made by taking samples of the sort of material which the learners are likely to read or hear, and counting the items that occur most often, and arranging them in descending order according to their overall frequency. Obviously, the larger the sample, the more reliable the frequency figures are likely to be and the best known published frequency counts are based on a very large corpus (e.g. *The General Service List*).

There are, however, difficulties with taking frequency as a basis for selection and grading. The most frequent words are few in number. Indeed, the 1,000 most frequently used words make up about 95 per cent of the total number of words in any randomly chosen corpus of language. Another problem arises when we consider what we mean by a 'word', since one and the same written form may have many different grammatical functions. Furthermore, high frequency words typically have a multitude of meanings, so some decision has to be made about which particular meaning of a given item is the most frequent.

Related to the multiple meanings of a word is the criterion of *coverage*, which refers to the number of things which can be expressed by any given item. If there are two more possible words of similar frequency, the one which covers the greatest number of uses is preferable. For instance, a verb like *go* will have a far wider coverage of meaning than other verbs of movement, such as *travel*, *move* or *walk*. Coverage is an important criterion because it enables the selection of a restricted quantity of vocabulary with a wide range of meanings. It is this principle which is behind Ogden and Richards's *Basic English*, although, taken to extremes, the 'system will break down because the language that it produces will conflict with what people actually say' (Howatt 1965:10).

Range, a third criterion, is also complementary to that of frequency. Words found in a large number of texts within a given corpus have a high range. By contrast, some words may occur in only a limited number of texts within the total corpus, so that their range would be restricted. Obviously, both frequency and range need to be taken into account in vocabulary selection to ensure that items selected are representative of a wide sample and so that high frequency is not merely the fortuitous result of high occurrence in a restricted area of the total corpus.

Another criterion for selection is *availability* or *disponibilité*. This term refers to the readiness with which a word is remembered and used by native speakers in certain situations. For instance, *salt* and *pepper* are equally available to an English speaker, even though they rank very differently in terms of frequency. Taking availability into consideration is important because it draws upon the native speaker's knowledge in a way which may not be revealed by other selection criteria.

The final criterion Mackey (1965) lists applies to both selection and grading: *learnability*. He gives five factors which are taken into account when considering the learnability of a word, although similar considerations apply to structures as well. The first factor is that of similarity of the L2 word to its L1 equivalent, e.g. French *classe* and English *class* or German *schule* and English *school*. Secondly, there is the demonstrability of a word, an important factor in its teachability. In general, concrete terms are easier to demonstrate (and easier to understand) than abstract ones. For instance, a concrete noun like *car* is easier to learn than an abstract noun like *transport*. Thirdly, we have brevity, on the assumption that long words are more difficult to learn than short ones. According to this measure, *car* should be an easier word to learn than *automobile*. A fourth factor is that of regularity of form, e.g. a new verb with a regular past tense will be easier to learn than a new verb with an irregular form. Finally, there is the learning load represented by a new word. Some items will be easy to learn because one or more components are known already. Mackey gives as an example the word *handbag*. If both elements are already known separately, the effort required to learn the new word will be low. Similarly, if some constituents of a new structure are already known, the learnability of the new structure should be increased.

Mackey also points out what will have become obvious, that 'some items may be justified by one principle but not by another', and that some conflicts may have to be resolved so as to permit the selection of items for teaching.

There are two further criteria which Mackey does not mention, but which can taken into account. The first of these might be termed *opportunism*, by which is meant that some things are available within the immediate situation or are felt by the teacher to be useful to the students. Opportunist items include such pieces of classroom vocabulary as *blackboard* (or *whiteboard*), *pen*, *book* and *paper*, while *cassette recorder*, *video* and computer are likely to be part of the beginner's vocabulary requirements in the up-to-date language school. Few, if any, of these words are likely to be high in a frequency list, yet the need for them is obvious and their selection on opportunist grounds can be justified.

The second influence on selection and grading is that of *centres of interest*. These can range over a wide variety of areas, including such categories as transport, food, clothing, work, leisure, travelling and entertainment. Clearly, selection of vocabulary made on this basis should be informed by a survey of the students' interests – a notoriously difficult area of study and always a slippery basis for organizing a syllabus.

Structure Selection

The term 'structure' is generally used to include not just sentence structures or patterns, but other formal features of language at lower levels, notably the noun and verb phrase and inflections of both nouns and verbs. I will use the term in all of these senses.

The selection of structures could, in principle, be subject to the same criteria as those which have been outlined for the selection of vocabulary. However, frequency has not been applied to the selection of sentence patterns with the same enthusiasm as it has to the selection of vocabulary (but see Greens 1973 and Turano-Perkins 1979) though, as we shall see shortly, frequency counts have been applied to the selection of elements at a lower rank than the sentence or clause. Likewise, range and availability do not appear to have been used as a basis for structure selection. Coverage is relevant, however, since some structures allow for a wider range of substitution within a given pattern than others.

The final criterion, that of learnability and teachability, is relevant, since the selection of sentence patterns appears to be motivated by two principles. The first is that the simpler patterns are more easily learnt than the more complex ones. The idea that difficulty should influence selection and grading can be traced back to Palmer, but as McDonough (1980:311) points out,

> psychologists have objected that there is no reason to assume that linguistic complexity is itself a cause of learning difficulty because many constructions that appear complex in terms of counts of elements or underlying rules are used by native speakers with no hesitation or greater difficulty in execution than apparently simpler ones, in appropriate context. . . . This is not to deny that constructions do differ in complexity and learnability, rather it is to claim that the only measure of learnability is actual learning and not predictions derived from linguistic description alone.

The second principle involved in learnability and teachability is that the structures which are most different from those of the native language will be those that are most difficult to learn. However, several factors have contributed to the decline in the significance attached to contrastive analysis as a basis for organizing a language syllabus. As a linguistic procedure, contrastive analysis was married to behaviourist psychology as a learning theory with its emphasis on the systematic shaping of responses through the careful ordering of elements to be learnt. The rising awareness of universal developmental sequences in learning a second language has been linked to a cognitive view of learning in which the learners themselves may determine the optimally efficient order of acquisition. The effect of this has been that little systematic attention has been given to contrastive features in structural selection and grading, even though reference to such features has not been abandoned, as we shall see.

When we come to elements at a lower rank than the clause, we find that there are a number of frequency studies, including several on the verb phrase. One of the most substantial accounts is that of George (1963), whose findings are largely confirmed in the work of Duskova and Urbanova (1976) and Kramsky (1972). What George and his colleagues found was that the most frequently occurring tenses in their chosen English corpus were the Simple Past narrative, the Simple Present actual, the Simple Past actual and the Simple Present neutral. George, it should be noted, distinguishes between different tense uses under each main tense heading. 'Actual' refers to 'at this or that time', 'neutral' has no specific time reference, while 'narrative' refers to a sequence of events.

George's survey also took into account the occurrence of different verb forms: stem (or bare infinitive), stem + s (the inflected third person simple present form) and stem + ed (the preterite or past tense form). Out of every 1,000 verb-form occurrences, the following items accounted for 575.

Form	*Use*
stem	imperative
	after imperative 'don't'
stem/stem + s	simple present actual (referring to 'now')
	simple present neutral (without time reference)
stem + ed	simple past narrative
	simple past actual ('at that time')
	past participle of occurrence
	past participle of state

The verb survey also revealed that the Simple Present tense referring to 'now' was much more frequent than the Present Progressive by a ratio of twenty-four occurrences to one, a finding which confounds expectation and conflicts with the occurrence of each tense in many structural syllabuses. Turano-Perkins (1979), in a smaller investigation based on a corpus of TV interviews, confirmed the frequency of the Simple Present tense.

George and Kramsky also investigated the noun phrase, and discovered that the predominant type was simple, with little modification. These findings are confirmed by Quirk et al. (1972) who found that 'less than one-third of the 17,000 noun phrases in a sample are "complex"' within the range of complexity that they defined.

Regarding the implications of such findings, George claims that 'a great formal simplication is possible by selecting for inclusion into the early parts of a teaching program those verb forms which have a high frequency of occurrence in the ordinary use of the language' (George 1972:24). A similar principle can be applied to the noun phrase as well.

George was concerned with simplification of input to promote efficient and effective learning. The linguistic evidence that he draws upon – notably in the frequency studies – has largely been ignored, while his proposals for careful grading of input are out of step with more recent thinking. However, with the return to structural syllabuses as the basis for some popular coursebooks, the principles advocated by George may yet provide a useful basis for grading, though one course based on these principles has been less successful than some of its rivals, no doubt because the application of a set of principles in pure form yields materials which conflict with such factors as teacher and student expectations, interests and needs.

Grading: Structures

Kelly (1969) credits Palmer with laying the foundations for modern ideas on grading. Palmer (1917/1968:240) states that

> there will be found to be five bases of gradation – that is to say, five different considerations governing the choice of matter and the order of presenting it. These . . . are:
>
> (a) Frequency
> (b) Ergonic combination
> (c) Concreteness
> (d) Proportion
> (e) General expediency

Palmer's 'ergonic combination' is what we would now call structural combination, while proportion refers to the balance of receptive and active.

Palmer (1917/1968) also stressed the importance of grading 'in accordance with the capacities of the average student, to work from the easier toward the more difficult forms of exercise, to select the more used in preference to the less used ergons [structures], and to avoid abrupt transitions.' Thus, for Palmer, the prime consideration in grading was not linguistic, but rather the ability of the student to cope with the various aspects of the foreign language.

However, as we have already noted, judging ease and difficulty is no simple matter since this is a question of learning rather than linguistics. There are, indeed, quite different considerations in grading when the criteria are psychological rather than linguistic. This can be seen in applying the criteria of combinability, grouping and contrast, which are based on linguistic considerations.

'Combinability' means that simple structures can be combined to form longer and more complex structures. Given the hierarchical nature of linguistic structures, this is an obvious criterion for grading. A structure such as the simple noun phrase, e.g. determiner + noun, can be combined with a preposition to form a preposition group, and the preposition group can be combined with another noun phrase to form a post-modified noun phrase, thus:

the book
          on the table
the book on the table

Combining and rearranging clause elements can yield more varied and complex patterns, too.

X is V+ing	Maria is reading
Is X V+ing?	Is Maria reading?
Q word is X V+ing?	Why is Maria reading?

Clearly, combinability is an important factor in grading structures since building up more complex structures in later stages of a syllabus will depend on the combinability of structures introduced earlier.

Grouping, the second criterion, may bring together structures which are similar on one level but different on another. On linguistic grounds, such grouping may seem justified since substitutibility of elements within a structure is an important structural feature. Thus, within the pattern Subject + Verb + Complement, a number of substitutions are possible, e.g.

This is a car
This is an American car
This is American
This is big

George (1972:105) points out that such grouping can lead to what he calls 'cross association', which may be clearer from the example he provides:

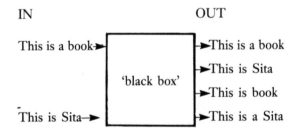

Where the student is already predisposed by the nature of the L1 to omit various structural features of English which, as George observes, are usually redundant in terms of communicating a message (thus the omission of the indefinite article before a singular count noun, such as 'box', does little to damage the message), grouping together such items as those given above may lead to the type of erroneous output which appears in his example. If such grouping together of structures does produce errors, then clearly, grading requires careful thought as well as the kind of knowledge which comes from observation of student output. The implication is that some elements may be better separated rather than grouped together in potentially confusing association.

Another criterion for grading is that of contrast. As noted in our historical review, contrast is an important feature of the structural linguist's method of identifying elements in a language. Furthermore, there are many contrasts within any language system, such as the contrasts found in plurality and singularity, past and present tenses, perfective and continuative aspects, and so on. Such contrasts are, like the grouping together of similar structures, essentially a linguistic phenomenon and although in terms of the linguistic system contrast may be necessary for full understanding of the elements so contrasted, from the psychological point of view the learner may be confused rather than aided by having items presented in contrast.

So, then, the picture which emerges on grading of structures is by no means clear-cut because there is obviously a conflict between linguistic and psychological considerations. Linguistic criteria must be augmented by psychological criteria based on evidence from students' output. It was the failure to take account of such evidence which, in part, led to disenchantment with structural syllabuses. However, it could be argued that such disenchantment was premature and that with more careful use of evidence from learners' output, structural grading based on psychological principles would have yielded better structural syllabuses. What is striking is that, in spite of the fact that until recently there was no empirical evidence to guide structural grading,

> syllabus designers seem to have a relatively homogeneous idea of the order of difficulty of various grammatical devices of simple English. Some kind of empirical validation of this, or empirical challenge, is required, because despite gradual replacement of structural criteria by communicational criteria of sequencing in recent textbooks, the presentation of grammatical constructions is still ordered according to intuitive ideas of relative difficulty. (McDonough 1980:318)

In fact, empirical evidence which could challenge intuitive ideas of relative difficulty is now available in the findings of SLA research. An early attempt to work out the implications of such findings for organizing language syllabuses was made by Valdman (1974), who discussed whether the process of pidginization could be used as a basis for grading teaching material. The result would be a 'little language' which could be exploited from the earliest stages for actual communication. The problem would be, of course, that this little language would contain stigmatized forms, which could become fossilized. To avoid this, Valdman proposed the 'Focus Approach', which Pienemann (1985:51) summarizes as follows:

1   The learners are allowed to use reduced and deviant forms in communicative activities.

2   However, these forms will not be brought into focus in the syllabus.
3   The learners are exposed to a 'fully formed input filtered only by the application of pedagogical norms'. (Valdman, 1977:68)
4   The syllabus will be graded according to what is easy to acquire.

Pienemann himself points out that, in fact, 'natural order' and textbook grading of structures (albeit of a very restricted range) are not widely divergent, and, following Hatch (1978), he compares the two:

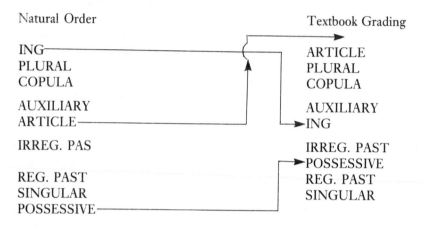

Natural Order

Textbook Grading

Natural Order	Textbook Grading
ING	ARTICLE
PLURAL	PLURAL
COPULA	COPULA
AUXILIARY	AUXILIARY
ARTICLE	ING
IRREG. PAS	IRREG. PAST
	POSSESSIVE
REG. PAST	REG. PAST
SINGULAR	SINGULAR
POSSESSIVE	

Other structures, notably inversion as part of interrogation, tend to occur later than in many textbooks – or than for the demands of real life communication. Asking questions is an early need for most learners, whether in natural or tutored contexts, but such questions tend to demand grammatical development, such as subject/verb inversion and the use of 'dummy' do, which is beyond the learners' existing stage of grammatical competence.

With this in mind, Pienemann (p. 55) outlines some general guide-lines based on natural grading:

1   Do not demand a learning process which is impossible at a given stage (i.e. order of teaching objectives be in line with stages of acquisition).
2   But do not introduce deviant forms.
3   The general input may contain structures which were not introduced for production.

He points out that conflicts will arise between these criteria, but that one way round such conflict is to vary the focus of the language and to bring about a match between input and intended output. Thus, at that stage in the progression at which inversion is required, it would be applied in the general input, although 'inversion is neither instructed at this point nor would I suggest reacting, e.g. by "correction" to the corresponding "deviant" interlanguage forms which are bound to occur at this stage' (p. 65).

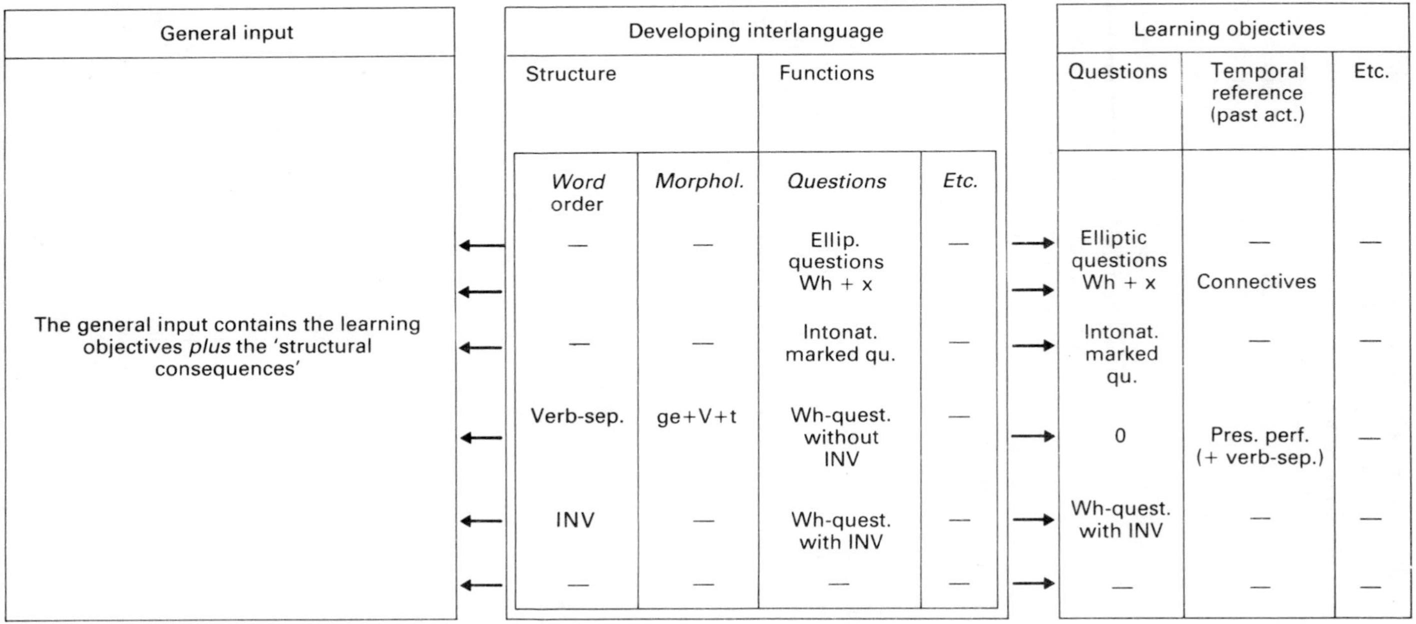

Figure 4.2 Communicative syllabus and interlanguage development (from Pienemann 1985)

In order to allow learners to perform the function of 'asking' from the earliest stage, Pienemann suggests introducing non-inversion question forms (e.g. intonation questions which preserve statement word order). Typically, these are not introduced for some time (if at all) in traditional structure-based syllabuses. He proposes incorporating such a grammatical grading within a communicative syllabus, and figure 4.2 is his illustration of the proposed implementation (p. 66).

> The syllabus is split into two parts: the general input (to the left in [the figure]) and the learning objectives (the right). According to the tenets of communicative syllabus construction, the learning objectives are systematized in notional/functional terms ('asking', 'temporal reference' etc.). The structural devices to fulfil these notions/functions are taken from the developing interlanguage system.

This is in line with the principles summarized above. Moving from top to bottom of the table in figure 4.2 'represents the chronological axis of both the interlanguage development and the progress in formal instruction.'

What Pienemann has proposed is a marriage of a natural order grammar syllabus with a notional – functional syllabus; the requirements of the latter are met by focusing on grammatical forms which are not beyond the current level of language development of the learner. He summarizes the advantages of his approach as:

1   L2 items are focused on in the order they are learnable.
2   L2 forms are introduced which have proved to be communicatively effective in natural L2 development.
3   The focus on meaning can be maintained in the instruction, while the required L2 items are selected and graded according to the above principles.

Obviously, Pienemann's proposal leaves unanswered a number of questions, one of them being the precise sequence of natural acquisition of grammatical items beyond the very restricted dozen or so items so far investigated. Another point which Pienemann does not consider is the role of such unanalysed chunks in language acquisition, as discussed by Peters (1983a and 1983b), who suggests that learners make communicative use of such holistic, grammatically unanalysed phrases or sentences which are 'beyond their competence'. Thus it may be that what is called for in a syllabus is a combination of grammatically tuned and grammatically unanalysed input and output whereby learners are able to communicate (if in a restricted way) in the target language, their competence and performance gradually expanding as their own grammatical system evolves as a result of increasingly rich and complex input and challenging communicative demands.

It is clear that abandoning teaching and following 'natural order' is not the answer, even if natural order as revealed by SLA studies may ultimately provide a guide to the sequencing of input and what can reasonably be expected of output from learners at any given stage of second language learning. It is also clear that learners' output will (and does) lag behind input in terms of grammatical development. In other words, learners will continue to make errors. A well-planned grammatical syllabus will be organized in such a way as to 'catch' the learners when they are ready to proceed to the next developmental stage. Attempting to force them to learn a grammatical item before they have reached this stage of readiness may, in fact, lead to a distortion of their evolving competence. Unfortunately, the state of research on the one hand and of the art of teaching on the other does not as yet enable us to fine tune language grading to match the developing competence of the learner.

Conclusion

I have suggested that syllabuses fall into two main categories: Type A and Type B. The former focuses on content, the traditional domain of syllabus, and both the traditional structural as well as the more recent notional–functional syllabuses belong to this class. Tradition, largely following the lines laid down by Palmer, rather than empirical evidence, has determined the basis for selection and grading of vocabulary and structures in syllabus design.

Although the principles of selection and grading have been widely exploited in the design of language syllabuses, evidence from learners' output, which has formed one of the main sources of data for SLA research, was largely ignored because the prevailing view during the heyday of structural syllabuses was that errors were instances of deficient learning or of interference from the L1. George, while not rejecting L1 interference as a factor, noted that the presentation of structures in combination or contrast could promote error, and pointed out the need to avoid such 'cross associations'.

More recent research into SLA has indicated a natural acquisition order, thus giving rise to the possibility of developing structural selection and grading principles in tune with this natural order. Pienemann has suggested modifying grading to bring the two in line, though without requiring learners to produce correct forms before they are ready to do so. While non-deviant input will be provided, focus on correct forms in learner output will be planned to coincide with the learners' stage of readiness to produce such forms. As yet, however, the kind of detailed evidence on which to base such a progression is lacking, although the accumulation of research in SLA may result in the evolution of new criteria for organizing language input to learners to avoid some of the learning problems which appear to have arisen from syllabuses planned according to traditional criteria for structural sequencing.

Suggested Reading

Selection and Grading

Contrastive analysis, once an important principle in structural syllabus design, is reviewed by James (1980) in his book of that title. A very detailed and comprehensive account of selection and grading is provided by Mackey, *Language Teaching Analysis* (1965), while a less intensive but more readable account appears in chapter 7, 'Language teaching and language learning' of Halliday, McIntosh and Strevens (1964), *The Linguistic Sciences and Language Teaching.* McDonough (1980) is virtually alone in considering the psychological aspects of sequencing.

Syllabus Design

Howatt's clear discussion of course design is included in *The Edinburgh Course in Applied Linguistics*, edited by Allen and Corder (1974), while in his *Introducing Applied Linguistics* Corder (1974) also devotes a chapter to syllabus organization, and apart from demonstrating the complexity and difficulties of grading structures, suggests a scheme in which elements are recycled at intervals throughout the syllabus. In *Linguistics in Language Teaching*, Wilkins (1972) gives a critical review of the organization of structural syllabuses, showing how the terms in which such syllabuses are specified tend to be ambiguous and imprecise.

George's discussion of selection and grading appears in *Common Errors in Language Learning* (1972), an application of his principles being provided by McEldowney (1976), with their realization in a course book, *English Right from the Start*, being made by Hore and Hore (1982).

Hornby's *The Teaching of Structural Words and Sentence Patterns* (1959–66) presents a classic example of structural syllabus design. An updated structural syllabus has been prepared by Alexander, Allen, Close and O'Neill in *English Grammatical Structure* (1975).

Second Language Acquisition (SLA)

In 1974, Valdman made an early response to the findings of SLA research, while Pienemann's more recent proposals are in *Modelling and Assessing Second Language Learning*, edited by Hyltenstam and Pienemann (1985). Other contributions to this discussion have been made in a seies of articles by Long (1975, 1981, 1983) and by Pica (1983, 1984, 1987).

For a way into the rapidly expanding literature on SLA (of which these are instances), refer to Hatch, *Second Language Acquisition: a Book of Readings* (1978); Ellis, *Classroom Second Language Development* (1984) and *Understanding Second Language Acquisition* (1986); Faerch and Kasper, *Strategies in*

Interlanguage Communication (1983); Krashen, *Principles and Practice in Second Language Acquisition* (1982); McLaughlin, *Theories of Second Language Learning* (1987); and Ritchie, *Second Language Acquisition Research* (1978). Apart from presenting a well-grounded account of the field, McLaughlin also puts the work of Krashen into perspective.

Pedagogical proposals based on SLA research have been announced by Krashen and Terrell, who promise more than they deliver in *The Natural Approach: Language Acquisition in the Classroom* (1983). More carefully considered, if more modest, indications of classroom applications are discussed by Bygate (1987) in his book on speaking.

5 Where, What and How: Other Bases to Syllabus Design

Introduction

In chapter 4 I suggested that there are two main approaches to syllabus design, and we reviewed the traditional structural basis to content syllabuses, noting the as yet imperfectly realized implications of SLA research for grammatical sequencing and grading. In this chapter I shall continue the survey of content syllabuses, ending up with a discussion of skills-based syllabuses, which represent something of a half-way-house between the content syllabuses of Type A and the process syllabuses of Type B.

Situational Syllabuses

CONTENT

|

SITUATIONAL
Contextual focus

In chapter 2 I referred to Hornby's so-called 'situational' method, in which classroom situations were used to demonstrate the meaning of a new language item. In his use of the classroom as a setting for presenting language and meaning, Hornby was adapting a feature of direct method teaching, and such demonstrations of language items, using real objects and activities which can be performed within the classroom, have become part of the repertoire of conventional language teaching procedures.

The other use of the term 'situational' matches the layperson's view of situation, that is, it refers to the contexts in which language and behaviour occur in the 'real world', outside the classroom. The relationship between language and context, long recognized in the British tradition thanks to the work of Malinowski and Firth, has – quite intuitively – long formed the basis of many phrase books produced for travellers and traders.

Basically, in considering the various aspects of a situation, we are concerned with

the setting   (Where?)
the participants (Who?)
relevant objects within the setting (What?)

Thus, to take an example, we might have the following:

Setting	at a bank
Participants	bank clerk, customer
Relevant	travellers' cheques, passport,
Objects	bank forms, currency

Such a combination of elements will be associated with fairly predictable language, in lexical, structural and functional/interactional terms, e.g.:

A: Good afternoon. Could I cash some travellers' cheques, please?

B: Yes. What currency are they?

A: Sterling. They're Thomas Cook cheques.

B: Will you fill in this form, please? And can I have your passport?

Variations on the above will soon suggest themselves, based on experience, although in such service-encounters the range of possibilities will be relatively restricted.

In a situationally based syllabus a series of situations will form the main organizing principle. Often, the situation will be closely linked with a practical activity or task of the kind which tourists might have to undertake. Typically, a restricted range of language will be covered, the emphasis being on getting things done rather than learning the language system; some attention may also be given to grammar, but usually only to the extent that it is helpful in generating further utterances of the type represented in the model.

In fact, it is difficult to find any publications organized on an exclusively situational basis. As will probably be obvious, it is not easy to take situations as the main element in syllabus planning because there are difficulties with the very category itself. A 'situation' can be defined with varying degrees of precision or generality and the more broadly the category is defined, the less useful it is likely to be. Thus, a general situational category like 'banks' provides such a wide spectrum of possibilities as to be practically useless. It becomes necessary, therefore, to specify the situation with more precision. Then there is the danger that the situation will be so special and the language so situation-specific that the content will have relevance to only a limited number of students.

An example of a situationally based course for tourists will illustrate some of the features involved. The BBC have developed the useful 'Get By In' series, and the list below is taken from *Get By In Italian* (1981). Each unit is organized under a general heading, with subheadings for specific activities. As will be clear, a series of typical tourist situations is used in conjunction with associated activities. Thus we have shops, restaurants, streets, the station, the post office and hotels as typical settings, with buying things, asking the way and ordering a meal as typical activities within these settings.

Ordering and paying
Helloes and goodbyes
Ordering a drink
Simple numbers and money

Shopping around
Buying an ice-cream
buying food for a picnic . . . ham, cheese, bread rolls
Buying stamps
Buying a wallet

Travelling around
Asking the way . . . to the cathedral, the station, the post office
Catching a train – tickets and platform
Catching a bus

Getting somewhere to stay
Booking into a hotel
Getting a place at a campsite
Opening times

A meal and a chat
Ordering a pizza meal and wine; the bill, toilets
Meeting people
The weather

Once the situations have been selected, a language syllabus can be devised, based on the language associated with the situations concerned. The basis for grading and sequencing the syllabus will be less obvious than in a purely structural syllabus, since there are no clear criteria for grading situations. The syllabus designer may, therefore, simply order them according to a chronological sequence based on arriving, staying and departing, or group situations together according to similarity, so that service-encounters dealing with everyday needs might go in one section, while cultural activities (museum visiting, theatres, etc.) might go in another. Alternatively, a structural grading of the associated language might be used as a guide to the sequencing of situations.

In fact, the category of situation has become one of several which the syllabus designer usually takes into account, and the typical coursebook will be based on such a combination of categories. Indeed, the concern with authenticity and realism which has exercised materials writers during the past two decades has ensured that situations as well as functions have been an integral part of most language syllabuses.

Topic-based Syllabuses: Selection and Grading

When linguists refer to an idea as 'pretheoretical', they are, in effect, saying that the concept in question is messy, imprecise and insufficiently rigorous as a basis for scientific study. Such, in general, is the attitude towards 'topic', which is regarded as 'a very attractive pretheoretical notion' (Brown and Yule 1983). Attractive though the concept may be, there are, as Brown and Yule show, a number of difficulties with it. Simply defined, topic is what is being talked or written about. Unfortunately, there are no formal characteristics which enable any particular topic to be defined unambiguously, unlike grammatical categories which, by and large, can be defined in terms of objective formal features. (For instance, a noun, among other things, has a plural form, marked in regular nouns by the –s suffix.) Topics are defined by meaning, not form, and meaning is a notoriously slippery concept to work with.

A second problem, deriving from the difficulties of dealing with meaning, is that defining what a stretch of speech or writing is about may be very difficult in itself. Brown and Yule (1983:73) point out that 'there is, for any text, a number of different ways of expressing "the topic". Each different way of expressing "the topic" will effectively represent a different judgement of what is being written (or talked) about in a text.' There are also other problems. Topics can be thought of in varying degrees of generality, some so general as to be meaningless. Thus, topics like travel and shopping can mean many things to many people and ultimately almost anything could be included under such content headings. By contrast, topics can be limited to things which are so minutely particular that it becomes difficult to decide whether the focus is topic (in the general sense of subject matter) or vocabulary (in the specific sense of labels for things, actions and experiences). Meanwhile, the interchangeability with which 'notion' and 'topic' appear to be used creates further confusion.

Yet, in spite of all these problems, topic continues to be a category which most Type A syllabus designers use, even though few syllabuses are entirely topic-based. There are, however, two justifications for a topic focus for the language syllabus. One justification is broadly educational, as argued by Abbott (1987), who suggests that learners (specifically European children in his example) 'could learn a great deal *through* English', and that 'much of the content of the English syllabus could well consist of a revision, illustration and broadening of other parts of the school curriculum.' Although he does not refer to Widdowson in his discussion, Abbott appears to be thinking along similar lines by advocating learning the language through exposure to content. In a content-based syllabus, the geography or history lesson becomes both a vehicle for language learning, as well as a means of providing content of educational value within the total school curriculum.

The second justification for topic-based syllabuses is a purely motivational one. In their search for new and stimulating bases for courses at advanced levels, some syllabus designers and text book writers turn to topic. Such was the motivation of Fein and Baldwin (1986) and their colleagues teaching a pre-university course in the USA. They report that their students 'had no intrinsic interest in English' and, seeing the English requirement as necessary for university admission, simply 'went along with the skills-based approach'. So 'members of the faculty saw the content-based approach, with its incorporation of the many features of college courses, as a way of motivating such students, as a way of providing "free validity" to their English instruction.'

The result was a course organized on a modular basis, each module was equal to one content area (i.e. topic) and lasting approximately three weeks of the ten-week quarter. Modules and sub-topics for one level are (Fein and Baldwin 1986:2):

1   'Marketing' (creating products, advertising, marketing abroad, consumer protection).
2   'The Environment' (ecology, man's negative and positive impact on the environment, problems of the future).
3   'The Brain' (physiology, behaviour modification, memory, abnormality, cognition, and altered states of consciousness).

Having identified their topics, they then selected and organized the readings which were to form the basis of input for each module. Selections were made which

1   did not require simplification;
2   represented a variety of sources, types of sources (books, newspapers, magazines) and points of view;
3   were neither too long nor too technical.

Although interest, need, utility and relevance appear to be the main criteria in selecting topics, it is probably the case that the interests of the syllabus designer will also be an important and covert influence, a point acknowledged by Fein and Baldwin, who conclude their account by pointing out that 'in a field where burnout is all too common, teachers have the opportunity to replenish their energies by expanding their own knowledge of a variety of exciting subjects' (p. 2). Whereas in structural grading there are some linguistic criteria, there is no established theoretical basis for the grading of topics. Fein and Baldwin and their colleagues adopted the following criteria for content selection:

1 Pedagogic merit, by which they avoided topics likely to become too similar to introductory university course material. Topics with an academic orientation relevant to a broad spectrum of students were given priority.
2 Affective considerations, by which stimulating topics were selected, which would also expose students to various aspects of American culture.
3 Practicality – basically, what materials could easily be found.

Another criterion which can be applied to topic grading is depth of treatment (cf. Reynolds 1981). We have already noted that topics can be considered in terms of specificity so that in grading it is possible to move from the more general and superficial to a highly specific and detailed treatment. Grading by depth of treatment will, therefore, probably involve such considerations as length of texts to be dealt with and conceptual features, the latter being concerned with the familiarity of the conceptual field to the learners, its conceptual complexity and the number of mental operations involved in dealing with textual material.

At this point, it is difficult to keep conceptual factors separate from task factors; in other words, in-depth treatment of a given topic may call for performing increasingly complex skills involved in the comprehension or construction of discourse. Fein and Baldwin (p. 2) note the importance of providing a range of skills activities appropriate for their students: 'Care is taken to sequence the skills, from the receptive (reading and listening) to the productive (speaking and writing). In addition, the teacher can make use of supplementary exercises ranging from vocabulary reviews to error analysis activities.' A factor which Fein and Baldwin do not mention is the utility of given topics as a vehicle for language. The problem here is that topics can be relegated to an instrumental role, being simply a way of operating the language rather than an end in their own right. It is also important to realize that reactions to topics are particularly influenced by the attitudes of both syllabus designer and students – cf. Fein and Baldwin's 'affective considerations' – and while few stake-holders will question the choice of language items in a syllabus, the selection of topics can arouse considerable controversy on religious, moral or political grounds.

Another development in topic-based syllabuses is the use of literature as a source for language work. Language-based approaches to the study of literature are not, in themselves, an innovation (cf. Leech 1969, Widdowson 1975), but there has of recent years been a growing interest in the teaching of language through literature (Brumfit 1983), in which literary texts (embracing works which fall outside the traditional literary canon) are used as a resource for language. The focus is not on the literary canon as classically defined, nor on the study of literary forms and genres and criticism. Rather, literature and the topics which are embodied in literary texts are incorporated into the syllabus on a thematic basis. Texts sharing a common theme but drawn from a variety of sources (including imaginative writing) will be exploited as language material (Brumfit and Carter 1986), as exemplified in a textbook by McCrae and Boardman (1984).

In general, topic selection and ordering will be determined by educational rather than linguistic criteria, as the value of topic lies in the provision of meaningful and relevant content to stimulate motivation and lead to opportunities for meaningful discussion. The teacher can still derive language focused work from the textual material, of course, though when the material is organized by topic rather than considerations of linguistic grading, the language exposure may be somewhat random and only 'roughly tuned' grammatically. However, in so far as the content is both significant and comprehensible to the learner, such rough tuning may be less important than the fact that learners are being provided with the kind of language input that may stimulate successful language learning – a point to be taken up in the discussion of process and procedural syllabuses in chapter 7.

Skills Based Syllabuses

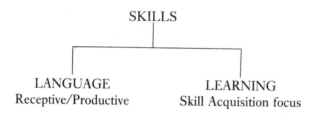

In this section I will consider two ways of looking at skills: firstly, in terms of the traditional division into receptive and productive skills, and secondly, in terms of the similarities between language and skilled behaviour. I will also suggest that there is some overlap between these two views which might usefully be incorporated within syllabus design.

Language Skills

Traditionally, the so-called receptive and productive skills – listening and reading, speaking and writing respectively – have been regarded as the 'four skills' in language syllabus design and it is these which fall into the first category in the diagram above. In syllabuses for general (as opposed to specific) purposes, these four skills have been given more or less equal weighting, although a glance at any general language textbook will usually show that of the four skills speaking will have been given more weighting than any of the others, even though reading and writing will have been used as a means of presenting and practising the language.

The realization that equal weighting for all four skills is not appropriate to all learners is one of the insights provided by ESP and needs analysis. The traditional idea that science students, for instance, needed a 'reading' knowledge of German is at the basis of the principle of defining different skills requirements for different purposes. The development of needs analyses in association with ESP in the first instance, and subsequently for the so-called general learner, has strengthened differentiation among skills and levels in such examinations as the Royal Society of Arts Examination in the Communicative Use of English as a Foreign Language.

In this examination, students can opt for different levels of performance in the four skills, so that it is not necessary to achieve uniformity in all of them. Thus a student for whom reading is an important requirement can aim at a higher level of performance than in, say, speaking, which may be less important – or the student can even opt not to be tested in speaking. Similar differentiations are to be found on the Graded Objectives in Modern Language Teaching. Another change is the greater significance attached to listening and speaking as examinable skills so that nowadays most public examinations contain listening and speaking components.

These changes have been reflected in the development of supplementary skills materials by most publishers, so that language teachers now have the opportunity of using a core course book augmented by a range of skills-specific materials. In curriculum terms, the opening up of supplementary skills materials has greatly broadened the options available to teacher and learner, with a considerable expansion of aims and objectives as well as of learning experiences and evaluation requirements.

In spite of the greater awareness and importance of specific language skills, less attention has been given to designing skills syllabuses than to structural or functional syllabuses. There are, however, signs of change, partly because of the already noted growth of interest in these skills, and partly because work in applied linguistics, psychology and education is providing interesting new insights into the skills of reading (e.g. Carrel 1983, Goodman 1967, Olshavsky 1977, Pugh 1978) and writing (e.g. Freedman, Pringle and Yalden 1983, Nystrand 1982, Pellegrini and Yawkey 1984) in particular. One result of these new insights is that views on the very nature of reading and writing are changing. Another consequence is that there is a redirection from what may be broadly called product-focus to process-focus in teaching reading and writing. In other words, instead of attending to the text (either as a product to be read or written), interest has shifted to the ways in which readers interpret texts and to the processes whereby writers compose them. Such a change of focus is in line with the general trend in curriculum studies and I shall return to a consideration of such process skills in the account of the process syllabus in chapter 7.

Language and Cognitive Skills

All language use involves the mastery and deployment of numerous skills other than linguistic ones. Activities such as writing and speaking can be broken down into their sub-skills; some will be linguistic, others will be the kinds of process skills referred to in the earlier discussion of the four skills. Although the evidence from skills psychology suggests that holistic rather than atomistic practice of skills may be more effective when synchronization of sub-tasks is important, it has also been noted that concentrating on sub-tasks may be better when there is a wide range of them. Thus the identification of sub-tasks may be a useful stage in syllabus design as a prelude to organizing the various skills in a graded sequence.

Munby (1978) has provided an extensive, though non-graded, taxonomy of language skills, which can form a useful starting point for such a specification. His list of language skills is, of course, only one component of several in his syllabus model (to be discussed in the section on needs analysis in chapter 6). The list is specified in terms which partially resemble behavioural objectives. Each skill is stated in terms of a verb:

understanding
expressing
interpreting
extracting
recognizing
indicating
expanding
planning
initiating
maintaining
terminating

The verb is followed by a noun phrase object:

information
the script
relations within the sentence
the discourse

More specific detail is supplied in the modifying phrase or adverbial which follows:

explicitly

of a language

using especially, elements of sentence structure

how to initiate the discourse

Typical examples of language skills specification are:

understanding explicitly stated information

manipulating the script of a language:

forming the graphemes

catenating grapheme sequences (spelling system)

using punctuation

using indicators in discourse for

introducing an idea

developing an idea (e.g. adding points, reinforcing argument)

Munby's taxonomy, exhaustive though it is, has its limitations. It is not organized hierarchically (Widdowson 1983:52), although it is quite clear that some of the skills are of a lower order and subsumed within others, while the relationship of the skills to language use also remains unspecified. Nor does the taxonomy distinguish between language skills in the sense of being able to use the *language code* (as in articulating stress patterns within words); *cognitive skills* (such as planning and organizing information in expository language); and *study skills* (such as skimming to obtain gist). (See Yalden 1983 for an adapted version of Munby's skills taxonomy.) Furthermore, although Munby lists such composition skills as planning and organizing information in expository language, and using rhetorical functions, he does not specify other composition skills such as generating ideas and revising. Nor is any reference made to the skills involved in drawing upon existing world knowledge and schemata in both reading and writing, or to the heuristic skills (cf. Hughey, Wormuth, Harfiel and Jacobs 1983) which are increasingly seen as being important in writing.

In terms of behavioural objectives, the list is also deficient in that it does not specify the conditions under which the skills are to be used nor the degree of skill to be exhibited. In fact, by a cumbersome matching up of skills with other specifications in the model, some such statement could be arrived at. In principle it is thus possible to state that the skill of understanding explicitly stated information would occur within a specified physical, occupational and psychosocial setting, in interaction with a given set of addressees, through specified channels of communication, involving interlocutors of a given regional and social class origin, and to specified standards of length, speed and complexity.

Even accepting these limitations, Munby's list of language skills provides a useful checklist of sub-skills involved in skilled language use, both in general and in respect of the four receptive and productive skills. For writing, by way of illustration, his list yields about 24 language skills, including some of those already noted above. In addition to his list, there are other skills which research into writing processes suggests should be incorporated in a writing syllabus. These include:

using invention and discovery techniques to generate ideas;

organizing ideas according to various criteria, including the writer's own writing plan as writing proceeds;

identifying and developing a thesis;

identifying and developing a theme or viewpoint;

providing thematic unity to a text through the use of lexical and grammatical devices such as synonymy, collocation and parallelism;

establishing a shared frame of reference with the reader by identifying shared and privileged knowledge.

As should by now be clear, organizing these various skills into a graded syllabus is likely to be difficult. Some skills, such as manipulating the script of a language, would be regarded as basic and therefore preceding others, such as providing thematic unity to a text. One set of criteria for grading might be concreteness versus abstractness of the skills – characteristics which are, of course, difficult to measure. One set of skills could be established on a linguistic basis, such as expressing relations within the sentence, for which formal criteria could be invoked, while another set of skills, based on conceptual criteria, would include generating, planning and organizing.

Because writing (in the sense of composing) involves numerous skills operating both sequentially and in parallel, it would be important to avoid specifying a writing syllabus as a series of unrelated sub-skills. Instead, writing activities could be specified in which the focus on sub-skills would change from one task to another. Thus, any part of the syllabus would specify a number of skills and the degree of importance of any sub-skill could be indicated for each part. Likewise, the importance and difficulty of various skills would lead to their being recycled throughout the writing syllabus. Obviously, this begs the question of how importance and difficulty can be established. In part, this will depend on the view of writing espoused by the syllabus designer; and it will also derive from experience with students similar to those for whom the syllabus is being prepared.

We have seen that, in principle, skills syllabuses could be based on two categories of skill, of which the second, derived from skills psychology, is as yet only imperfectly realized. There is, however, a coming together of the traditional 'four skills' and those such as behaviour in the specifications offered by Munby and others. The skills which are specified can be grouped into several classes: language skills, cognitive skills, composition skills, and study skills. The conditions and levels of performance for these skills can be specified, though attempts to achieve the precision called for in behavioural objectives are likely to be cumbersome and difficult and ultimately impossible to operate. Even so, the grouping together of sub-skills and a varying focus on these skills throughout a language programme could provide a basis for a skills syllabus. Such a syllabus – or syllabuses, given the range of skills to be covered – would, however, form only one component in a language syllabus since there are other aspects, such as features of form and meaning, which would also have to be covered by a comprehensive syllabus.

Conclusion

Although the syllabus types reviewed here are very disparate, each has a contribution to make to the design of a fully realized, integrated syllabus. Language structure cannot of itself form the complete basis, unless it is as an object of study, when the language system rather than its use becomes the focus of learning. Language use must be contextualized, and any interactive or social use of language occurs in a situation involving institutionally defined relationships which influence stylistic and interactional features. Thus the category of situation is an important element in syllabus design, although it does not by itself make a sound basis for organizing a language programme.

Even when language has been contextualized, the participants must have something to talk (or write) about, and the category of topic provides the basis for this aspect of content. Topic can, like situation, be considered at greater or lesser degrees of generality and it is a difficult category to define precisely. At their most general, topics can be grouped under thematic headings at a macro level, while at their most specific, they can be very particular subjects at a micro level.

Arguments have been put forward for the educational value of content-based syllabuses in which topics from other parts of the curriculum can provide educationally worthwhile content as a vehicle for language learning. Such content-based programmes can also serve a motivating function. The use of very wide-ranging literary content, organized on a topic or thematic basis, has also been advocated by those who propose using literature as a vehicle for language input.

Finally, the traditional four skills and the cognitive skills involved in the expression of purpose and meaning, and in the creation and interpretation of messages, provide other bases for syllabus design. Again, they constitute only one aspect of a complete syllabus and need to be viewed in relation to the other categories already outlined in this chapter and chapters 4 and 6.

Suggested Reading

Language and Context

Neither situational nor topic based approaches to syllabus design have spawned much in the way of literature. For an accessible discussion of the relationship of language and context, see Trudgill's *Sociolinguistics* (1974), while for an account of the relationship between speech situation and style, see O'Donnell and Todd's *Variety in Contemporary English* (1980) and Gregory and Carroll's *Language and Situation* (1978). A key work in the discussion of language variety is Crystal and Davy, *Investigating English Style* (1969).

Content Based Syllabuses

For a discussion of a content basis to the language syllabus, see Widdowson, *Learning Purpose and Language Use* (1983), while for language-based approaches to literary stylistics, refer to Widdowson, *Stylistics and the Teaching of Literature* (1975). A collection edited by Brumfit (1983) focuses on the issues of teaching English literature outside of Britain, while Brumfit and Carter, in *Literature and Language Teaching* (1986), provide an up-to-date review of the field. An interesting example of theme-based literature material may be found in McCrae and Boardman (1984), *Reading Between the Lines*, whose content is grouped under such themes as war, authority, rebellion and ambition.

A very good account of the differences between spoken and written language is provided by Brown and Yule (1983), who in *Discourse Analysis* also devote chapters to the role of context and topic.

Skills

On skills psychology, see Reed in Lunzer and Morris (eds) (1968), Holding (1965) and Welford (1976). For a discussion of skills and language learning, see Herriot (1970), *An Introduction to the Psychology of Language*, Levelt (1975), Johnson (1986) and McDonough (1981), *Psychology in Foreign Language Teaching*. For the realization in teaching material of many of the composition skills reviewed in this discussion of writing, see White (1987b).

6 Type A Syllabuses: Notional–Functional

Introduction

In this chapter we come to the most recent form of content-based Type A syllabus: the notional–functional syllabus. Essentially a product of the 1970s, a notional–functional approach introduces two important elements to syllabus design: firstly, a notional or conceptual aspect, which is concerned with such concepts as time, space, movement, cause and effect; and secondly, a functional aspect, with which the intentional or purposive use of language is described and classified. Neither notions nor functions were in themselves an innovation, because language teaching has always been concerned with teaching concepts (e.g. possession: 'This is my book') and functions (e.g. using interrogative forms to ask for information, or the past tense to report events). What was new was the proposal that syllabuses could take notional–functional categories as an organizing principle. Thus, syllabus organization would no longer be determined solely by grammatical considerations, but would have to take communicative categories into account as well.

Where functional categories become a principal feature of language syllabus content, the issue of needs analysis soon follows. Whereas no learner could actually be said to 'need' the past tense, many learners might need to be able to report events and narrate stories. So, associated with functional syllabuses, though by no means unique to them, has been the incorporation of needs analysis as a stage in notional–functional syllabus design, and a discussion of needs analysis will form the final part of this chapter.

Waystage and Threshold Level

The prototype notional–functional syllabuses are the *Threshold* (Van Ek (1975)) and *Waystage* (Van Ek and Alexander (1977)) syllabuses prepared by the Council of Europe. 'Syllabuses' is, however, something of a misnomer, since they lack some of the critical features of a syllabus according to Brumfit's definition (chapter 1). It is notable that in neither of them is the content presented in a graded and sequenced order, so that what we have is simply a checklist of items under such categories as 'language functions' and 'topic'.

There is more to these lists, however, than meets the eye, since they are the product of applying the criteria for grading functions listed on page 48: need, utility, coverage and interest. Thus, the lists which appear in the Council of Europe syllabuses are not simply random selections of functions, topics and exponents. That this is so can be inferred from the topics and functions chosen for inclusion in Waystage, of which the following are examples:

Topics	*Functions*
personal identification	identifying
health and welfare	reporting
food and drink	greeting people

Unfortunately, the Waystage listing suffers from some of the flaws inherent in a functional approach. The first problem is impossibility of defining functions with precision and clarity. Although speech-act theorists (Austin 1962, Searle 1969) have proposed conditions whereby a given speech act may be defined as performing a given function, no reference is made to such specifications in the Council of Europe syllabuses – nor, indeed, in any other similar listings. The absence of a specification of conditions (or contextual factors) which limit or determine the interpretation of a given function means that there is at best, some ambiguity, and, at worst, total misunderstanding over what is meant by such functions as *expressing intention, expressing one is/is not obliged to do something* or *expressing dissatisfaction*.

The second difficulty, related to the first, is that the interpretation or definition of a function is, in considerable measure, determined by context, including the other language in that context. Indeed, the functional interpretation we place on virtually any utterance depends upon the situation, the role of participants, the various purposes of the speakers so far, and much else besides – including cultural knowledge and knowledge of the world. Further complications are that, firstly, one language function may be expressed in many different ways; and, secondly, one exponent may express more than one function. There is not, in short, a one-to-one relationship between context and function, or function and exponent. This may be clarified by looking at the following examples:

Example 1

We're thinking of going to see the new Woody Allen film tonight.

How about going to see the new Woody Allen film tonight?

If you're free tonight, shall we go and see the new Woody Allen film?

Would you like to see the new Woody Allen film tonight?

Have you seen the new Woody Allen film? Because if you haven't, you could come with us tonight.

Example 2

A: What about the camera?

B: It's in the cupboard in my study.

A: What about the camera?

B: I don't think I'll take it.

All of the exponents in Example 1 will immediately be recognized as forms of invitation, although some of them might also be interpreted as exponents of the function of making a suggestion. Without further knowledge of the context, it is impossible to decide which function is being expressed. Thus there is considerable lack of congruity between form and function.

The two exchanges in Example 2 provide further demonstration of this lack of congruity, together with the fact that one and the same exponent can be interpreted in quite different ways, depending on the context and the participants' shared knowledge and assumptions. Clearly, in the first exchange, participant B has interpreted A's question as a request for information, specifically about the location of a camera. In the second exchange, B assumes that A is making a suggestion, specifically to take his or her camera with them.

The third difficulty with functional selection and grading is very closely connected to the issues we have just noted: language functions do not usually occur in isolation, a point emphasized by Crombie (1985) in her discussion of what she terms 'binary discourse values'. For instance, the functions of accepting and declining an offer or invitation usually occur as part of an exchange in which offering or inviting appear in a preceding stage, thus:

A: Invites B to the cinema.

B: Accepts A's offer.
   or
   Declines A's offer.

The value or meaning of B's utterance depends upon the value or meaning of A's. Thus, the value of *accept* or *decline* within such an exchange depends upon the relationship with *invite*. The binary units which occur above may be followed by further units, each linked in a similar way.

Either

B: Accepts A's offer.
   Asks for further details.

Or

B: Declines A's offer.
   Gives reason for declining.

It is unusual for any stages in an exchange to occur in isolation, unrelated to other steps or segments in the exchange. Warnings, insults and threats would be among the few instances of such segments having unitary rather than binary value or function (Crombie 1985:5).

Curiously, in the Waystage, there is no reference to the binary nature of most functions so that, while the functions of 'accepting' and 'declining an offer or invitation' are listed, 'making an offer or an invitation' is not. Thus, if applied unthinkingly, the Waystage functional list could lead to the bizarre situation in which a language learner might know how to recognize and produce an acceptance or refusal, but not be able to make an offer!

One way of avoiding treating language functions simply as an unrelated list of items is to follow Crombie's (1985) approach, and regard them as binary values (or mutually dependent paired functions). The pairing of segments is realized at several levels of abstraction. Thus, she suggests that we can take notional relations, such as cause–effect, or discourse relations, such as question/reply, or clause structure, such as interrogative and declarative, or even specific linguistic items, such as Q (question) word *what*. The outcome of her proposals is what she calls a *relational syllabus*. Although the emphasis on the relationship between functions and structures in discourse is admirable, her proposals do not appear to have overcome the problem of achieving functional coherence with structural control.

Function and Form: the Problem of Combining

What is certain is that the exponents and the structures used to express various functions may be highly varied in frequency and complexity. Thus, there will almost inevitably be a conflict between principles of simplicity, combinability, teachability and learnability when applied to exponents and structures on the one hand, and need, utility, coverage and binary relations, applied to functions, on the other. Further criteria in addition to those traditionally applied to structural selection may also have to be evolved. Canale and Swain (1980), for instance, have suggested five categories in addition to that of grammatical complexity: transparency with respect to the communicative function of an utterance; generalizability to other communicative functions; the role of a given form in facilitating acquisition of another form; acceptability in terms of perceptual strategies; and degree of markedness in terms of social and geographical dialects (Yalden 1983:126).

The problems inherent in structural grading while operating within a functional framework can be seen in some of the Waystage items:

Identifying	This is + Noun Phrase
Expressing preference	I'd prefer + Noun Phrase/Pronoun
	I'd like + Noun Phrase/Pronoun

Inquiring about want/desire   Would you like + Noun Phrase/Pronoun?
Do you want + Noun Phrase/Pronoun?

Typically, in a structurally graded syllabus, the modal verbs such as *should* and *would* are introduced after such modals as *shall* and *will*, which means that the actual structures required to operate the two functions given above would not appear at an early stage. However, need, utility and coverage might dictate that these two functions and the exponents and structures here associated with them should occur early in the syllabus. In fact, this very problem has had to be faced by coursebook writers in the post Waystage–Threshold era, and one solution is to introduce such exponents as *would you like* and social formulae as grammatically unanalysed units, standing outside the structural sequence found elsewhere in the syllabus.

Mixing and Matching

Another solution is to interweave functional and structural elements. Various proposals for such interweaving have been put forward, giving rise to a range of communicative syllabus types (Yalden 1983). Basically, the range of types arises from the differing combinations of structural and functional elements, which can be summarized diagrammatically thus:

A	B	C	D	E	F
++++++	* * * * * *	+++***	+ + +	+ * + *	* + * +
++++++	* * * * * *	+++***	+ + +	* + * +	+ * + +
* * * * * *	++++++	+++***	* * *	+ * + *	* + * +
* * * * * *	++++++	+++***	* * *	* + * +	000000
++++++	* * * * * *	+++***	+ + +	+ * + *	000000
++++++	* * * * * *	+++***	+ + +	* + * +	* + * +
* * * * * *	++++++	+++***	* * *	+ * + *	+ * + *
* * * * * *	++++++	+++***	* * *	* + * +	* + * +

Key ** = functional, ++ = structural, oo = free, unspecified

In type A, a substantial functional component is followed by an equally substantial structural component. There is not necessarily any connection between the two components; each could be quite independent of the other. It makes sense, however, to establish a link between them so that the structural component would develop grammatical and lexical features which had already been presented and practised in the functional component. The role of the structural component would be to systematize the grammar, which would not have been presented in a grammatically ordered sequence within the separate functional component. In short, there is a change of focus from one component to another, with the functional one providing 'roughly tuned' grammatical input, and the grammatical one focused on selected grammatical items with, possibly, an emphasis on formally correct output. (See the earlier discussion in chapter 6 of Valdman's and Pienemann's syllabus proposals.)

Type B is similar to A, but here the order of elements is reversed, with the structural preceding the functional. In this case, the learner would first be systematically presented with language forms. These would then be followed by a functional/communicative phase in which some or all of these structural elements would be used to perform whatever communicative acts had been planned for that section of the syllabus. In type B, organized and focused structural input would be followed by a communicative phase in which structures would be roughly tuned.

In type C there are two parallel streams, one grammatical, the other functional. It would be possible, as in types A and B, to have no connection or integration between the functional and grammatical elements, but in fact the conception here is of the two elements acting in unison, with the content of one reflecting and interacting with the content of the other. Learners are thus given a systematization of the grammatical input they receive in the functional element.

Type D is a variant of A and B, but here the separate functional and structural components are arranged in shorter sections. In effect, this might mean having a functional lesson followed by a structural lesson or vice versa, whereas in types A and B the relationship between the two elements is seen in terms of unit or sets of units, so that in actual practice a functional element might cover several lessons or even weeks of work, the structural element being of equivalent length. The spreading out or bunching together of structural and functional elements will be influenced by the syllabus designer's or teacher's theory of learning and knowledge of learners' preferences.

In type E there is a combination of the two elements in a spiral, with the structural and functional elements integrated in such a way that there is revision and recycling of both as we move up the spiral. A spiral or cyclical model emphasizes revision and expansion, a feature not implicit in types A to D. A good syllabus, like a good curriculum, should incorporate recycling so that the learners are given an opportunity to revise items previously learnt.

The cyclical or spiral syllabus does not merely provide a return to an earlier point, however, for the concept of recycling embodies the idea of adding something new to what has been learned before. For instance, a given function could be reintroduced in a new setting, new exponents of the same function might be presented, an expansion of stylistic variation provided, or the function linked with a different topic or topics. Indeed, given the number of different elements which can potentially be incorporated into a syllabus, recycling provides the syllabus designer with an opportunity to 'mix and match' elements in a variety of ways. It also makes it possible to fine-tune grammatical content and to change the focus as the students proceed through the syllabus.

Finally, type F is identical to type E, but with 'free' elements in which teachers are at liberty to include whatever they wish. If they feel that, however desirable a carefully planned syllabus may be, the learner should be exposed to a rich selection of language input which has not been adapted or simplified for pedagogical purposes, then it is essential to allow for such exposure by building in 'free' stages whose content would not be specified in advance. Indeed, both objectives and content would derive from the preceding stages, but by having free space, there would be opportunity for flexibility, catching up, innovation and adaptation. Indeed, there is a good argument for designing a syllabus so that the specified sections are stated in relatively general terms to provide an overall structure and sequence for the learning/teaching programme, while simultaneously allowing for opportunities to respond to formative feed back. Such provision is in line with the give-and-take which tends to be part of any pedagogical programme. (See chapter 7 on the process syllabus for further discussion on this point.)

A further solution to the problem of reconciling functional and structural demands on the syllabus designer is outlined by Yalden (1983) in her *Proportional Syllabus*, which offers a close interweaving of structural and non-structural, systematic and non-systematic elements over time, as illustrated in figure 6.1.

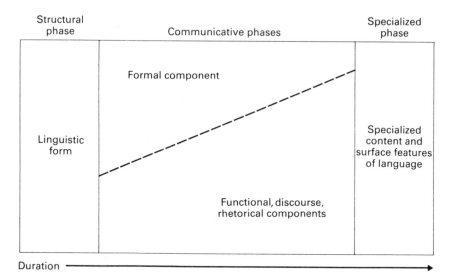

Figure 6.1 The proportional syllabus
(from Yalden 1983)

Identifying Form: Function Relationships

In carrying out the mixing and matching implied in most of the syllabus models just received, it would be useful to have some information on the typical exponents of particular functions in various contexts. In an earlier discussion of grading, I noted that there is some empirical evidence regarding the frequency of structures, but there is a dearth of such evidence for functions. Applied linguists with an interest in register study have attended to the formal characteristics of certain varieties of the language (see Chiu 1973, White 1974a, 1974b), while specialists in English for Specific Purposes have also looked at such features (e.g. Selinker, Trimble and Trimble 1978). The vogue for such studies has declined, however, and has not been revived, even though Wilkins (1979) has noted the need for observational research into the realizations of communicative categories.

One consequence of the lack of such empirical research (though see Sinclair and Coulthard (1975) on classroom discourse) is that functional syllabus and textbook writers tend to depend on intuition when it comes to selecting exponents and structures for the functions they have chosen. On the one hand, exponents may be chosen with half an eye to such traditional structural criteria as simplicity and combinability, while on the other, they may be selected on the basis of such criteria as authenticity or frequency. Unfortunately, it is rare to find these latter criteria being evaluated by actual observation.

As yet, other criteria based on language acquisition studies (see Ellis 1985), have not emerged for functional grading. This is partly because much of the acquisition research has focused on a distinctly limited range of morphological features and little attention has been given to the functional development of language (but see Halliday 1975, Wells 1985). Even here, though, there are problems: a natural order of acquisition of given functions by a child learning its native language does not logically provide a basis for grading and sequencing language functions for the SL learner, while the differences in both the needs of the SL learner and the situations in which the target language is used will give rise to further differences between the functional development of first and second languages.

Functional Syllabuses: Conclusion

The selection and grading of items for functionally based syllabuses relies on such considerations as the needs of the learners, both in terms of classroom functions and in the 'real world', usefulness, coverage or generalizability, interest or relevance and complexity of form. Issues of matching functional and formal selection and grading have proved to be problematic. Various models have been created with a view to providing a satisfactory mix of form and function, though there is an absence of any evaluation of the models proposed. Similarly, syllabus designers lack any empirical evidence upon which to base their selection of structures and exponents when working within a functional framework, and to date there has been an unsatisfactory reliance on intuition.

What may be provided by the syllabus models reviewed above is variety of forms of organization which can be matched to various exigencies, while the implications of FLA and SLA research are that some variation in syllabus organization along the lines discussed here might very well match, in broad terms, the sequence of SLA. In particular, there are planning implications in the account of SLA by Peters (1983a and 1983b), who suggests that there is a stage involving unanalysed chunks and sequences which are used functionally and appear to be stored in the memory pending later grammatical analysis. If, in fact, learners do operate two different but complementary and interactive systems – memory and syntactic – in tandem, there would be some justification for maintaining two different strands in a language syllabus, one of which would be broadly functional/communicative, the other analytical, with content from memory feeding into the syntactic system for analysis. Such a two-level model of language learning fits into the two-element syllabus models just discussed.

Following such a model, the learner would be presented with contextualized chunks of unanalysed language which could be used for communicative purposes in interactive practice. Subsequently, the student would be introduced to exercises in which the chunks already known and used would be analysed grammatically, and opportunities for producing new variations on the elements concerned would be provided. (The precise nature of the grammatical work is left aside in this discussion. One important consideration would be whether such work was inductive or deductive in nature.) Variants on the spiral and other syllabus types summarized on p. 79 would readily lend themselves to such a combination and sequence of language focus.

Another context in which one of the above syllabus models would be used is in the all-too-familiar situation in which a group of learners is either strongly wedded to a particular approach (e.g. rule-based grammar manipulation) or is afflicted by a desire to reject the traditional. In the former, it would be unwise to abandon the familiar, and so retaining form-focused work would be essential as part of the transition to a meaning-based approach. For the latter, the adoption of a functional syllabus with a grammar safety net would fit the bill. In any case, given the mixed characteristics of most groups of learners, it is unlikely that the teacher could assume an all-or-nothing approach by switching over to a totally new type of syllabus. Thus, a hybrid or a proportional syllabus would provide a valuable and viable compromise.

Needs Analysis

Needs analysis, to return to the house-building analogy once more, has parallels with the curriculum = house plan, only in this case the plan is based on an existing dwelling, which is to provide the basis for a dwelling owned by someone else. Briefly, in needs analysis the teacher or planner investigates the language required for performing a given role or roles. The specification derived from this forms the plan for the language syllabus. Thus, it is rather as if an architect were told to look at someone else's house as the basis for the dwelling he or she is about to plan for the client.

The resulting needs analysis specifies the ends which the learner hopes to achieve. What a needs analysis does not specify is the means by which the ends will be reached. In other words, a construction system is not described. For such a plan, a *means* analysis is required. The means analysis will concern itself with the resources (in terms of people and materials) available for the realization of the product specified by the needs analysis. Whereas in the early 1970s much attention was given to needs analysis and the specification of objectives, recently there has been a realization that means analysis is equally important, since without a clear understanding of resources and constraints the teacher/planner may face difficulties in achieving the goals specified in the needs analysis.

The impetus for needs analysis came from recognition of the link between language code and language use as manifest in the notional–functional approach. When, previously, the focus of language teaching had been on the code, it was not possible to define learners' needs except in terms of the language system itself. Thus, in this sense, a learner 'needed' the affirmative before the negative or interrogative; or 'needed' the present tense indicative before the past; and so on. Once, however, the functional use of language is admitted, the learners' needs take on an entirely different perspective because these needs are determined not by the content of the language system but by the exploitation of that code by users in the world of affairs.

Thus, the purpose for which language is to be used becomes a key consideration in defining the content and objectives of a language syllabus. And once considerations of purpose are admitted, a number of other factors must be taken into account. It is no great step from this point to the realization that what is required is a sociolinguistic description of the language use needed by a given set of learners when carrying out the target roles of which language is a crucial part. In this way, the essentially descriptive categories outlined by Hymes (1966) become the basis for a predictive account of learners' needs.

Not surprisingly, the development of needs analysis as a stage in syllabus design and as a set of procedures evolved in association with languages for specific purposes (LSP), already noted in chapter 2. LSP is that branch of language teaching most closely allied to training in such fields as industry, commerce, science and technology. In LSP, the language is not being learned as an end in itself; it is being learned as a means, these being indicated in the SP of the title. As a branch of vocational training, LSP is thus associated with a battery of procedures and techniques which have evolved in this field.

Adopting a training model (see figure 6.2), Bell (1981) proposes a stage in

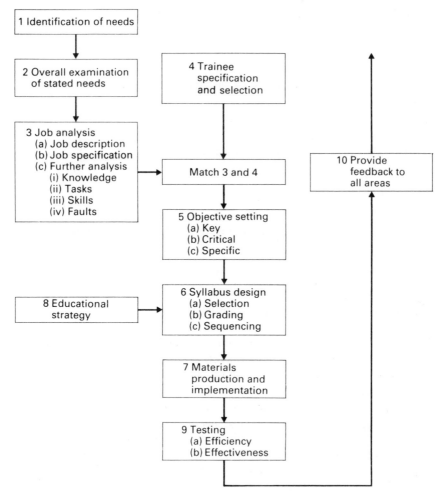

Figure 6.2 Ten steps in the design of training programmes
(from Bell 1981)

which job requirements and learner characteristics are matched, the deficit
between the two then defining the needs which have to be fulfilled on the
training programme. The question which now arises is, how are language
needs to be defined?

Essentially, this depends on establishing a number of categories whereby
language needs can be described. At its simplest, this would mean describing
needs in terms of

Who?

Where?

When?

Why?

What?

How?

In addition, other questions such as the ones below will refine the specification further:

A stranger? An equal? A superior?

A familiar situation? A stressful and noisy one?

During working hours? In the evening?

How often?

What purposes are involved? What degree of reciprocity is there?

What topics are to be dealt with? Are these specialized? general?

What medium (or combination of media) is involved?

Are productive and receptive skills involved?

What level of performance is required?

What kinds of levels of cultural knowledge are required?

Answers to questions of this kind were sought by Richterich and Wilkins (1975/80) and Richterich and Chancerel (1977/80) in their Council of Europe projects concerned with the definition of needs for adult learners. Mindful of the fact that 'one of the characteristics of the adult learner is his desire to learn rapidly something he can use immediately', Richterich and Wilkins (1975/80:46) proposed defining language needs and content by obtaining quantitative and qualitative statistical data from polls and surveys. 'Analysis of content means observing and examining the oral and written use made of a language by a given person or class of persons, and then deducing objective needs which are foreseeable and generalizable' (p. 48). They point out that a person about to learn a foreign language 'has only a vague idea, if any, of his future needs', and therefore a survey of the language needs of a pre-determined category of adults should be carried out by analysing the language use 'among persons already using the language in the same field as the category of persons concerned' (p. 49). They also advocate surveying the learner group 'in order to discover their motivations and their opinions as to their needs'.

The Council of Europe project was concerned with the definition of needs for European adult language learners as a means of standardizing specifications across the member states – essentially a bureaucratic approach which has its counterpart in the various forms of standardization which have characterized the Council's commercial counterpart, the EEC. Such standardization for 'general' adult learners is, as the authors acknowledge, very difficult.

Less difficult is defining needs for learners with specific requirements. A very influential proposal for this was published by Munby (1978), whose language skills in *Communicative Syllabus Design* have already been mentioned. His approach, which is summarized in figure 6.3, has been described by Hawkey (1979:8) as directed towards ESP contexts,

> informed by functional views of language and biassed towards a sociolinguistic interpretation of competent language use. Hymesian notions of contextualised language use and Hallidayan views on the functions of language were thus reflected in a systematically organised, sequential, cumulative and comprehensive set of procedures for defining the communicative needs of a particular potential language user.

He points out that it is important to recognize what the model 'did and did not claim to do'.

> In broad terms, it took only two steps – needs profile and target syllabus – towards course design. It did not take account of implemen-

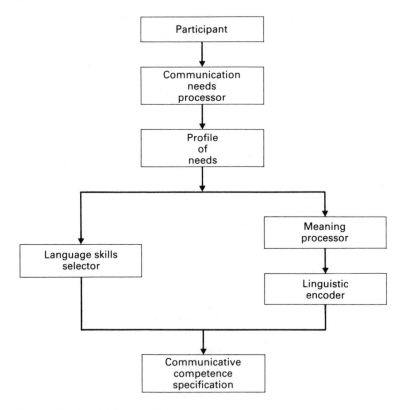

Figure 6.3 Model for specifying communicative competence
(from Hawkey 1979)

tational constraints: the syllabus specification could be adjusted later. A distinction was therefore drawn between target syllabus and pedagogic syllabus. It did not specify how data should be collected and analysed. It did not claim to generate directly language realisations. The first step was to define: who will be using English, for what purpose, where, with whom, in which media, using which dialects, at what level, to perform what activities, to convey which tones. The second step was to identify the skills, notions, functions (and possibly forms) which were required in order to satisfy the user's requirements. (Hawkey 1979:8)

The procedures derived from the Munby model involve systematically working through a series of steps in a 'Communication Needs Processor', beginning with a profile of the learner (called 'participant'). Next, the purposive domain (e.g. educational, occupational) is identified, together with the setting, both institutional and psychosocial. Next come interaction (the social relationships involved) and instrumentality (the medium, mode and channel). After this the dialect (both for understanding and production) is defined, followed by target level. This is specified in some detail, including the size, complexity, speed and flexibility of language for receptive and productive purposes, together with the conditions under which it is used, such as tolerance of error and stylistic failure. Finally, there comes the communicative event (e.g. attending lectures, negotiating with contractors) and communicative key (the style of interaction, such as sociable, co-operative, thoughtful).

Munby's model has been the subject of criticism (e.g. Davies 1981, Mead 1982) on both theoretical and practical grounds. It would be tiresome to catalogue these criticisms, but two are worth taking note of, in addition to the criticism of the non-hierarchical nature of his language skills specification, already discussed in the section on skills-based syllabuses in chapter 5.

The first point is that the Munby model does not address itself to the political, economic, administrative and personnel factors which inevitably influence planning and outcomes. In fact, Munby quite firmly states that the consideration of such constraints must be deferred until after the syllabus content specification, based on learners' needs, has been arrived at. Although such an approach reduces the complexity of the syllabus design process, by deferring *means* analysis, it begins by ignoring the current situation, which may prove to be the most important factor in the whole equation. More recent work in ESP by Holliday and Cooke (1982) and Holliday (1983) has raised the status and significance of means analysis, serving as a reminder that any syllabus design proposal exists within the wider context which is such an important part of Skilbeck's situational curriculum model. Thus, means analysis should be regarded not as a subsidiary, but as an equal stage in the syllabus planning process.

The second criticism, related to the exclusion of implementational constraints, is the tendency of the Munby model to encourage needs analysis in the study or office instead of on the shop floor, as is clear from the examples which Munby himself provides. Whereas the Richterich approach to needs analysis encourages surveying the user community, Munby's model seems to encourage a 'hands-off' approach whereby the needs analyst, using the 'Communication Needs Processor', analyses by remote control. The danger is that the analyst will impose his or her own perception and interpretation of needs on the learner.

It is only by checking with the user community and with the learners themselves that a rounded picture of needs can be obtained. There are, of course, a number of practical difficulties in the way of doing so. The first problem is actually gaining access to the user community whose language use forms the basis of the learners' needs. Stories of attempting to record oil rig operatives on the job are legion, and may serve to highlight the difficulties of on-site data gathering. Although there is a long tradition in industrial training of job analysis, this has tended to focus on psycho-motor rather than linguistic skills, so the needs-cum-job analyst will be ploughing a new furrow when waving his (or, even more problematically, her) tape recorder under the nose of an oil rigger.

Approaching the learner may be less onerous, and quite large-scale attempts have been made to engage would-be learners in a definition of their *wants*. Clark (1979) reports a survey carried out in Lothian among secondary school pupils, in which they were polled on such questions as:

What language did they want to learn? (French, German, etc.)

What reasons did they have for learning it?

Which jobs did they have in mind in which a foreign language would be useful?

Which areas of language (in particular, immediate v. deferred use of the language and role relationships)?

Which modes of communication?

What listening/reading/writing activities?

What physical settings?

Which spoken communicative activities/functions?

Which topics?

The answers to this survey became an important source of information for Clark and his colleagues in planning a new secondary schools language syllabus which would match the aspirations and expectations of the pupils. The result is a graded objectives syllabus of the kind now becoming popular in MLT in Britain.

Eliciting such information from clients, sponsors and prospective learners remains a problem, however, as may be obvious from questionnaires in which respondents are asked to rank the importance they give to such language functions as:

expressing want, desire, intention

expressing bewilderment

forbidding someone to do something

Although examples of many of the functions may be provided, e.g. blaming (It's your fault . . .), the unfamiliar terminology can prove confusing to informants. In any case, there is, as I have already noted in the discussion of language functions, some ambiguity in the definition and realization of any function, the context playing a crucial role. Thus, a questionnaire of decontextualized functions, catalogued rather in the manner of language structures, may not prove to be very helpful when attempting to define learners' needs, whereas having the informants talk through those situations and episodes in which they are required to use the target language may prove more enlightening to the needs analyst. Unfortunately, such procedures do not form part of the typical needs analysis literature.

As will have become obvious during the discussion of the basis and outcomes of needs analysis, the specification of learners' needs tends to be made in behavioural terms. Indeed, the Council of Europe's specification was quite consciously formulated in this style. Such use of behavioural objectives raises another issue, that of the pre-specification of outcomes in precise terms to which the course designer, teacher and learner are expected to conform. The controversy surrounding behavioural objectives has already been aired in chapter 3, from which it will be recalled that there is implicit in this argument the conflict between language teaching as training for ordained outcomes on the one hand and education for unexpected outcomes on the other.

There is, however, another side to needs analysis because, as Johnson (1982:41) points out, it 'enables us to discriminate between various learner types, and to produce syllabus inventories (and courses) especially geared to their needs', although, as he observes, this only works satisfactorily 'as long as we are dealing with groups having the same needs.' In languages for general (as opposed to specific) purposes, it is rarely possible to predict the needs of all learners. One solution to this difficulty is to attempt to define a common core of functions relevant to all learners. It is precisely this which the Council of Europe project attempted to do. The functions listed in this common core include those which are associated with the general area of social interaction rather than with specific occupations. Thus, all doctors or secretaries or dentists or engineers will greet, introduce and ask for information. Richterich and Chancerel (1977/80) point out that needs analyses will contribute information not only before the course, but during it as well. The formative effects of needs analysis thus overlap with the formative influence of evaluation, to be discussed in chapter 9. Indeed, many of the concerns and procedures of needs analysis and evaluation are similar. Each is concerned with informing decision-making about the aims, objectives, content and methods of a learning programme. Although needs analysis has tended to be regarded as a pre-course stage, I see it as an on-going process which will help both learners and teachers by providing feedback according to which succeeding stages of a programme can be modified, and in doing so, needs analysis can make provision for the unexpected outcomes which, as we have noted, are seen to be such an important aspect of education.

Type A Syllabuses: Conclusion

What Type A syllabuses have in common is a basis in content. In this respect they conform to the traditional definition of a syllabus as an organized statement of content of things to be learnt. All syllabuses are based on principles of selection and grading, although these will vary according to the content of the syllabus. Syllabuses which give priority to grammatical form (i.e. structural syllabuses) will be based on such criteria as frequency, simplicity, learnability and teachability. Syllabuses which have meaning as their priority will tend to be based on the needs of the learner, which vary according to whether they are short, medium or long term.

SLA research has, as yet, had little impact on content syllabuses, although it is clear that the concept of a natural order of acquisition must be taken into account in syllabus development in the future. It is also clear that abandoning attempts at selection and grading would be premature. Rather, a reconsideration of selection and grading in the light of SLA findings would seem to be advisable. While input to the learner would lack the grammatical fine-tuning characteristic of traditional structural syllabuses, such syllabuses would vary the language focus to match the developmental progress of the learners, since attempting to teach items well beyond their existing competence is wasteful and ineffective. However, provision would also have to be made for capitalizing on learners' capacity to acquire, store and use unanalysed chunks as a preliminary to processing these items as part of grammatical development.

With the substitution of functional for structural content, needs analysis has become an important stage in syllabus design. The principles of needs analysis are sociolinguistically based, and procedures involving both the user community (i.e. the target language users) and the learner have evolved. Many of these overlap with evaluation procedures, and in so far as needs analysis is on-going, it merges with formative evaluation as a means of shaping both syllabus and course. Both make use of similar techniques, including questionnaires and interviews.

Although needs analysis has tended not to give much attention to situational constraints on the content, scope and methodology of the language curriculum, recent trends have emphasized the importance of means analysis as a stage in language curriculum development. By attending to the present situation rather than the situation in the future, such a shift has matched the concerns of needs analysis with those of situational analysis and thus the concept of needs-based syllabus design has been greatly extended and enriched, albeit at the cost of adding a new set of variables.

While content-based syllabuses have become the norm, there are other approaches to syllabus design, one based on topic and the other on skills. The former falls within the content-based category, while the latter forms an intermediate point between Type A and Type B syllabuses. In fact, a complete syllabus specification will include all five aspects: structure, function, situation, topic, skills. The difference between syllabuses will lie in the priority given to each of these aspects, any one of which can become the leading or organizing principle upon which the others are dependent.

The more elements which are included and specified in a syllabus, the richer it is, and the more complex the process of specifying the syllabus becomes. Furthermore, the richer the syllabus, the less choice is given to the teacher and learner, thus raising basic issues regarding the educational effects of the behavioural objectives which are commonly associated with such syllabus specifications. Ultimately, such syllabuses can become so rigid a scaffolding that there is little room for adaptation, improvisation and growth. An alternative basis, which attempts to make provision for such flexibility and growth will be found in Type B syllabuses, the subject of the next chapter.

Suggested Reading

Overview

A review of the state of the art of language syllabus design from the viewpoint of the late 1970s was published by Shaw in a review article in *Language Teaching Abstracts* in 1977. A more recent review, containing a very good selection of papers by Widdowson, Candlin, Breen and Yalden, has been edited by Brumfit (British Council 1984a) in the *ELT Documents* Series, and indeed it is Brumfit's definition of syllabus from this source which has been cited in chapter 1. Another collection of articles in the same series may be found in *ELT Documents 108, National Syllabuses* (British Council 1980). Meanwhile, the latest overview of syllabuses is found in Breen (1987).

Notional–Functional Syllabuses

The best introduction to notional–functional syllabuses is provided by Wilkins's *Notional Syllabuses* (1976). To find out what the Council of Europe's proposals contained, see *The Threshold Level*, Van Ek (1975) and *Waystage*, Van Ek and Alexander (1977). Their syllabus proposals stimulated a lot of discussion at the time, as is reflected in the fact that much of an issue of *Applied*

Linguistics was devoted to this topic: vol. 2/1 (1981). It includes papers by Brumfit, Paulston and Wilkins. For further discussion of notional categories in language teaching, see Crystal (1976).

A criticism of the notional–functional basis to syllabuses by Widdowson is found in a collection of his papers, *Teaching Language As Communication* (1978). A lucid review of syllabus design, including notional–functional syllabuses, has been contributed by Furey to *Trends in Language Syllabus Design*, edited by Read (1984). A discussion of the design and procedural issues arising out of the move to semantically based syllabuses appears in Johnson, *Communicative Syllabus Design and Methodology* (1982).

For an example of the application of functional theory to syllabus design, see Jupp and Hodlin, *Industrial English* (1975). Examples of syllabuses also appear in Yalden, *The Communicative Syllabus: Evolution, Design and Implementation* (1983) and *Principles of Course Design for Language Teaching* (1987). For a discussion which moves from syllabus to materials design, see Dubin and Olshtain, *Course Design: Developing Programs and Materials for Language Learning* (1986).

Realizations of the functional syllabus in published materials can be found in such representative series as *Strategies*, by Abbs, Ayton and Freebairn, and Abbs and Freebairn (1977 onwards); *Network*, by Eastwood, Kay, Mackin and Strevens (1980); and *Main Course English*, by Garton-Sprenger, Jupp, Milne and Prowse (1979).

Needs Analysis

Munby's *Communicative Syllabus Design* (1978), though open to criticism (see Davies 1981 and Mead 1982), has provided a widely adopted and adapted model for identifying learners' needs. A seminar, in which the Munby model was put to the test, took place in 1979 and the outcomes were published by the British Council (1979) as one of their Dunford Seminar Reports. For a data-based approach to needs analysis, see Freihoff and Takala (1974), while for an evaluation of approaches to needs analysis, see Cunningsworth (1983).

7 The Type B Tradition

Introduction

In chapters 4, 5 and 6, I reviewed the characteristics of and principles underlying Type A syllabuses, which are based on the pre-specification of content. I also reviewed skills-based syllabuses and noted the importance of incorporating a skills component into the language syllabus. I now turn to the Type B tradition, which represents a move, already implicit in the skills approach, from content to processes of learning and procedures of teaching – in other words, to methodology. I shall begin by reviewing some of the principles underlying the Type B tradition, and then go on to look at the process and procedural syllabuses in some detail.

Methods-Based Syllabuses

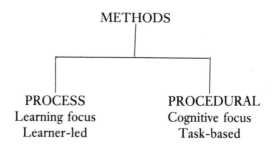

Under the Type B tradition, I have classified two rather different types of syllabus united by a common basis in methodology rather than in content. In most other respects, the syllabuses are very dissimilar, however, being based on rather different approaches. Of the two, only the procedural syllabus has as yet been evaluated. In India its originator, Prabhu, has tried out this type of syllabus on an experimental basis in a number of classrooms. By contrast, the process syllabus, advocated by Breen and Candlin, has as yet to be evaluated, one of the difficulties undoubtedly being that it is by its very nature learner-led rather than teacher-directed (as is the case in the procedural syllabus).

But what does 'learner-led' mean in this context? And what is the difference between a teacher- and a learner-led syllabus? Briefly, there are a number of bases upon which a syllabus can be developed. Traditionally, syllabuses are content- and teacher-led, that is, a teacher (using the term very broadly) selects and organizes the content, following those criteria which have been reviewed in the discussion of Type A syllabuses in the preceding chapters. A more radical approach involves basing the syllabus on methodology (or means), in which tasks rather than content form the focus. While the aim of such a syllabus is to promote effective language learning, the emphasis is on tasks through which language is used and learned. Such a syllabus is still teacher-led, however, since the teacher is in control of the selection and organization of the tasks.

A learner-led syllabus, by contrast, will take the direction determined by the learners, so that it is impossible to predict in advance exactly what route the syllabus will follow, since it is the pace and direction set by the learners that will dictate its shape. The fact that learners do follow some kind of internal syllabus has been referred to on a number of occasions, and it is this kind of learner-led syllabus which constitutes the basis of the programme to be followed.

To return to the house-building analogy, a learner-led process syllabus is rather like building a house a section at a time, with only a general idea of what the final dwelling will be like. The only aspect which is likely to be agreed on in advance is the ultimate outcome, though even that will have to be negotiated among participants before construction. This does not mean that the teacher is completely powerless, entirely at the mercy of the learner. What it does mean is that a very different view of the teacher's and learners' roles is implied by such an approach, and, as we shall see later in discussing innovation, such redefinition can be a powerful factor in inhibiting change. In this, among other considerations, we may discover a reason for the striking shortage of tangible examples of the process syllabus.

Approaches to Learning

Both the process and procedural syllabus are influenced by views on the way learners learn a language. An accumulating body of research into learners and learning (see below) has given support to the idea that some learners are more efficient language learners than others and that different people have different ways of learning. In one sense the picture has been clarified; in another, it has been made more complicated.

The growth of interest in the learner has been one spin-off of the Chomskyan view of language, from which has evolved a reassessment of the role of error in both native and second language learning. Instead of being viewed as 'vicious tendencies', errors could be viewed as evidence of learning, and, indeed, the systematic study of learners' errors has revealed that in both L1 and L2 learners proceed through progressive stages, each governed by a consistent set of rules whose salient characteristic is that they differ from the rule system of the adult form (in the case of children acquiring their L1) or the target language form (in the case of second language learners). In SLA, 'Interlanguage' is the term given to this language system which is independent of both L1 and L2.

Paralleling the linguists' concern with the processes of language acquisition has been the development of a similar interest among educationists and educational psychologists (e.g. Entwhistle 1981) in learning processes, based on cognitive theories of information processing and learning. From a concern with finding out how learners learn, it is no small step to organizing a learning programme around the enabling skills thus identified. Such an approach to curriculum will be means- rather than ends-based, although some notion of target performance skills must be taken into account, because an exclusive concern with means can lead to the provision of a directionless set of learning experiences.

There are three main sources of information on the way learners go about learning a language. The first consists of that body of research which is often subsumed under the heading 'Good Language Learner Studies' (e.g. Naiman et al. 1978, Pickett 1978). The second is a collection of investigations based on subjective data derived from introspection and self-report (e.g. Cohen and Aphek 1981, Hosenfeld 1976, 1977, Wenden and Rubin 1986). The third falls outside the field of language learning as such, and is based on investigations into cognitive styles and strategies on the one hand, and into students' approaches to learning on the other (e.g. Witkin et al. 1962, Entwhistle 1981).

Of the two approaches to syllabus design subsumed under Type B, the process syllabus shows the greater influence from these sources of information on how learners approach learning. Indeed, as we shall see, organizing the syllabus around learners' learning preferences is an important feature of the process syllabus proposals. In comparison, the procedural syllabus shows more direct influence from SLA theory and research.

The Process Syllabus

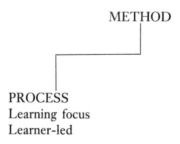

METHOD

PROCESS
Learning focus
Learner-led

The rationale for the process syllabus is an educational rather than a linguistic one and this is reflected in the proposals Breen and Candlin have put forward, the latter pointing out that 'targets for language learning are all too frequently set up externally to learners with little reference to the value of such targets in the general educational development of the learner' (Candlin 1987). Candlin (1987) and Breen (1984:86) both repudiate a means–ends approach to curriculum, observing that 'even a predesigned plan . . . is inevitably and continually *reinterpreted* by ourselves and by our learners.' Furthermore, they say, there is always a disparity between intention and reality, and Candlin (1984:32), while acknowledging that such a tension between 'what is' and 'what should be' can be valuable, asserts it can only be so 'if the should-be is personal and unchartered, not imposed and pre-defined.' The similarity of this view to Stenhouse's is not accidental, since Candlin quite overtly draws upon his curriculum philosophy (as described in chapter 3).

Candlin (1984:34) goes on to argue for an interactive syllabus 'which is social and problem-solving in orientation rather than one which transmits preselected and often predigested knowledge' and he suggests a *retrospective* syllabus, the product of the kind of negotiation and evolution which actually goes on in the learning milieu. Indeed, it is likely that most teachers, if asked to compare initial plans with eventual outcomes, would acknowledge that what they and their students actually did during the course of a year did not exactly match what they thought they would do. Inevitably, there is a process of give and take (or negotiation) which determines the eventual journey and possibly even the destination. Candlin's proposal is, in part, to build this process of negotiation into the system rather than to ignore it.

Candlin summarizes his proposals in figure 7.1, in which the planning of language learning and teaching occurs at two levels: curriculum and syllabus:

Figure 7.1 The process model
(from Candlin 1987)

At the level of curriculum guidelines we would find statements about learning in general and learning of particular subject-matter, indications of learning purpose and experience, targets and modes of evaluation, role relationships of teachers and learners, as well as banks of learning items and scripts with accounts of procedures for drawing on these, exploring and expanding their boundaries. (Candlin 1987:5).

The joint planning between teacher and learners concerns 'everyday decision-making', which leads to three kinds of syllabus: (1) language learning, (2) content and (3) actions – 'of what was explored and how that was accomplished' (Candlin 1987:6): 'What we have, then, as [the figure] indicates, is a dialectic process between the level of guidelines and the level of syllabuses, by means of which the accounts of classroom work can effect curriculum change.' Breen takes such proposals a step further in a model which moves away from knowledge of abilities and skills for communication and from ends towards means. He suggests that, in addition to a content syllabus, there should be a second kind of syllabus, co-existing and supporting the first. This second kind of syllabus 'would be a plan relating to the teaching and learning process made available by the classroom' (Breen 1984:54). The process syllabus he advocates would involve the learners in designing the programme of learning, and the approach attempts to deal with the question, 'How might we best realize and involve the learner's own principles or organization when confronted with new knowledge?' Such a syllabus will be concerned with joint participation by teacher and taught, with the procedures to be adopted and followed in negotiating content, methods and objectives, and with the decision-making related to these. In short, the syllabus addresses the question, 'Who does what with whom, on what subject-matter, with what resources, when, how and for what learning purposes?' Figure 7.2, from Breen (1984), provides his own summary of the process syllabus, in which it can be seen that there are a number of levels through which participants proceed in a continuing, cyclic process.

As outlined by Breen, the syllabus appears abstract and, to many teachers, either incomprehensible or unworkable. This is unfortunate, because, whatever impression may be given by the terminology and the diagram, the proposals are not as alien as they might at first seem. Any teacher even vaguely familiar with individualized learning and the organization and use of resource centres will find much that is familiar, since both of these involve identifying learner needs, wants and preferences and directing the learners to appropriate resources.

What Breen is proposing is in many ways an extension of such a practice, but whereas individualized learning and resource centres have tended to be something extra attached to an existing programme, here they would become part of the very basis of the syllabus. At Level 1, the class and teacher will negotiate general aims, procedure and content, thus providing an overall direction to their activities. The processes of discussion and participation

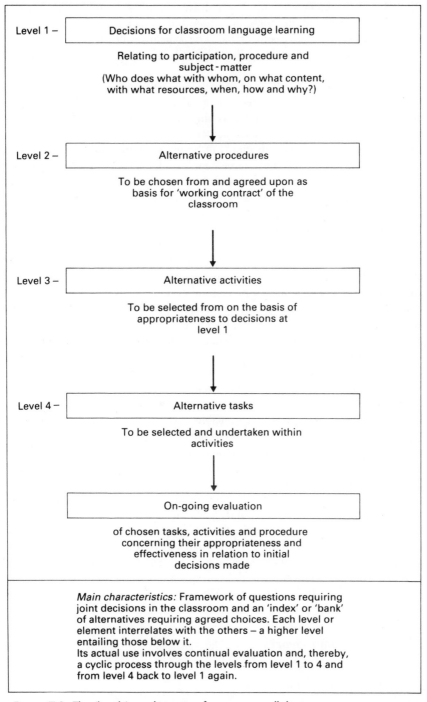

Figure 7.2 The 'levels' or elements of a process syllabus
(from Breen 1984)

through which agreements are reached are regarded as important, because they will involve genuine communication and personal commitment within what is termed the classroom arena. The syllabus will, in other words, be based on opportunities made available by the classroom and the processes of learning.

In the second level, the teacher and students will agree on procedures to be followed in reaching their agreed upon aims, while in Level 3 alternative activities will be chosen in so far as they are appropriate to the aims and procedures agreed in Level 1. Each activity will embody a range of tasks, from which, again, a negotiated selection will be made. Throughout the processes of discussion, selection and agreement, students and teachers will be evaluating the tasks, activities and procedures in the light of their original aims and plans, made at Level 1. Such evaluation will be continuous and formative, informing decision-making at each stage and, if necessary, resulting in alterations to earlier decisions or changes to the choices about to be made.

One can imagine such a process syllabus in action. At the beginning of a course, teachers would review their knowledge of the students – their characteristics, their previous language learning experience, their past results and future needs. The students' perception of their needs would be elicited by questionnaire and discussion, as would their preferences for content, skills and learning activities. It might be, for instance, that the students were particularly keen to be able to understand public announcements in the target language, possibly because of recent experience on recent or planned travel abroad. Students and teachers could together decide what kinds of public announcements were envisaged, how well the students wished to be able to comprehend them, what difficulties they had had or anticipated, and so on. Discussion could then focus on available materials and how they might be exploited, e.g. in the language lab, in small groups in the classroom, as a whole class activity, etc. An agreement would be reached on how, how much and when such listening materials would be used and how teachers and students would evaluate successful learning.

After this stage participants would begin work, following the agreed methods of classroom activity and teaching materials. Evaluation of the learning experiences would take the form of discussion involving both learners and teachers, and such matters as the match between methods and student learning strategies and techniques could be aired, and solutions to the learning problems could be shared. Such questions as the following would be asked (cf. Candlin 1985, citing Dam 1985):

What are we/am I doing?

Why are we/am I doing it?

How do we/I go about it?

What can it be used for?

Through such discussion, both the content and the processes of learning would become part of the language learning experience. At the same time, the learners would be assuming some control over the direction and methodology of the teaching/learning programme.

Clearly, the stimulating proposals which Breen and Candlin have put forward are a manifestation of progressivism, and they draw on the curriculum philosophy articulated by Stenhouse as well as the ideas set out by such radical educators as Freire (1970), whose concepts of praxis and dialogue are an integral part of Breen and Candlin's approach. However, like all such utopian proposals, there will be problems of implementing them in the world of everyday affairs, and it is as well to consider what some of these contraints might be.

The first problem is that there exists no evaluation of such a model in practice. The fact that language curriculum evaluations are thin on the ground does not invalidate this criticism – all proposals for curriculum development should be evaluated at every stage, and the process proposals are not exempt from this requirement. Secondly, as with Stenhouse's process curriculum proposals, the process syllabus calls for considerable professional competence and confidence on the part of teachers. Although curriculum development (of which syllabus design is an aspect) may be a good vehicle for teacher development (by extending professional skills through INSET (in-service education of teachers), there are situations where such development is at worst not feasible or at best is very difficult (cf. Kouraogo 1987).

This brings us to the third criticism: there is inadequate provision within the proposals for relating the syllabus to the context in which it will occur. There may be many cultural barriers to the implementation of such a syllabus which, by its very nature, tends to challenge conventional or accepted notions of authority. Fourth, and related to this last point, is the redefinition of roles which such an approach to syllabus design entails. It is not only the teacher who has to change roles – the students do too. Even in a situation where students may hope for or demand more participation in decisions to do with their learning, accepting such participation requires the assumption of responsibility and effort, neither of which may be willingly shouldered by students when the time comes (see Rudduck 1973, for instance.) Furthermore, the abdication of certain areas of authority by the teacher may be very unwillingly undertaken.

Quite apart from these problems, there are other practical ones as well. Such a process syllabus involves the abandoning of the single textbook, the mainstay of many language courses in which the textbook equals the curriculum. It is difficult to see how a process syllabus as outlined by Breen and Candlin would be compatible with the traditional reliance on a textbook, even when it is supplemented by skills-based materials. Instead of using one main textbook, the teacher would be required to draw on a bank of materials, some of which could and would probably be published textbooks and supplementaries. Questionable though reliance on a textbook might be, it is a tradition which dies hard, while in many situtaions the coursebook is all the hard-pressed or underskilled teacher has to rely on. What price the process syllabus, then?

Finally, we come to the question of aims and objectives. As we noted in chapter 3, behavioural objectives are regarded with suspicion or even distaste by some educationists, though such suspicion may derive more from the source of the objectives than from the aims themselves, as there is a tendency for objectives to be defined by authorities other than the teachers, still less the students. This places teachers in a dependent and non-participatory role within the decision-making process, and such a posture is, within the ideology underlying a process curriculum, untenable. One response is to reject the presetting of ends and to concentrate on means.

Within language teaching, such a position seems equally untenable, given the means–ends nature of language pedagogy (cf. Stern 1984:421, 501). Although the process model does not advocate ignoring aims, the emphasis on process and procedures rather than on outcomes could result in an aimless journey. There is little point in substituting a pedagogical magical mystery tour for a reasonably well-defined educational destination and such a warning may need to be kept in mind when replacing prescription by negotiation.

The Procedural Syllabus

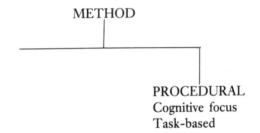

METHOD

PROCEDURAL
Cognitive focus
Task-based

The procedural syllabus is associated with the work of Prabhu, who has developed a 'learn*ing*-centred' (as opposed to learn*er*-centred) approach to language teaching. Working at the Regional Institute of English in Bangalore, Prabhu shared the growing dissatisfaction with the Structural–Oral–Situational method which had been developed and disseminated as the pedagogic orthodoxy in the 1960s. Taking the work of Palmer, among others, as a theoretical inspiration, Prabhu has evolved an approach which is based on the principle that the learning of form is best carried out when attention is given to meaning, and since 1979 in India 8 classes of children ranging in age from 8 to 13 years have been taught by the methods developed by Prabhu and his colleagues. Early in 1984, the project was cautiously but favourably evaluated by Beretta and Davies (see below), and their report was published in *ELT Journal* a year later. Meanwhile, and almost inevitably, some controversy has surrounded the project, finding expression in a paper by Greenwood (1985).

There are several notable features to the Bangalore/Madras Communi-cational Teaching Project (CTP), as it has come to be known. Unlike some theorists (e.g. Krashen), Prabhu has been very modest about the wider application of his approach, which is based simply on the findings of the project. Also, unlike the process syllabus discussed earlier, the Bangalore project and the procedures to which it has given rise have been subject to public scrutiny. Indeed, it could be said that a project which has for the most part been described in relatively obscure publications (mostly emanating from the Regional Institute, Bangalore) and which has involved about 300 children and less than a dozen teachers in southern India, has generated a disproportionate amount of professional interest. Fortunately, Prabhu has himself now provided an account of the project which will be available to an international audience (see Prabhu 1987) and it is from this source that I have largely drawn.

At the basis of the CTP are tasks which engage the learner in thinking processes, the focus of which is completion of the task rather than learning the language. Such task-based teaching is intended to enable the learners, in due course, to achieve 'grammatical conformity in their use of language' which is believed 'to arise from the operation of some internal system of abstract rules or principles'. This process of 'internal system-development' was believed to go on 'at a subconscious level of their minds', and the system-building would be

> activated or furthered by immediate needs to understand and express meaning but, once activated, capable of going beyond what is strictly called for by those immediate needs, achieving grammatical conformity in addition to communication. Learners engaged in task-based activity are, at any given time, meeting the demands made on their understanding and expression by bringing into play such internal systems as they have developed so far (which, being in formative stages, may lead to miscomprehensions or ungrammatical expression) but, in doing so, they are also developing those systems a little further.

I have summarized the CTP model below.

Task	→ Learners' Cognitive Processes →	Task completion
Conscious	Meaning-building	Meanings understood or conveyed
Unconscious	System-building	Grammatical system developed

'Task-based teaching', says Prabhu (pp. 69–70)

operates with the concept that, while the conscious mind is working out some of the meaning-content, some subconscious part of the mind perceives, abstracts or acquires (or recreates, as a cognitive structure) some of the linguistic structuring embodied in those entities, as a step in the development of an internal system of rules. The intensive exposure caused by an effort to work out meaning-content is thus a condition which is favourable to the subconscious abstraction – or cognitive formation – of language structure.

He points out that the acquisition of any element in language structure is not 'an instant, one-step procedure' for 'it may take several instances of intensive exposure to different samples of language before any abstraction is made, or cognitive structure formed, and particular instances may or may not lead to any such result.' Indeed, it is only 'recurrent effort at comprehension [which] thus leads to recurrent deployment and to the gradual growth of an internal linguistic competence.' Prabhu repudiates any attempt to develop the language system by formal means, pointing out that it is not the job of language teaching to discover the various aspects of the internal system (this is the linguists' job), but to *develop* the system in the learners:

> the internal system developed by successful learners is far more complex than any grammar yet constructed by a linguist, and it is therefore unreasonable to suppose that any language learner can acquire a deploy-able internal system by consciously understanding and assimilating the rules in a linguist's grammar. (p. 72)

He emphasizes the point that 'teaching a descriptive grammar is likely – as has pointed out at various times in the history of language pedagogy – to promote in learners an explicit knowledge of that grammar, rather than a deployable internal system.' Prabhu also draws attention to the mismatch between the organization of a descriptive grammar and the organization of the learner's internal system – a point which I have already noted in references to research into language acquisition. He notes that the assumption that 'the development of the internal system is a discrete item, additive process . . . goes counter to the highly plausible perception in interlanguage studies that the process is a holistic one, consisting of a sequence of transitional systems.' Thus, a linguistically graded syllabus is rejected in favour of a task-based one, in which the tasks are selected and graded in terms of cognitive complexity. The language selection which arises from such a sequence of tasks will be based on 'the needs of the activity/discourse and manageability for learners'.

The Tasks

Since a great deal of what is done in the procedural syllabus is related to tasks, a list of some of the tasks used in the CTP may serve to illustrate the basis of the approach in recognizable terms. Here are some of the tasks given by Prabhu. The numbering follows the order in his list, thus reflecting the sequencing of the tasks.

1 Diagrams and formations

    a Naming parts of a diagram with numbers and letters of the alphabet, as instructed.

    b Placing numbers and letters of the alphabet in relation to one another, as instructed, to arrive at particular formations.

    c Placing letters and numbers in given crossword formats; constructing/completing such formats, as instructed.

5 Maps

    a Finding, naming or describing specific locations on a given map.

    b Constructing/completing a map from given descriptions/instructions.

    c Deciding on the best route from one place to another; giving directions.

    e Deciding on the best form of transport (given information on bus routes, fares, etc.).

    f Making decisions on good/bad siting (e.g. of a new hospital or school).

10 a Working out the money needed to buy a set of things (e.g. school stationery; vegetables), from given price lists and needs.

    b Deciding on qualities to be bought with the money available; inferring quantities bought from the money spent.

    c Discovering errors in bills; inferring when an underpayment/overpayment must have taken place.

    d Deciding between alternatives in shopping (e.g. between a small store nearby and a large one which involves lower prices but expenditure on transport).

    e Working out possibilities of saving, from information about incomes and expenses.

16 Stories and Dialogues

    a Listening to stories (of a 'whodunit' kind) and completing them with appropriate solutions.

    b Reading stories or dialogues and answering comprehension questions (particularly of an inferential kind) on them.

    c Completing or continuing given dialogues, as appropriate to given situations.

    d Identifying factual inconsistencies in given narrative or descriptive accounts.

18   Personal details

a   Finding items of information relevant to a particular situation in an individual's curriculum vitae.

b   Constructing a curriculum vitae from personal information.

c   Organizing/reorganizing a curriculum vitae for a given purpose/audience.

d   Working out ways of tracing the owners of objects, from information supplied by the objects.

These tasks will not strike most readers as being particularly innovative, since such tasks are the stock-in-trade of many language teachers. What is claimed to be innovative is the way the material is used. Instead of focusing on the language, the teacher (and learners) focus on the task, and such attention to language as occurs is in order to complete the task. Furthermore, although language errors are corrected, they are only repaired by the teacher offering (or eliciting from the rest of the class) the correct form; there is no attempt to focus on the language and to provide a rule of grammar or spelling. Such language repair is what Prabhu (p. 61) calls 'incidental correction', contrasted with 'systematic correction' in which there is 'a larger interruption of on-going activity to focus learners' attention to an error that has taken place by providing an explanation of a set of other instances in the hope of preventing a recurrence of the error.'

Each lesson consists of two stages: a pre-task and a task. It is the purpose of the pre-task to provide a 'public', teacher-directed run through of the task, but with different content, so that although it is similar, it is not actually the same as the task the pupils will do themselves later in the lesson. The pre-task enables the teacher to judge the pupils' comprehension of what is involved, and from this judgement the teacher can, if necessary, break the task down into smaller, more comprehensible and more manageable units. The task itself is 'private' and, although the pupil can seek help from peers or teacher, the idea is that it will be completed individually. Prabhu summarizes the sequence as follows:

> the pre-task and task pattern divides a lesson desirably into an initial period of whole-class activity, teacher-direction and oral interaction and a later period of sustained self-dependent effort by learners sustained reading (or sustained listening, when the task is presented orally by the teacher) and some writing. (p. 55)

What is important in such task-based teaching is the maintenance of the pupils' effort to understand, 'since it is this effort which brings about a preoccupation with meaning and a contingent struggle with language.' Because repeated failure would be demoralizing for the learner, the concept of a 'reasonable challenge' in the tasks is important. Learners 'should not be able to meet the challenge too easily, but they *should* be able to meet it with some effort.' The criterion for judging the reasonableness of a task was that approximately half the learners in the class should be successful on approximately half the task, as revealed by marking their work. It was also found necessary to have a regular change of task types after every few lessons for reasons of over-familiarity leading to 'fatigue'.

An important characteristic of caretaker language (as used by parents, teachers and other care-givers) as input to the learner is that, although there is simplification, caretakers rarely indulge in the kind of simplification which gives rise to ungrammatical language. However, in peer-group interaction in the target language, instances of such ungrammatical language are legion, resulting in the provision of 'junky input' (Selinker, Swain and Dumas 1975). One concern of the Bangalore project was to avoid the effects of such junky input during that phase of learning when, through opportunities for production, the learners' grammatical system is 'firming up'. This meant that, although opportunities for group work were by no means ignored, it was underplayed. The reasons for this are discussed by Prabhu:

> Deployment . . . is a process during which learners' internal systems get firmed up (in production as well as in comprehension) and revised or extended (in comprehension). Opportunity for revision or extension arises when there is a mismatch between the internal structures being deployed and those embodied in the sample of language being processed– when, that is to say, the internal system encounters 'superior data' or, in other words, samples of language which embody a more highly developed internal system. It is therefore important for learners' internal systems to be continually encountering 'superior data' so that the process of firming up is balanced by a process of revision and extension. Since differences between the internal systems of different learners are much smaller than those between the internal systems of the learners as a group and the teacher, sustained interaction between learners is unlikely to provide very much opportunity for system-revision. As a result, the effect of learner-learner interaction will largely be a firming-up of learners' systems.

The consequence can be the risk of fossilization of the learner's internal system.

Although 'voluntary consultation or collaboration' between learners was allowed, there was no pressure on learners to engage in such interaction (as there is in group work intended to promote interaction in the target language). Furthermore, Prabhu makes the perceptive point that not all learners like to have to take part in group work and may feel humiliated in front of their peers, even though they may accept loss of face in front of the teacher who is, in any case, regarded as a superior.

The Bangalore/Madras CTP: An Evaluation

Prabhu, as may be clear from the quotation I have taken from his account, puts forward a convincing and well argued case. What, though, are the results in practice?

One account of the Bangalore project had already been published by an outside observer (Brumfit 1984d) when Beretta and Davies undertook an evaluation of the project in 1984 (Beretta and Davies 1985). Their purpose in seeking an evaluation was 'to assess through appropriate tests, whether there is any demonstrable difference in terms of attainment in English between classes of children who have been taught on the CTP and their peers who have received normal instruction in the respective schools.' Beretta and Davies point out that, given the complexity and difficulty of designing a satisfactory research procedure to evaluate methodologies, the history of such *Which?* type comparative studies is not encouraging (a point also made by Cronbach (1963), some 20 years earlier). Because the CTP was not set up as an experiment (with matched control and experimental groups), Beretta and Davies had to use intact classes, rather than operate in a 'stripped down environment' (Beretta 1986a), with consequential limitations on the validity of their findings. Three hypotheses were raised (Beretta and Davies 1985:125):

1   There is a difference between the language abilities arising from form-focused teaching and those arising from meaning-focused teaching. Thus, we expected each group to perform significantly better on its own achievement tests.

2   Acquisition of non-syllabus-based structure is best achieved without focus on form. If this were true, experimental classes would do significantly better than control classes on the proficiency tests of contextualized grammar and dictation.

3   Structure acquired *without* focus on form is more readily available for deployment than structure learned *with* focus on form. For this to be confirmed, CTP groups would have to score significantly higher than control groups on the proficiency test of listening/reading comprehension.

They conclude that the requirements of the first and third hypotheses were fulfilled, while 'The second hypothesis . . . is partly borne out. . . . In short, the results reveal a pattern which is consistent with the first and third hypotheses, and in part consistent with the second (and central) hypothesis.' Finally, Beretta and Davies (p. 126) says that while admitting the limitations inherent in their study, 'we regard the results as being, on the whole, positive, and conclude that they provide tentative support for the CTP claim that grammar construction can take place through a focus on meaning alone.' In contrast to these cautiously phrased conclusions, one writer (Greenwood

1985) has been quite sceptical, suggesting that none of the accounts of the project had offered sufficient evidence to evaluate the claims made for the procedural syllabus and its associated methodology. The subsequent publication of the Beretta and Davies report and of Prabhu's own account of the project does not altogether diminish the doubt Greenwood voiced and, although theoretically the procedural syllabus has much in its favour – as Prabhu himself has so eloquently argued – commitment to a particular viewpoint can give rise to a vested interest which supports rather than evaluates the very principles the project set out to demonstrate. Is Greenwood observing that the emperor really has no clothes? Fortunately, the curious or sceptical reader has an opportunity to investigate the question further by referring to the publications I have drawn upon in writing this account. In any case, the debate on the procedural syllabus is unlikely to diminish.

Which Syllabus?

From our review of syllabuses, it will be clear that the would-be syllabus designer is faced with a rather bewildering choice. Although attempts can be – and indeed, have been – made to combine different types, as in hybrid and proportional syllabuses, there is a basic incompatability between Type A and Type B which might make some combinations or compromises unworkable. Thus, it is difficult to imagine how a structurally based syllabus could be combined with a process one without compromising the theoretical principles upon which each is based, since the pre-selection and ordering of structures which lies at the heart of a structural syllabus are quite incompatible with the avoidance of such a pre-specification in a process syllabus.

The answer to the question, Which syllabus? will be influenced by two factors. Firstly, it will be recalled that, in his definition of syllabus, Brumfit (1984:75) pointed out that 'It is a document of administrative convenience and will only be partly justified on theoretical grounds and so is negotiable and adjustable.' This means that the choice and definition of a syllabus will be influenced by policy rather than principle, a point which curriculum developers ignore at their peril. Decisions about syllabus will, therefore, be subject to the values and aims of the learning system itself. Such influences are less to do with what has been demonstrated by theory and associated research than with what is based on custom, belief and convenience. Any curriculum choices tend to be compromises reached by negotiation (Weston 1979) among individuals with divergent interests (Jenkins and Shipman 1976). Furthermore, from the point of view of introducing a new syllabus, the evidence from innovation studies (to be discussed in chapters 8 and 9) suggests that compatability with *current* practices is a characteristic of successful innovations.

When we come to the theoretical justification of a syllabus – the second factor – we find ourselves in very deep water, since the evidence accumulated from SLA research throws considerable doubt on traditional justifications for Type A syllabuses. The general tenor of such research findings is that it is *methodology* rather than organization which may hold the key to successful language teaching – and learning. Reference to the characteristics of an optimal learning environment, outlined by Ellis (1984), will reveal that at least half the features concerned fall under the heading of 'procedure' rather than 'design', although some will be linked to design decisions.

On the question of empirical demonstration of the effect of organization and procedures on learning outcomes, with the exception of the Bangalore experiment there has been no really concerted effort to evaluate any approach in actual operation, although there is a growing body of research into the effects of procedure on language learning in tutored settings (e.g. Aston 1986, Doughty and Pica 1986, Long 1981, Long and Porter 1985). While there are difficulties in comparative 'Which?' type research, as I noted earlier, we should not be deterred from requiring both rigour and caution in adopting a new approach simply because it is theoretically more satisfying; nor because some research, with little ecological validity as far as typical learning milieux are concerned, lends weight to a theory that there is a natural order of acquisition or that children pass through a period of learning holophrases or unanalysed utterances.

Theory-driven practice can be unworkable because practice is so complex, as the ultimate failure of audio-lingualism, based on linguistic and psychological theory, has revealed. Most language learning takes place in the classroom, which can disturb the predictions based on evidence acquired under controlled or experimental conditions. Attempts directly to work out the implications of language acquisition research in the classroom – either in terms of syllabus design or pedagogical procedures – may not yield the results anticipated, and for this reason we must be cautious.

We must also take account of what language teaching aims are. These aims may be of two kinds in an educational system: firstly, to acquire a knowledge of the second language system and culture; secondly, to acquire the ability to perform with some degree of fluency in the second language, that is, to develop communicative competence. These are two very different aims, and the design and procedures for one will not be appropriate for the other – a lesson which should be clear from the historical review in chapter 2.

If priority is given to language as product, a Type A content syllabus will be most appropriate. If, however, priority is given to the process of developing second language competence, a Type B syllabus will be preferred. Within these two general syllabus types, a choice may be made between sub-types, according to the needs and circumstances of the learner. Thus, a notional–functional syllabus, in which – at least initially – the focus is on useable chunks of language, will be appropriate when the aim is a limited fluency in the target language. If, however, the aim is to develop a flexible and adaptable control over the target language, a process or a procedural syllabus is likely to be more appropriate. In the end, a hybrid syllabus will probably result, not simply because of theoretical considerations, but because, in the day-to-day world of teaching, this will be the compromise which satisfies most interest groups, and I personally would find it difficult to argue against such a pragmatic solution.

In any case, the choice of syllabus type will be determined initially by the aims of the education system. Clarity of aims, as will be emphasized in the discussion of managing curriculum development in chapter 9, is essential. Once aims have been clarified, the choice of syllabus type should be made with a full awareness of what is and what is not possible within the constraints of each syllabus. Confusion over such matters simply leads to frustration and disappointment. For instance, a notional–functional syllabus is not the best choice if the aim is control of formal accuracy, and policy-makers need to be aware of this. If, however, both accuracy and fluency are aims, consideration must be given to a combination of functional and formal syllabuses of the hybrid or proportional type.

Even with such considerations in mind, disappointments and frustrations will still arise. I think this is inevitable if too narrow a view is taken of language teaching. Language teaching is concerned with more than the choice of the 'best' syllabus, and an excessive amount of time and effort can be devoted to the selection and ordering of content, while giving insufficient attention to questions of methodology; to the numerous factors which should influence choices of design and procedure; and to the practical issues of implementation. What I am suggesting, in fact, is that to focus on content is too restricted and that the language educator needs to draw on the principles and procedures of curriculum studies and to apply principles of effective management, the latter being the subject of the following two chapters.

Suggested Reading

Good Language Learner Studies

A seminal paper in the good language learners studies is Rubin (1975), while two important studies are Naiman et al., *The Good Language Learner* (1978) and Pickett, *The Foreign Language Learning Process* (1978). Observational studies include Wong Fillmore (1982) and Saville-Troike (1984).

Introspection

Investigations based on introspective data have been published by Hosenfeld (1976, 1977) and Cohen and Aphek (1981) and Cohen (1986). A more recent study by Wenden (1986) is in the same tradition. A collection of papers on this topic, *Learner Strategies*, has been edited by Wenden and Rubin (1987).

Process and Procedural Syllabuses

Unfortunately, little has been published on process syllabuses, so we must rely on largely on Breen's (1984) and Candlin's (1987) accounts of it. We are rather better off for descriptions of the procedural syllabus, as there are accessible and readable accounts by Johnson (1982) and Brumfit (1984d), as well as a lengthy description by Prabhu in *Second Language Learning: A Perspective* (1987). A more critical discussion has been written by Greenwood (1985).

For grading tasks within a syllabus for spoken language, see Brown, Anderson, Shillcock and Yule, *Teaching Talk* (1984).

8 Language Curriculum Design: Process and Management

Introduction

In earlier chapters, I reviewed the historical background, as well as some of the main approaches, to curriculum design and language syllabuses. I have also noted that while a syllabus is essentially a specification (predominantly of content), curriculum design is a process embracing aims, method and materials which may be specified in a plan, either of future intentions or of existing practices. Any such process will involve choices and decisions, while any process involving people and resources will require the exercise of management. Furthermore, any proposals for renewal or change immediately take us into the area of innovation studies.

It is with such issues that this chapter will be concerned, as a prelude to the final chapter, which will deal with management and evaluation. My own experience, as well as that of many others working in the field of language curriculum, confirms the importance of looking beyond the traditional concerns of the syllabus designer, whose main influences are derived from applied linguistics. Although applied linguistics provides a basis for approach, design and procedure, putting into effect any decisions regarding design and procedure takes us right out of applied linguistics and straight into innovation management. This is because decisions about language curriculum rapidly cease to be decisions about ideas and become actions which affect people. On such matters, applied linguistics is silent, and it is in order to benefit from experience in other fields that this and the following chapter have been written. My hope is that they will provide a useful introduction to what I believe to be crucial to the concerns of anyone dealing with language curriculum development and syllabus design.

Language Curriculum as Innovation

The introduction of a new textbook, changes in forms and procedures of assessment, the substitution of new methods for old, the provision of new equipment (e.g. video recorders, computers) are all aspects of curriculum innovation, though they are often dealt with in a largely unplanned manner. Yet, as Hoyle (1970:2) has observed, 'the cost, complexity and radical nature of current innovations perhaps renders inappropriate the reliance upon the rather ad hoc and individualistic response that one has had in the past.' One of the problems when considering innovation is that it is concerned with a hugely complex area. At one level, we are dealing with systems which can range in scale from the international to institutional, while at another we are dealing with individuals, the private and the personal. Thus, while we can consider innovation in relation to the various effects and forces which operate within a system, we need also to consider innovation from the viewpoint of the individuals who will be most affected by it: the teachers and learners.

Furthermore, innovations are rarely, if ever, disseminated in a 'pure' form, for dissemination almost always involves re-invention, that is, 'the degree to which an innovation is changed or modified by a user in the process of its adoption and implementation' (Rogers 1983:175). It is important to recognize the widely observed tendency of innovations to be modified during the dissemination and adoption process, and the failure to do so lies behind the questionable practice of developing so-called 'teacher-proof' materials in an effort to protect the purity of ELT innovations.

What is innovation and how does it differ from change? *Change* is considered to be any alteration in something between time 1 and time 2. Change can occur spontaneously and does not involve conscious planning or intention. *Innovation*, by contrast, is defined as involving *deliberate* alteration – intention is a crucial element. A number of definitions of innovation have been offered. Miles (1964:13), for instance, has emphasized organizational behaviour, while the definitions offered by Rogers and Schoemaker (1971:19) and Rogers (1983:11) highlight the personal perception and interpretation of innovation. This phenomenological view characterizes much of the most insightful work on educational innovation (Hurst 1983:52–3; Fullan 1982).

Drawing on these earlier definitions, Nicholls (1983:4) defines an innovation as 'an idea, object or practice perceived as new by an individual or individuals, which is intended to bring about improvement in relation to desired objectives, which is fundamental in nature and which is planned and deliberate.' Nicholls goes on to point out that there are a number of difficulties associated with innovation. The first is that, because innovation (as she defines it) is fundamental in nature, it will involve changes in teachers' attitudes and practices. This, as has already been pointed out with regard to language curriculum, can be seen as probably the most important single factor, and one which serves as a reminder of the private and personal aspects of innovation. It is recognition of this which informs the normative–re-educative strategy of innovation, to be discussed later.

The second difficulty is that innovation will almost always lead to an increase in teachers' workloads. Such an increase can occur at all stages: in preparing for the change (through staff meetings, workshops, in-service courses); in planning lessons and materials; in the classroom itself (through having to adopt new roles and techniques); and after the lesson (in the marking of assignments and tests or processing questionnaire or interview data). Any important change in language curriculum will – indeed, should – involve such extra work.

There will also be an economic cost in terms of time and funds. Innovations may require extra preparation time, the costs involving not only paying teachers for extra time spent on such activities, but in footing the bill for new materials and equipment. Time and cost may also be involved in setting up and running research and trialling projects, monitoring outcomes and disseminating findings. In fact, such expense is characteristic of the Research, Development and Diffusion model of innovation, to be discussed below.

Finally, there is the question of evaluation. Since innovations are normally introduced so as to 'be more efficacious in accomplishing the goals of the system' (Miles 1964:13), there is some obligation on those involved to demonstrate that improvement has in fact occurred. Such evaluation may require the system to open itself up to outside appraisal, thus raising issues of accountability, which, as I noted in the discussion of behavioural objectives, can be regarded as a threatening experience by those subject to the evaluation. Furthermore, even within an individual institution, evaluation can raise uncomfortable issues which its members might prefer to keep submerged.

Thus, we see that curriculum innovation is likely to be fraught with difficulties from the outset, as any change agent will rapidly discover, even when proposing an innovation as seemingly innocuous as a new composition marking system or the use of cassette recorders – let alone a new language syllabus.

Innovation within a System

We have seen that at one level, innovation occurs within a system. What, then, is a system? Miles (1964:13) defines it as 'a bounded collection of interdependent parts, devoted to the accomplishment of some goal or goals, with the parts maintained in a steady state in relation to each other and the environment by means of (1) standard moves of operation, and (2) feedback from the environment and the consequences of system actions.' Miles, like many other writers concerned with educational systems, points out that they have special characteristics which, among other things, make the management of innovation different from those systems – notably commercial, industrial, and agricultural – in which it has been studied. In educational systems it is difficult to measure outputs precisely, whereas, of course, in the other systems referred to, the measurement of both inputs and outputs is done with great precision. A further important feature of educational systems is that products – that is, students' learning – are supposedly to be assessed over a long span of time. After all, at least 11 years' compulsory education is the norm in developed countries, while the effects of such education are to be viewed in an even longer term, possibly a whole lifetime.

Another significant difference between educational and other systems is that in the former there is a narrow difference between lay and professional competence. Everyone has had some experience of an educational system, and thus everyone claims some expertise in education. In an earlier discussion I noted the important role of stake-holders. While in a commercial or industrial organization stake-holders might be reluctant to claim technical or professional expertise because of the apparently specialized nature of the organization's activities, many people are prepared to put forward their views on education in general and language teaching in particular, and on how their children should be taught because, of course, everyone can draw on personal experience of being educated and many people have experience of trying to learn another language. Only a few people can draw on comparable experience of running a production facility or managing a retail outlet.

It is with people that we come to a crucial factor: organizations are made up of people, not things, and although systems and organizations can be described in terms of structural and functional elements which can be depicted in organizational charts, in an organization, as Paisey (1981:10 quoting Emmet 1967:184) emphasizes, it is *people* who inhabit the institution, and an organization consists of 'networks of relationships between people acting and reacting on each other, sometimes in accordance with intended ways of furthering the purpose of the organization; sometimes in ways which are intended, though not always in terms of the official purpose; and sometimes in ways not intended by anyone.' Thus, organizations contain rational as well as non-rational elements, a fact which emerges in the subjectivity members of an organization bring to their perception of the organization and of innovation. Most crucially, an educational organization is operated by the persons who are themselves the instruments of change. Without their willingness and participation, there will be no change. And, it might be added, without the participation of the pupils there will not be change, either. Furthermore, because innovation will almost always involve some evaluative element, teachers can resist the changes that are required, even if, on rational grounds, they might agree with the proposals concerned.

Within any complex society, there will be a large number of interconnected systems, which Miles lists under four main heads:

Non-professional structures

Government agencies

Commercial structures

Directly educative systems

Each of these influences the other, and Miles notes the importance of commercial considerations when old investments and new products are at stake in any innovatory process. Also, as Richards (1984) points out, the feasibility with which language teaching innovations can be converted into publishable materials has a profound effect on their dissemination and take-

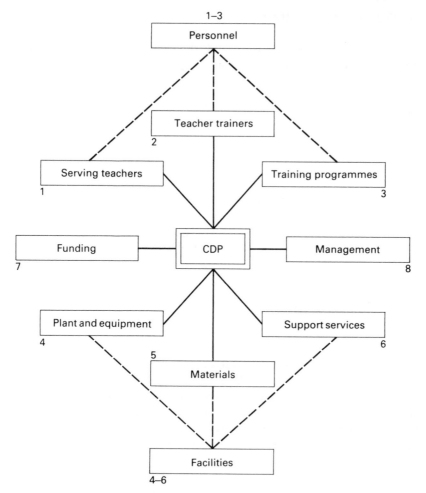

Figure 8.1 Interlocking systems affected by a curriculum development
(from Bowers 1983)

up. Thus, the commercial viability of an innovation in terms of published materials provides an instance in which commercial and educational systems interact.

The complexity of any educational system has been well illustrated by Bowers (1983), who likens it to a spider's web in which a touch at any one point sets the whole network in motion (see figure 8.1). He also shows how decisions made at one point will have a knock-on effect at other points in the system, which in turn may restrain or even inhibit such decisions. To take one instance: decisions to introduce a new textbook will lead to questions about in-service teacher training, which will then result in questions about resources – time, money and the availability of trainers. And so on.

The Process of Innovation

There are three main elements and three main stages in innovation, summarized in a diagram adapted from Bolam (1975).

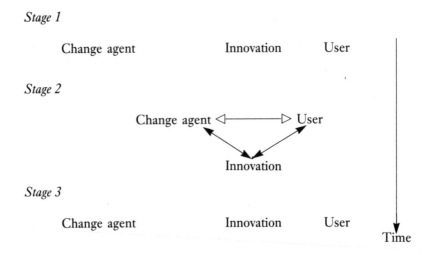

The role of the change agent is to initiate the innovation and to assist in its adoption. The agent may not, in fact, be the originator of the innovation, but in terms of the receiving system or institution it is the change agent who is the message-bearer. In practice, the change agent may be the principal, the director of studies or a staff member who has been on an in-service course or even an author or publisher with new materials. The role of user is that of receiver and adopter of the innovation.

Initially, the three elements – change agent, innovation and user – may exist independently. In fact, change agent and user may be one and the same, although the roles of each are different. Also, change agent and user may occupy identical or separate parts of the system. Where the change agent is separate from that part of the system into which the innovation will be introduced and 'installed', the innovation itself will be external to the receiving user and institution. Where, however, the change agent and innovation are both members of the same institution, the innovation may be internally developed, although an outside agency may be called in as consultant or adviser.

If an innovation is indigenous to an institution, the process will tend to be from the bottom-up, whereas an innovation introduced from outside may follow a top-down process. Much will depend upon by whom and how the innovation is identified, specified and introduced. In school-based curriculum development (as discussed by Skilbeck 1984a), the innovation will have been initiated by members of the institution, whereas in a national and centrally controlled curriculum development, the innovation will have its origins outside the receiving institution, whose role will be that of receiver and implementer rather than that of initiator and developer.

Once the change agent, innovation and user become focused on the innovation, there is an interactive stage during which the two parties concerned will negotiate the installation of the innovation. It will be at this stage that what may have started as a national or regional initiative will be translated into operational terms within the individual institution, leading ultimately to change in the classroom itself and in the practices of teacher and students. Finally, when the innovation is 'successfully and durably installed', the three elements may revert to the same kind of relationship as indicated in the initial stage and the whole process can be repeated.

Innovation in schools takes place within an organization, and account will have to be taken of the antecedent context, the process whereby organizational innovations are implemented and maintained (cf. Rogers 1983:374–8), and the fact, as Miles (1964:18) points out, that 'innovations are *always* operant in relation to a given social system; they affect one or more parts of the system crucially, and are in a very real sense rejected, modified, accepted and maintained by existing forces in the immediate system.'

Indeed, the different interests of members of the system – teachers, pupils, administrators and other stake-holders – lead Weston (1979:39) to invoke the concept of *negotiation* in curriculum development within the social system of the school – a view reminiscent of Brumfit's point regarding the negotiability of the syllabus, quoted in chapter 1. In Weston's view (1979:39), members of this social system are 'constantly working out their own understanding and relationship to the system', while the process of curriculum development involves 'a probing for common ground by groups and individuals with divergent interests but some shared meanings as fellow-members of the same system.'

Thus, we may view the context in which curriculum development and innovation occur as one of divergent interests and conflicting forces (Jenkins and Shipman (1976:42)). In such a dynamic setting, innovation is seen as something which is not necessarily complete or finished, a point stressed by Miller (1967:17): 'Too often an innovation is introduced as "the answer" rather than as something good but not perfect that can be improved with experience and careful study.' This is very apposite if we think of curriculum innovation as being on-going and developmental rather than as the installation of a ready-made and complete solution to an educational problem or the answer to a teacher's prayers. Indeed, the adoption of a new language textbook or new hardware (video and computers being two instances) may mistakenly be seen as being 'the answer', whereas it may be only the beginning of a process of adaptation, adjustment and refinement. The innovatory process is a complex one, and just as several models of curriculum have been put forward, so, too, several models of innovation have been suggested, and it is to these that we shall now turn.

Three models of the change process, from Huberman (1973)

RD and D	*Problem-solving*	*Social interaction*
1 Invention or discovery of innovation	1 Translation of need to problem	1 Awareness of innovation
2 Development (working out problems)	2 Diagnosis of problems	2 Interest in it
3 Production and packaging	3 Search and retrieval of information	3 Evaluation of its appropriateness
4 Dissemination to mass audience	4 Adaptation of innovation	4 Trial
	5 Trial	5 Adoption for permanent use
	6 Evaluation of trial in terms of need satisfaction	

Emphasis on

Developer	Receiver	Communicator

Dissemination Strategies

One-way media for information and training	Two-way involvement between sender and receiver	Variety of transmission media

Models of Innovation

The three main models of innovation, as described by Havelock (1971), have been summarized on page 121. It is important to realize that these are models, and therefore do not necessarily represent any actual state of affairs. Such models involve a simplification of actual events, and·it may be difficult to match any particular instance with the characteristics of any one model. Even so, these models do provide us with a scheme for helping to make sense of innovation. I shall summarize each model in turn before discussing strategies for innovation.

Research, Development, Diffusion/Dissemination (RD and D)

The RD and D model has been regarded as a successful basis for development in such fields as agricultural innovation and the adoption of new industrial processes. In a period in which the shortcomings of education were criticized, the application of such a model to curriculum development had obvious attractions and so during the 1960s and 1970s, large-scale, national projects were established on an RD and D model, in the USA, Europe and Australasia as well as in the newly emerging countries of Africa and Asia (Skilbeck 1985). It is a model of innovation which coincides with the ideology of reconstructionism, which emphasizes cultural renewal, improvement and rational planning.

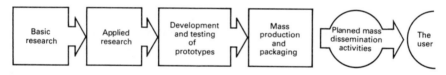

Figure 8.2 The research, development and diffusion model
(from Havelock 1971)

Of the three models, this is the closest to an engineering approach to innovation, as may be clear from the stages from which the model takes its name and from figure 8.2, from Havelock (1971). Classically, a team is assembled and it undertakes

needs assessment

specification of objectives

analysis of alternative strategies and treatments

choice among alternatives in field situations

continuing evaluation and refinement

production

dissemination and installation

Typically, such RD and D projects have devoted themselves to the production of materials or the development of new methods, and the package, conventionally in the form of published materials, is disseminated to the mass audience who are the intended users of the innovation. In language teaching, the Council of Europe Threshold Level is an instance of such an RD and D model motivated by a reconstructionist ideology. Ministries of education in both developed (e.g. the Netherlands) and developing countries (e.g. Malaysia) have adopted or adapted the notional–functional basis of the T-level in centrally controlled RD and D style innovation, and ministries as well as commercial publishers have not been slow to produce appropriately organized materials which can be disseminated and installed following either a power-coercive or an empirical rational dissemination strategy.

Based on the assumption that there is a rational sequence of activities from research, to development, to dissemination, the RD and D approach involves a high level of initial development costs before dissemination takes place. It also implies that planning on a large scale has occurred and the model involves a division of labour, with a clear separation of roles and functions, among which the consumer's role is seen to be a passive one. Indeed, it is assumed that because the user will be motivated by enlightened self-interest, the innovation (typically either a new textbook or new methods, or both) will be adopted with alacrity.

There are, however, problems with the RD and D model. Although it is essentially a linear-sequence model, it has been suggested (Wrigley 1973) that in education, research and development are never linear but are always interactive. Also, while there is an implied separation of specialist-researcher and teacher-user, in fact, the two may intermingle in development teams. Furthermore,

> Despite the verbal and at times ideological promulgation of RD and D, in the UK setting it is difficult to find examples of large-scale curriculum projects where there is at the beginning a substantial research phase out of which emerges a design which ultimately provides a product for widespread dissemination. (Skilbeck 1985:267)

Another problem arises over the dissemination and take-up of the product. In a 'free market', in which teachers have an open choice, the RD and D body may face the prospect of limited interest in and acceptance of their product – an outcome not unknown to the publishing trade. Yet, in such a free market setting, making use of the product mandatory will be unacceptable, whereas in a system where teachers have no choice of materials other than those specified by the ministry of education, dissemination and take-up will be less of a problem, at least in terms of textbooks actually being installed in the schools. Thus, in many countries where decisions regarding language curricula are taken centrally, ELT textbooks sponsored by the ministry of education are distributed throughout the system.

The tendency for such RD and D projects to be closely associated with government may prove to be a limitation in several respects. Because such projects tend to look to central funding for finance, and because such central funding almost inevitably derives from government, questions of control can arise together with difficulties stemming from the tendency of governments to be less rather than more generous with funding. Ultimately, of course, government can withdraw financial support altogether, as happened in Britain with the Schools Council in the early 1980s. Another problem with the close association of such centrally funded development bodies with government is that they may be viewed simply as a creature of government. If, too, the teacher is regarded as a passive consumer, the situation can become politicized, with rejection on one side and attempts at coercion on the other.

Perhaps, however, the most important constraint on the effectiveness of an RD and D strategy is the lack of what Rogers (1983) calls *homophily* between change agents and clients. Homophily is 'the degree to which pairs of individuals who interact are similar in certain attributes' (Rogers 1983:26). Heterophily 'is the degree to which pairs of individuals who interact are different in certain attributes, such as beliefs, education, social status, and the like.' As Rogers notes, the relationship between change agents and clients, when characterized by heterophily, limits the diffusion process. In ELT, such a situation frequently arises when the change agent (such as an expatriate project leader or a school inspector based in an urban office) who is associated with a centralized diffusion agency, is seen belong to a different world from the teachers who are required to take up the innovation.

It would not be right, though, to conclude that the RD and D model is entirely inappropriate and has no further use. Large-scale RD and D can provide important insights and can have – indeed has had – valuable spin-offs. It would be quite irrational to deny the beneficial influence of the Council of Europe's T-level project, for instance, or to denigrate the centrally developed and disseminated publications which have been stimulated by this initiative. In all cases, though, experience shows that no proposal for action will ever be realized unchanged, as is well demonstrated by the variety of materials claiming to be either notional–functional or communicative in basis which have appeared all over the world since the mid 1970s.

The Problem-solving Model

In the problem-solving model of innovation (see figure 8.3 from Havelock 1971) can be seen an expression of progressivism and the approach to curriculum development advocated by Stenhouse, who takes the view that all teachers should assume some responsibility for researching their classroom work and that this is an important part of the teacher's professionalism. A problem-solving approach is also at the basis of action research, whose aim is to make use of research in modifying and improving curriculum practice, thus having a direct relationship to innovation and reform. Indeed, the term 'action' research embodies the aims of this approach – the commitment to action, to the elimination of problems and to the growth of practical

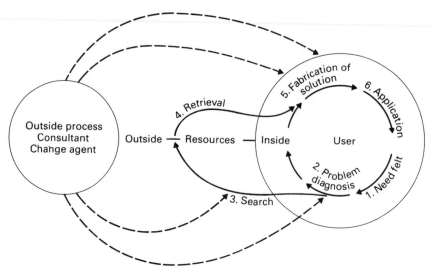

Figure 8.3 The problem-solving model
(from Havelock 1971)

understanding and the improvement of practice – while the focus of action research is on the identification of problems by teachers themselves rather than on those defined by an outside consultant or change agent.

The first stage in the problem-solving model involves problem identification in a highly specific manner, the users' needs being paramount in this process: what the users think they need is the primary concern of any would-be consultant or helper and the diagnosis of their needs has to be an integral part of the total process. The outside change agent should be non-directive and adopts the role of counsellor rather than instigator or director, since it is believed that self- (or client-)initiated innovation will have the strongest user commitment and the best chances for long-term survival – a point emphasized by Everard and Morris, citing Lavelle (1984), who has noted that innovation is more likely to be successful when perceived as necessary by those in the school, rather than by outsiders.

Such an approach means that innovations are likely to be highly appropriate to the context in which they occur, but there is the danger that a head teacher and staff can impose their own values on the school. Furthermore, there are limitations to the technical skill of teachers, particularly in terms of research skills. However, the application of action research methods may overcome such limitations, particularly as action research involves the planned and systematic collection of appropriate forms of data and not just a muddle and impressionistic gathering of evidence. Also, action research aims to improve practice by stimulating reflection upon action in the light of theory derived from practice. We shall return to such questions in the final chapter when discussing evaluation.

Within the context of current ideological concerns, the problem-solving model is closely allied to both the process and situational models of curriculum described in chapter 3, while, with its emphasis on a bottom-up rather than top-down approach, it fits in with much contemporary thinking on the importance of school-based and teacher-initiated research and development. Furthermore, in the ELT context, Holliday (1983) has applied many features of the problem-solving model to ESP curriculum development in a way which has drawn attention to the importance of carefully basing any ELT curriculum initiatives in the local context.

The Social Interaction Model

By its very name, the third model highlights the influence and importance of social relations in the transmission and adoption of innovation. Within the social network, communication and the communicator are key factors, while the role of the change agent is also significant.

In this model (see figure 8.4 from Havelock 1971), the individual user or adopter belongs to a network of social relations which largely influence his or her adopter behaviour. The place of the adopter within the network is a good predictor of the rate of acceptance of new ideas. Briefly, the more central the adopter is within the network, the higher the rate of acceptance. Informal personal contact is a vital part of the influence and adoption process (Rogers 1983), so such a model of innovation will match a decentralized system of management in which influence rather than coercion is the means whereby new ideas and practices are disseminated and taken up.

Group membership and reference group identification are major predictors

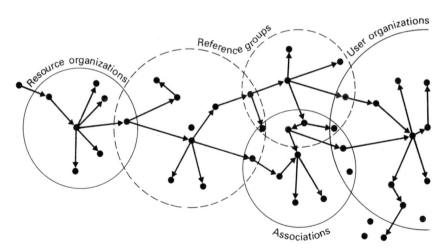

Figure 8.4 The social interaction model
(from Havelock 1971)

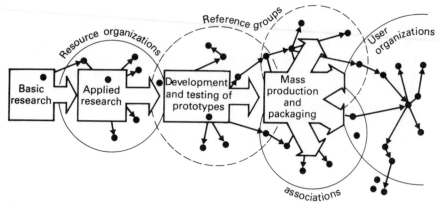

Figure 8.5 Research, development and diffusion takes place in a social context (from Havelock 1971)

of individual adoption, while the presence of an opinion leader (Rogers 1983) and the relation of the leader to the group is also important. (An opinion leader is the kind of individual of whom people say, 'If so-and-so thinks it's good, it must be OK.') The rate of diffusion through a social system follows a predictable S-shaped curve pattern (see chapter 9), during which the stages of awareness, interest, evaluation, trial and eventual adoption are followed.

The social-interaction model may well be an appropriate way of accounting for the diffusion of some innovations in ELT, although the diffusion process in this field awaits study and explanation. The role of opinion leaders in the profession, teachers' centres, informal local groupings and professional organizations (such as TESOL and IATEFL) will all have their place in developing the kind of networks described by Havelock (1971), whereby users and resource persons are put in contact so that the benefits of innovations resulting from RD and D can be diffused to would-be users; or, through collaboration and helping projects, a change agent can assist users to identify and resolve their own problems, following a problem-solving model.

In figure 8.5, Havelock (1971) illustrates how the flow of knowledge from research to practice takes place via social networks, rather than through a series of logical steps, while Rogers (1983) has shown how dissemination follows cliques and social networks. What figure 8.5 does not make clear is what Havelock himself emphasizes (1971:42), that 'social interaction is not merely a matter of passively receiving from others; it is also a matter of give-and-take, of mutual influence and two-way communications.' The reciprocal nature of dissemination and the non-passive role of client or user are features which would-be language curriculum innovators are unwise to ignore (Fullan 1982).

Strategies of Innovation

From *models* of innovation, we now turn to innovation *strategies*, the assumptions which underlie them and the limitations and benefits which each might offer. No doubt anyone who has been involved with innovation in language teaching – whether at classroom or managerial level – will recognize aspects of each model. The three strategies concerned have been proposed by Chin and Benne (1976), and, like the models of innovation, they are an idealization and do not necessarily represent what actually occurs in any given innovatory process. What can be gained from summarizing these models is alerting would-be language curriculum innovators to the assumptions which underlie their own approaches to innovation, thus helping them avoid some of the problems which can arise when a given strategy is adopted. It may also become clear that certain strategies are more likely to evolve in some contexts than others, and that one of the problems may derive not just from the innovation itself but from the attempts to employ an innovatory strategy which does not readily match characteristics of the context – part of the 'ecological' issue noted by Holliday (1980, 1983) and the sociopolitical factors discussed by Markee (1986) in their accounts of innovation management in ESP.

The three strategies are

Power-Coercive

Empirical-Rational

Normative-Re-educative

Power-Coercive

The first type of innovation strategy is based on the application of power in some form – political or otherwise. Knowledge is seen as a major ingredient of power, and knowledgeable people are viewed as legitimate sources of power, with the desirable flow of power being from those who know to those who do not through processes of education and the dissemination of valid information. Where there is resistance or reluctance, political and economic sanctions as well as moral force may be used, and where there is anything like differentiation of opinion or power within a society or organization, this strategy tends to be divisive.

One of the attractions of a power-coercive strategy is its simplicity and ease of use where the innovation is supported or proposed by those in authority, such as the head teacher or departmental head. However, coercive power is 'a decreasingly effective strategy for gaining real commitment', although as Everard and Morris (1985:223) point out, 'there are times when it helps to overcome initial resistance, and it can then give way to more acceptable and enduring methods of winning hearts and minds.'

Persistence in applying a power-coercive strategy may lead to opposition by some, who can adopt the same strategy in retaliation. The result is non-productive conflict and power competition.

A power-coercive strategy is likely to go hand-in-hand with a so-called 'Theory X' management style (McGregor 1960) 'which is seen in the autocratic behaviour of the individual who enforces his own pre-determined decisions by manipulative means which compel alienative or calculative responses in others' (Paisey 1981:114). We shall consider the relationship of management style with innovation strategies in chapter 9. Meanwhile, let us turn to the second innovation strategy: the empirical-rational.

Empirical-Rational

This approach, as its name suggests, is based on two main assumptions:

1 That people are rational;
2 That people will follow their rational self-interest once this has been revealed to them.

A change is proposed by an individual or group which knows of a situation that is desirable, effective and in line with the self-interest of the individual or organization concerned. Because people are assumed to be rational and motivated by self-interest, it is also assumed that those concerned will adopt the proposed change if it can be rationally justified and if they will gain by the change. As Everard and Morris (1985:171) observe,

> The first reason why those who initiate change often fail to secure a successful conclusion to their dreams is that they tend to be too rational. They develop in their minds a clear, coherent vision of where they want to be at, and they assume that all they have to do is to spell out the logic to the world in words of one syllable, and then everyone will be immediately motivated to follow the lead.

And they quote a characteristically acerbic rebuff to such a notion from George Bernard Shaw (p. 171): '"Reformers have the idea that change can be achieved by brute sanity."'

Chin and Benne (1976:30) point out that 'a clearer view of the process of diffusion must include the actions of the receiver as well as those of the transmitter in the transactional events which are the units of the diffusion process.' It is therefore essential to take account of the receivers' perception of things; not to do so is to risk failure. Indeed, the empirical-rational strategy assumes a relatively passive recipient of input, and in this, together with inadequate attention given to communication difficulties and role conflicts, lies one of its main limitations. Furthermore, the empirical-rational approach has evolved within bureaucratically organized enterprises which are characterized by a *role* culture (Handy 1978), in which the organization's purposes are given priority and there are codified procedures for carrying out roles and functions. Finally, empirical-rational strategies have been concerned more with the diffusion of 'thing' than 'people' technologies, which, as will have become clear, do not really match the requirements of educational systems.

The feeling that the empirical-rational approach is inappropriate in education is cogently summed up by Nicholls (1983:33): 'The fact that many educational innovations exist which can be shown to offer certain advantages but which are not taken up by teachers suggest that empirical-rational strategies are not appropriate in all cases.' Such a conclusion does not mean that attempts at introducing innovation should entirely abandon an empirical-rational basis. Indeed, Everard and Morris (1985:171) make the point 'that rationality has to be applied not only to defining the *end* of change, but also the *means*.' Furthermore, as Barrow (1984:225) observes, perhaps rather optimistically, 'it is easier to sell a well-thought-out plan to those with requisite understanding than it is either to sell such people an ill-thought-out plan, or to sell the well-thought-out plan to those without understanding.'

In any case, there will usually be stages in an innovatory process during which an appeal to the rational self-interest of teachers (and learners) will be both necessary and effective. Furthermore, in contexts where initiatives are expected to come from a central authority – as in a RD and D model – an empirical-rational strategy may encounter less resistance than an approach which conflicts with traditional roles and expectations. In practical terms, an empirical-rational strategy will take the form of directives, seminars, newsletters and resource or teachers' centres through which teachers are informed of innovations. The introduction of new syllabuses and textbooks by a ministry of education may be promoted by an empirical-rational strategy, whose appeal to the academic administrator is obvious.

However, an empirical-rational approach will have to be supplemented by other strategies if an innovation – such as a new textbook – is to be effectively installed, and it is to the third of these strategies that we now turn.

Normative-Re-educative

At the basis of the normative-re-educative model is the assumption that people are self-activating and non-passive. As rational and intelligent beings, people must participate in their own re-education, which involves normative as well as cognitive and perceptual changes. Normative change will involve alteration in attitudes, values, skills and significant relationships. It will involve, therefore, more than changes in the knowledge, information and beliefs that inform action and practice. In other words, the implementation of changes in teachers' practices will involve changing their own theory of teaching. Without such changes, change will be superficial and short-lived.

Normative-re-educative approaches involve direct interventions by change agents. Such interventions are based on a consciously worked out theory of change and of changing and they involve intervention in the life of the client system, whether that system is a person, a small group, an organization or a community. There are common elements to normative-re-educative approaches.

Firstly, there is an emphasis on the clients' system and the clients' involvement in working out programmes of change and improvements for themselves. In education, this means that teachers are involved in planning and introducing change – they assume the role of change agents. Secondly, the problem the clients face is not assumed automatically to be one that can be met by more adequate technical information, though such a possibility is not ignored. The problem may lie in the values, norms and the external and internal relationships of the client system and may require alteration or re-education of these as a condition of solving the problem.

In language teaching, improvements in results may not follow the provision of courses on more effective methodology or other revisions to curriculum. If the problem is inherent in some aspect of the organization – such as streaming by ability levels, timetabling of classes, power relationships between staff members – the provision of more technical information is unlikely to have an ameliorating effect because the problem is not one which can be solved by such information. It is a case of an inappropriate solution being applied to the wrong problem.

The third feature of normative-re-educative approaches is that the change agent must learn to intervene mutually and collaboratively along with the client into efforts to define and solve the clients' problem(s). Clearly, such intervention requires tact, skill and confidence. If the change agent is an outsider, commissioned to intervene, he or she will need to be fully briefed on the situation. If there are internal conflicts or schisms, the change agent will have to take care to identify them and not be recruited to one side or another. If the change agent is an insider, the dangers of being identified with a particular interest or power group are obvious, and it will take considerable care to avoid being so identified. Partly for this reason, it is a good idea to have an outside change agent since they are more readily viewed as neutral.

Finally, both change agent and clients have a wide range of resources to draw upon in bringing about change. It is important that these resources are used selectively, relevantly and with care in learning to deal with the problem which they face and with problems of a similar kind in the future. Some techniques for raising people's awareness and sharing problems can be very effective; but they can also get out of control or raise further problems which can have uncalled-for side effects. Thus, the change agent and clients have to choose with care from the various options which are open to them.

The implications of this are emphasized by Chin and Benne (1976:33):

These approaches center in the notion that people technology is just as necessary as thing technology in working out desirable changes in human affairs. Put in this bold fashion, it is obvious that for the normative-re-educative change agent, clarification and reconstruction of values is of pivotal importance in changing. By getting the values of various parts of the client system along with his own, openly into the arena of change and by working through value and conflicts responsibly, the change agent seeks to avoid manipulation and indoctrination of the client, in the morally reprehensible meanings of these terms.

As to the effectiveness of normative-re-educative approaches, Nicholls (1983:33) points out that

> there is some evidence to support the claim that normative-re-educative strategies are the most lasting and most self-sustaining forms of innovation, particularly when outside consultants are used, but they are time-consuming and difficult and require knowledge and skills that might not be present in all schools and so might initially necessitate some form of external support.

On a practical level, adopting a normative-re-educative strategy will require two things: an awareness by members of an organization that there is an issue (or problem) which calls for a solution; and the ability to call upon an outside adviser or change agent who can work together with members of the organization to achieve a solution. In some situations, the outsider is already a member of the organization by virtue of being imported as part of a development or aid programme. In others, the adviser can be recruited by seeking advice from a teachers' centre or similar body. In either case, the legitimacy of the adviser–change agent must derive from the organization itself. Attempts to impose legitimacy are almost certain to be unsuccessful.

Conclusion

Many proposals for change in the existing curriculum will be proposals for innovation. Decisions for innovation may be prompted by a number of stimuli; but once such decisions have been made, the implementation of the innovation will be subject to influences from within the education system in which it is to be installed. Since any educational organization exists only by virtue of the people who constitute it, proposals for innovation will inevitably involve the members of that system.

Proposals for innovation will come from a change agent and will involve a user or users. The implementation of an innovation will involve organizational changes, which in turn require negotiation among members of the organization to provide the conditions in which the innovation will be accepted.

Three models of the innovatory process have been proposed: RD and D, problem-solving and social interaction. The RD and D model tends to involve large-scale change, with centralized research, development and diffusion agencies. The problem-solving model is more localized in application,

Curriculum ideology	Language/syllabus/method	Curriculum model	Innovation model	Innovation strategy
Classical humanism	Grammar-translation	Classical	Centre-periphery	Power-coercive
Reconstructionism	Audio-lingualism Notional-functional	Rational planning and objectives (Taba, Tyler)	Research, development, diffusion (RD and D)	Empirical-rational Power-coercive
Progressivism	Task- or methods-based, Process (Breen and Candlin) Procedural (Prabhu)	Process (Stenhouse)	Problem solving	Normative-re-educative

Figure 8.6 The relationship between ideology, curriculum models and innovation

emphasizing the definition and solution of problems which arise within individual institutions rather than across a complete system. The social interaction model emphasizes the role of the individual within a network of social and professional relationships in which personal influence provides a means whereby innovation is disseminated.

Models of innovation have their counterparts in strategies of innovation. Again, three models are proposed: power-coercive, empirical-rational and normative-re-educative. The power-coercive model is based on the manipulation of power which derives from the possession of knowledge and is likely to be linked to an autocratic style of management.

The empirical-rational model is based on the belief that people will act according to their rational perception of the benefits of an innovation. Associated with a 'role' organizational culture, in which there are established and prescribed modes of procedure, the empirical-rational model has the attraction of clarity and simplicity.

The normative-re-educative model involves a collaborative venture on the part of change agent and client, in which they work together in defining and meeting the client's needs. Innovation is seen to involve more than superficial or imposed change. It is recognized as involving changes in people's values and attitudes as well as practices, and it is only when these underlying aspects are engaged that innovation will be effective.

The relationship between curriculum ideologies, language syllabuses and methodologies, and innovatory models is summarized in figure 8.6. From the point of view of contemporary language teaching, it is reconstructionism and progressivism and their associated models which are of most relevance. It will be noted that I have indicated a power-coercive innovation strategy could be used in the dissemination of language curriculum proposals based on a reconstructionist ideology. In fact, different strategies will be appropriate to and may be used under different circumstances.

On the whole, though, innovations which are identified by the users themselves (rather than specified by an outside change agent) will be more effectively and durably installed than those which are imported from outside, since it is the teachers and students themselves who will have 'ownership' of and commitment to the innovation concerned if it has a grass roots or bottom-up rather than a top-down origin. For this reason, a problem-solving model and a normative-re-educative approach to innovation will probably be the most successful combination, in language teaching as elsewhere.

Suggested Reading

Innovation Studies

Rogers (in collaboration with Schoemaker) is one of the main authorities in the field, and the third edition of his book *Diffusion of Innovations* (1983) is fundamental reading. Although many of his examples are not from education, they illustrate basic points which apply in all fields, while his account of the failure of curriculum innovation in Troy School, Ohio, provides an important lesson to anyone concerned with introducing change into a school.

Within education, innovation has a growing body of literature, and a good way of entering the field is to read Nicholls, *Managing Educational Innovations* (1983), who draws on earlier publications by Miles (1963), *Innovation in Education*, and Gross, Giacquinta and Bernstein (1971), *Implementing Organizational Innovations*, in which the fully documented account of 'Cambire' school includes the questionnaires that were used for staff interviews. Havelock (1971), and Bennis, Benne, Chin and Corey (1976) outline models and strategies of innovation. A salutary discussion, entitled 'Innovation – bandwagon or hearse?', by Nisbet (1974) draws attention to some of the unexpected consequences of change.

A comprehensive critical review of the literature on implementing educational change has been carried out by Hurst (1983), while Fullan (1982) has produced a stimulating and authoritative account which must be regarded as a key reading in the field. A collection of papers dealing with curriculum change, including Skilbeck's account of three educational ideologies, Dalin's summary of strategies of innovation, Havelock's (1971) paper and Nisbet's (1974) discussion, has been edited by Harris, Lawn and Prescott (1985). In addition, there is another collection edited by Horton and Raggatt (1982) for the Open University.

Helpful discussions on the management of change appear in section 3 of Everard and Morris (1985), *Effective School Management* and chapter 7 of Rowntree's *Educational Technology in Curriculum Development*. A package of materials for in-service training on innovation is contained in *Making School-centred INSET Work*, Code P536, the Open University. This package contains a video case-study of curriculum innovation, which makes an excellent basis for a workshop in association with readings from the relevant chapters of Everard and Morris and Rowntree.

Innovation in ELT

For accounts dealing with ELT innovation, see *ELT Documents 116, Language Teaching Projects for the Third World* (British Council 1983) as well as *Dunford House Seminar Report 1985, Communication Skills Training in Bilateral Aid Projects* (British Council, 1986). Proposals for ELT Innovation with respect to INSET in a very poor third world country have been outlined by Kouraogo (1987).

Although ESP specialists, Holliday and Cooke (1982) make effective use of a horticultural metaphor to discuss the issues involved in ensuring that ELT programmes take root, while Markee (1986a and b) draws attention to the sociopolitical context of programme development on the one hand and the development of 'an appropriate technology' of course development on the other. Another relevant paper is Kennedy's article, 'Innovation for a change' (1987), which relates strategies of innovation to ELT curriculum development.

Two discussions which centre on the problems of innovation in ELT methodology and syllabus design respectively are Hutchinson and Klepac (1982) and Tongue and Gibbons (1983). Vivid accounts of the problems of innovation as they affect ELT teachers are provided by Early and Bolitho (1981), Kirwan and Swales (1981), Medgyes (1983, 1986) and Smit (1979). They make interesting reading in conjunction with Rudduck (1973 and 1984).

The Graded Objectives Movement in Britain has spawned a number of locally based initiatives in curriculum renewal, while the Schools Development Council's National Writing Project uses a combination of centrally organized support for locally based groups of teachers. For GOMLT, refer to the Centre for Information on Language Teaching, Regent's College, Inner Circle, Regent's Park, London NW1 4NS, while for information on the Writing Project, write to Newcome House, 45 Notting Hill Gate, London W11 3JB.

9 Innovation: Managing and Evaluating

Introduction

Curriculum development or renewal and the decision to design and implement a new language syllabus are aspects of innovation. Indeed, the decision to alter existing syllabuses or to develop new curricula – especially decisions to adopt new aims (or ends) and new methods (or means) – is a decision for innovation. Such innovations can, as we have seen, be stimulated by various motives, which can range from a desire for higher efficiency to a wish for greater individual development. It is as well to realize that any attempts to bring about curriculum changes in ELT are essentially essays in innovation and consequently, in the discussion which follows, language syllabus design and curriculum development will tend to be used synonymously.

Although, as Barrow (1984:224) observes, 'The truth is that there are no correct or easy answers to the question of how change should be implemented (that is why models are misleading and unhelpful)', it seems to me that to ignore the accumulated wisdom on the management of change in organizations is to risk making the very mistakes others have made in the past – and which, through ignorance, continue to be made. So, while there are no correct or easy answers, there are some guidelines which the language curriculum innovator or syllabus designer would be well advised to consider when involved in the management of change, and it these which form the subject of this chapter.

Models of innovation	Strategies of innovation	Organizational culture
RD and D	Empirical-rational Power-coercive	Club/Power Role
Problem solving	Normative re-educative	Task Person

Figure 9.1 Innovation and context
(Handy 1978)

Context

Innovations do not occur in isolation; they take place in a context. Schools, as organizations, constitute the major context in which innovations will be installed, so it is worth giving some attention to the culture of organizations, especially as organizational culture, innovation strategy and models of innovation will probably be interrelated, as I summarize in figure 9.1.

Handy (1978:186f.) describes four organizational 'cultures':

Club or Power

Role

Task

Person

A club or power culture is like a spider's web, with a central power source or authority figure, from whom influence radiates. (The owner-managed language school is a representative of this type.) A role culture is one in which the organization is a collection of roles or job boxes. Individuals are 'role occupants', with job descriptions which effectively lay down the require-ments of the role. Role cultures are managed rather than led, in contrast to the club or power culture. (Language schools which are part of a large chain will tend towards a role culture.)

Task cultures are job-or project-oriented. A group or team of talents and resources are applied to a project, problem or task, each task getting the treatment it requires, since, unlike a role culture, there is no standardization of procedures across the organization. Similarly, in a person culture, there is no standardization, structure is minimal, and individual talents are given priority. (Development units within a language school, or co-operatives specializing in tailor-made courses, will be characterized by a task or person culture.)

Few organizations are restricted to only one culture, since most are a mixture of all four. 'What makes each organization different,' says Handy (1985:13), 'is the mix they choose. What makes them successful is, often, getting the right mix at the right time.' Discussing the organizational culture of British schools, Handy suggests that, although members of secondary schools may think of themselves as ocupying a task culture, such schools are predominantly role cultures, while a primary (or elementary) school is a task culture. He also points out that large secondary schools may be 'afflicted by a sort of organizational schizophrenia', with a demand for role culture products while valuing a person culture ethos.

Such organizational schizophrenia may, indeed, be found in a school or an educational system characterized by plural value systems and, consequently, different organizational ideologies or cultures, in various parts of the organization. It is commonplace for ELT teachers to express an awareness of conflicting sentiments when comparing their own aims and means with those of teachers in other parts of the system, and it is not difficult to see how conflict can arise from a difference of cultures within one and the same organization. Such conflicts are exacerbated when there are more profound cultural differences arising from a mixture of nationalities – a not uncommon feature of ELT organizations, which, by their very nature, tend towards such diversity.

As far as innovations are concerned, they are more likely to arise in some organizational cultures than in others. Thus, organizations having task and person cultures provide a productive context for innovation, whereas a role culture, with its emphasis on routinized procedures, is less likely to be innovative. In a club or power culture, innovations will arise, but they will come from the centre and may depend for their success on the influence of the individual innovator or change agent.

Clearly, a centre–periphery style of innovation harnessed to a power-coercive strategy is likely to emerge in a power culture, whereas an RD and D style fits more readily within a role culture where the kind of role specialization characteristic of this model finds a natural home. By contrast, a problem-solving model linked to be a normative-re-educative strategy is likely to arise within a task culture.

A successful organization – whether educational or commercial – is charac-terized by innovativeness because, of course, innovativeness and adaptability to changing circumstances go hand-in-hand. Successful organizations are biased towards action and they avoid stultification by developing and changing rather than remaining routinized and standardized. Innovativeness is also associated with autonomy and entrepreneurship: 'Excellent organizations encourage ideas and never kill a likely one until it is tried out. Above all, they foster communication and the infectious spread of ideas and they never penalize failure *if* it is learnt from' (Handy 1985:29). As Miles (1964) notes, a healthy organization exhibits problem-solving adequacy. To this we might add that the healthy and successful organization is good at identifying new problems and setting people to work on them, a characteristic commented upon by Handy (1985:27), who says that 'Problem-finding is often a more creative and difficult task than problem-solving. It does *not* mean looking for problems for the sake of it; it does mean discerning key opportunities for the advancement of the organization.'

And such advancement will almost always mean innovation. In the school context, this means curriculum renewal of some sort.

Finally, a key factor noted in the literature on innovation management in all organizations is communication. In the context of ELT curriculum develop-ment context, Bowers (1983:115) points out the importance of communication in his account of the Ain Shams project.

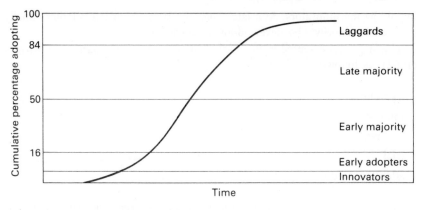

Figure 9.2 The innovation adoption curve
(from Huberman 1973)

Not only does the project team . . . need to communicate with the administrators and financial authorities upon whom the success of the project largely rests, as well as with those directly affected by the project (the teachers, the trainers, etc.). In addition, a project team needs to communicate *within* itself – to clarify the different preoccupations and preconceptions and values which individual members hold. . . . Too often, a team is set to work without the time for this professional familiarization, the opportunity to identify varying interests and strengths and put them to work in the context of the programme. And failure to recognize these differences of standpoint can lead to dissension later.

The same point is stressed by Nicholls (1983:75), who observes that innovation is also likely to provoke conflict, which will not disappear simply because it is ignored: 'However, the creation of a climate in which ideas can be discussed openly, criticized and rejected, while those putting forward the ideas are accepted within the group, is more likely to lead to successful innovation.' This view is remarkably reminiscent of the activities and attitudes which Stenhouse's humanities curriculum project set out to develop in the classroom, and of which process syllabus advocates in ELT also approve. In short, that which applies to the classroom should also characterize the staff room.

Stages in Innovation

The dissemination and adoption of an innovation – in language teaching as elsewhere – follows an S-shaped curve (figure 9.2). There is an early stage during which a very small percentage of innovators decide to introduce the new idea. This is followed by a second stage, during which the early adopters, who have noted that the innovation produces no harmful effects, take on the innovation. During the middle stage, the majority adopt quickly, influenced mainly by the innovators. At a late stage, the laggards or late adopters finally give in. A minority who never adopt lie outside the curve.

The stages represented in this S-shaped curve been summarized by Rogers (1962), as follows:

awareness

interest

evaluation

trial

adoption or discontinuance.

In the final stage, Rogers allows for acceptance or rejection, since it is not necessarily the case that an innovation will be taken up. Miles (1964) also provides for either possibility in a series of stages: awareness, indifference/ interest, denial/evaluation and trial, and he lists a number of forms and causes of rejection, including ignorance, the feeling that other things are equally as good, and such personal factors as uncertainty or fear.

Characteristics of Innovations

Rogers (1983:15–16) has emphasized that it is the receiver's perceptions of the attributes of innovations that affect their rate of adoption, and he has proposed a number of characteristics of innovations, as perceived by potential adopters, which are positively related to adoption rate:

1 Relative advantage
2 Compatability
3 Trialability
4 Observability
5 Degree of interconnectedness (i.e. interpersonal networks) in a social system
6 Complexity.

The final characteristic (6) is negatively related to adoption rate. No doubt all of these will strike a chord with anyone who has been concerned with almost any form of curriculum innovation in ELT. The fact is, of course, that some innovations are more trialable and observable than others. Video and group work are cases in point. Others, such as the introduction of a completely new syllabus or textbook, may be supported on the grounds of relative advantage (e.g. it will meet student needs more effectively than the existing syllabus), but may be less supportable on the grounds of trialability, since the evaluation of new syllabuses and textbooks is necessarily a lengthy process.

The question of compatibility will be applicable especially to teaching methods and classroom organization. A new method which requires radical reorganization of classroom procedures will tend to be less readily welcomed than one which demands fewer changes of this kind. Finally, the more complex an innovation, the less acceptable it will be. Thus, a language teaching innovation which calls for complex organizational arrangements (e.g. replanning timetables and introducing the use of multi-media, resource packs and diverse classroom groupings) is a recipe for rejection.

Trump's Five-Step Innovation Sequence

Trump (1967) has proposed a systematic five-step sequence:

1 Analyse co-operatively reasons for present practices;
2 Discover what people want that is different from what they are doing;
3 Make tentative decisions about the priority of proposed changes;
4 Plan the innovation carefully in terms of teacher preparation, student preparation, procedures to be followed and the anticipated effects of the innovation;
5 Determine the times and techniques for evaluation.

As Trump's list is concerned with educational innovation, and because it reflects essentially the same sequence of stages outlined in Skilbeck's Situational Model of curriculum development, it constitutes a useful agenda for planning and implementing a new language syllabus, materials, methods of assessment, or teaching methodology. Also, it emphasizes the collaborative, consultative character of the innovation process, and thus matches the precepts of the normative-re-educative strategy and the problem-solving model of innovation already discussed.

Management and Innovation

As will have become clear in the previous sections, management, both as a process and as a section of an organization, is important in implementing innovation – of which language curriculum renewal is, by definition, an instance. Although both the theory and study of management in educational organizations is in a formative phase (cf. Bush 1986), such studies as have been made so far (e.g. Bell et al. 1984, Gross et al. 1971, Nicholls 1983, Rogers 1983) demonstrate the importance of good organizational management in successful innovation. Indeed, it is effective management that provides the circumstances whereby innovation will arise, be taken up and successfully installed.

Innovation can occur in two different circumstances. In the first, it arises *within* an organization in response to the needs identified by members of the organization (though possibly, as I have noted in the discussion of the problem-solving model of curriculum development, with an outside consultant or adviser.) Typically, in such circumstances, someone within the organization will have identified a need for a new language syllabus or for changes in teaching methodology and will put forward proposals for change.

In the second, proposals for innovation occur when an *outside* or a superordinate agency defines and proposes the innovation, as happens in centrally organized curriculum projects or in those which are established as part of aid packages, of which Key English Language Teaching (KELT) projects are an example. Such proposals will usually be in the form of revised or newly created language syllabuses with or without new materials. In either case, the management and administration of a school or educational system will play a crucial role, since even bottom-up grass roots innovation will require forms of support which can only be provided by superordinate top-down parts of the system. Thus, an initiative developed by staff in a school can be nipped in the bud if the inspectorate disapproves, if extra resources are not forthcoming or if there are no rewards (in terms of promotion, pay, increased job satisfaction or other opportunities) for the innovators.

In either situation, as Gross et al. (1971) point out, only management is likely to have a whole view of the process; management must remain in close touch with things throughout, and they warn against assuming that an innovation has been adopted once it has been introduced – a common, but erroneous, assumption made by administrators in bureaucratic systems. Gross et al. (1971:210–11) also suggest that subordinates have a right to expect management to do certain things:

1   To take the steps necessary to provide them with a clear picture of their new role requirements;
2   To adjust organizational arrangements to make them compatible with the innovation;
3   To provide subordinates with necessary retraining experiences, which will be required if the capabilities for coping with the difficulties of implementing the innovation are to develop;
4   To provide the resources necessary to carry out the innovation;
5   To provide the appropriate supports and rewards to maintain subordinates' willingness to make implementational efforts.

The history of curriculum innovation in ELT is littered with instances of lack of success arising from the failure of management (whether at school or national level) to carry out the actions listed above.

In addition to making these provisions, an educational manager should

1   Take account of difficulties which teachers will probably be exposed to when they attempt to implement the innovation.

2   Provide for feedback mechanisms to identify and cope with barriers and problems arising during the period of attempted implementation.

Concluding their list of management responsibilities, Gross et al. (1971:215) say that 'The implementation of educational innovations, in short, not only requires alterations in behaviour expected of teachers but also changes in the role performance of management.' Implementational efforts can lead to frustration if obstacles are encountered and management does little or nothing to help overcome them. A consequence of the frustration which develops under such circumstances is that people who were initially favourable towards the innovation 'develop a negative orientation'. Once this happens, it is very difficult to retrieve the situation, as their own study illustrates and as will be attested by anyone who has tried to implement an innovation in ELT under circumstances where implementational efforts have been frustrated by inadequate management support.

A Systematic Approach

Managing innovation, which involves setting up and implementing new policy, is a highly complex business, and the numerous theories of management in general and of educational management in particular provide only a partial view of the process. Some models of educational innovation are believed to work better or to be more appropriate to some circumstances than others. Also, variations in organizational culture and school climate can provide contexts which may be more or less helpful to innovation. And we shall see that while rational models of management may provide a normative basis for action, actual practice tends to be less rational.

Here, then, we have a conflict. On the one hand, management principles stress the importance of trying to be reasonably systematic and rational in running any organization. Consultation and good communication, whereby all members of an organization are involved, are constantly stressed as being important. Clarifying goals, setting standards, monitoring progress are all aspects of good management, which in turn will help to sustain appropriate conditions for the continuing good health and adaptability of the organization in responding to environmental changes.

On the other hand, there are factors which inhibit rationality. The subjective views of members of an institution necessarily mean that there are many different perceptions of reality. Interest groups, coalitions and shifts of power mean that political factors may outweigh rational considerations. In addition, the sheer complexity of an organization – and especially one of any considerable size – enormously complicates the process of management. Should we, then, give up entirely any attempt to approach the management of policy change and innovation in a rational way? Should we simply abandon any attempt to control affairs with a modicum of systematicity? And should we ignore the lessons that can be learnt from experience and the accumulated wisdom of management theorists and practitioners? I would like to suggest that the answer is 'no', and that we should try to be at least moderately systematic in any approach to curriculum innovation.

In applying a systematic approach to introducing an innovation, we could begin to clarify our aims by describing what it is we hope to achieve. The clarification of aims can be thought of in three aspects. Firstly, we should ask ourselves the following questions:

'What is the innovation?'

Is it an innovation in hardware, software, materials, methods, forms of assessment, etc.?

'What do we mean by the terms that we use?'

For instance, what do we mean by *functional* or *communicative* or *task-based learning*?

'Why are we carrying out this innovation?'

Are we carrying it out because other stake-holders have told us to; or is it in response to problems that have arisen through a drop in student motivation or achievement; or is it to relieve teachers' boredom; or what?

'What is it for?'

Is it to improve learning in particular skills; is it to raise examination performance; etc.?

'Who is it for?'

Is it for the benefit of students or teachers? Is it for clients and sponsors? Who are the intended beneficiaries of the change?

'Do we actually need it?'

Can we really justify the innovation in terms of improvements and cost?

'What justifications are there for it?'

Can we give a principled justification for the innovation?

Basically, we need to go on asking and attempting to answer the question 'Why?'

Discussion of these and other questions will certainly be very time-consuming, but the time is well spent if, by establishing a forum which allows all parties to be aware of and involved in discussion and decision-making, a consensus is reached, thus laying the foundation for later stages.

Secondly, we should attempt to define the end results. What, in short, do we want to achieve? Although at this early stage the precise character of the end results cannot be specified, an agreement on the nature of the outcome is essential, since it is this specification which provides the goal towards which all members of the organization will be working. The specification will, of course, depend on the nature of the innovation. For instance, it could be a fully equipped and organized resource centre with materials catalogued and cross referenced with access achieved by means of a computerized key-word catalogue. Or it could be an A4 sheet specifying the main topics to be covered by a given class during the forthcoming semester. Or it could be a carefully graded sequence of learning tasks linked to a list of language functions and exponents to be covered by all students during a course of a specified level. And so on. What is important is that everyone agrees on the general features of the end result for the obvious reason that one wishes to avoid a situation in X months' time when it is revealed that everyone had a rather different idea of what they thought the outcomes of their efforts would be.

Thirdly, we have the question of evaluation. What are the success criteria or standards? What will demonstrate that we have been or are being successful? How can the end product be evaluated? Evaluation criteria should be built in right from the start, since it is important to know how to demonstrate improvement if, as we assume, an innovation is intended to be more efficacious in achieving organizational goals. Failure to consider success criteria at this early stage can result in problems later when, through lack of forethought, participants in the innovatory process apply inappropriate criteria or fudge things by adapting their criteria to the outcomes actually achieved. (Cf. the limitations of the evaluation of the procedural syllabus, referred to in chapter 7.)

The process of defining aims and of 'laying things open', as Bowers (1983) describes it, will usually be enormously time-consuming, although the evidence suggests that such time is well spent provided everyone is co-operatively involved in the discussions. It is as well, on a purely practical level, to keep records of what is discussed and agreed, and that these records (which should not be over-long and complicated, or nobody will read them) are circulated to all concerned (some of whom may well be absent from some of the discussions).

Another practical issue is that of time and outcomes. If it has been agreed that an innovation of whatever sort is to be carried out, it is essential that the task be achieved. To do this, a time scale and deadlines should be agreed, even if, because of slippage caused by unforeseen circumstances, the programme has to be changed and deadlines rescheduled. It will be someone's job to keep an eye on the schedule to ensure that there is as little slippage as possible and to remind everyone about deadlines.

This brings us to another important point: leadership. Although demo-cratically organized groups tend to work better than ones in which there is a top-down authoritarian structure, there does seem to be a need for an opinion-leader to support the innovation, and for someone to assume a co-ordinating role within a group, particularly when more than half-a-dozen people. Indeed, it may be difficult for even smaller groups to operate successfully over a prolonged period unless someone takes responsibility for chairing, co-ordinating, monitoring and record-keeping. Within a typical language school the co-ordinator can be the principal or director of studies, or it may be another member of the organization who assumes the co-ordinating role. It is not the role of co-ordinators to impose their own ideas about language curriculum on the group; rather, it is their role to elicit, clarify, encourage, summarize and to keep the group on target. In this, they should be assisted by the group and by other members who may assume other similar roles, such as record-keeper, information gatherer, researcher, and so on.

If materials production is envisaged, the co-ordinator's role becomes even more important, only then, the co-ordinator will assume the role of editor. Even ministry-sponsored materials production projects have been known in which there was no one to take on the role of editor, whose functions will include not only programme-planning and keeping writers on target, but will embrace such activities as reading and editing; seeing that materials are trialled (even if only among members of the writing team); establishing and maintaining conventions of format, rubrics and instructions; and generally providing coherence and unity to the publication. Indeed, the editor is the only person who (like any manager) will have an overview of the whole process – and the product.

To return to goal-setting, it is important to note that often, during this phase, people are very anxious to move straight into the next main phase, that of Getting Things Done. Sponsors and employers will usually be anxious to see some tangible evidence that their funding is being spent to good effect, and so minutes of meetings and things agreed will not usually be taken as evidence of such achievement. Such impatience and anxiety is understandable, but the Getting Things Done phase does depend on a clear definition of aims; thus pressure to move into action quickly should be tactfully resisted.

This may be amply demonstrated in the first step, which is concerned with information-gathering. In fact, an information-gathering stage may have been necessary *before* defining goals, as is clear from the first two steps in Trump's five-step sequence, outlined earlier. Information should be classified under two headings: *What We Already Know* and *What We Need to Know*, and to establish both will involve assembling relevant facts, ideas, skills, experience and resources. This will mean drawing upon existing knowledge and expertise and records. Some of the information will exist in people's heads, and will have to be elicited by discussion, interview and questionnaire. Other information will exist in records, such as existing syllabuses, teaching materials, examination results and test scores, comments from students and other interested parties, ministry reports and proposals, articles in the press, and so on. And a most important source of information will be concerned with skills and expertise within the group: who and what is good? People's existing expertise is an important resource and to ensure involvement, commitment and a sense of 'ownership', should be drawn upon.

Obtaining information which is needed for planning is, of course, crucial.

Decisions will have to be made about the precise nature of the information required and the means of obtaining it. It may be necessary to find out about such things as the students' previous language learning experience, the precise needs of the learners, costings and sources of funds in order to establish a budget. Some thought will have to be given at this stage to what will be done with the information once it has been assembled. How will it be processed, presented and interpreted? What options for action will be revealed? What risks will be discovered? How are people to react to the information? How will it influence planned outcomes?

Once decisions have been made about information known and needed, attention will shift to the *What Has To Be Done* and *Planning* phases. Here we are concerned with listing everything that needs to be done and with stating, in some detail, who will do what, how, when and where. It may seem obvious, but it is easy to overlook that even when only two peple are working together, failure to allocate responsibilities can lead to problems. With a group of people, this becomes an even greater risk. So, plans have to be agreed as to who does what, deadlines should be established, and records maintained and distributed. As will be clear, there is now a transition from the task culture of the initial phase of problem identification and objectives setting to the role culture of the planning and action phases. In Trump's terms, we have now moved on to steps 3 to 5.

Once plans have been fixed, we proceed to the *Action* stage. In fact, some actions may already have been carried out. It may be that what might be called an 'obvious action' should be performed early on. For instance, if an innovation is being mooted which will involve considerable expenditure (as would be the case with a change of textbooks), it would be sensible to carry out a financial feasibility study as a preliminary exercise, and this would involve some action in terms of obtaining relevant information, such as the ministry grant or projected income for the forthcoming year. In general, though, the action stage comes *after* the goal setting and planning stages.

During the action stage, monitoring of what is being done should be maintained. Indeed, it is important to schedule periodic review meetings so that everyone can report achievements to date, problems encountered and proposals for further action. This is what Roger Bowers calls 'keeping an eye on things'. Although the co-ordinator will have an important role here, all members of the group should accept responsibility for keeping an eye on things and for calling attention to problems.

Finally, we come to the review and evaluation stage. Reviewing, as just noted, is part of the continuing monitoring process which ensures that things are on target. Evaluation can be thought of in two stages: on-going or formative, which is a process of feedback; and final or summative, whereby outcomes are evaluated against the success criteria specified during the goal setting stage. In both cases, successes and difficulties can be analysed to provide the basis for improvement.

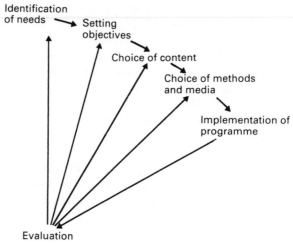

Figure 9.3   The place of evaluation
(adapted from Bramley 1986)

Evaluation

Evaluation is not, in itself, new. What is new is the incorporation of evaluation as feedback and as a formative process within language curriculum development, whereby it becomes an extension and elaboration of needs analysis, sharing with such pre-planning the use of many of the same information gathering procedures and techniques, such as questionnaires and interviews. Instead of being either overlooked, or at best added as an afterthought (as appears to have been the case with the Bangalore/Madras CTP), evaluation is now seen to be an integral part of language curriculum development, at whatever stage, and no one making proposals for any aspect of the language curriculum – be it aims, content or methods – can do so without carefully evaluating and justifying such proposals. In short, evaluation occurs at *all* stages, as illustrated in figure 9.3.

Historically, there has also been a move from the evaluator being a specialist somewhat outside a project, to evaluation (and the evaluator) being integral parts of the project, with formative and summative evaluation occupying a central role, feeding into decision-making at all stages. The importance of evaluation as a means of course improvement has been stressed by Cronback (1963:403), who believes that 'Evaluation, used to improve the course while it is still fluid, contributes more to improvement of education than evaluation used to appraise a product already placed on the market.' Such evaluation should be concerned with 'observing effects in context' (Cronbach 1975) rather than with making predictive generalizations. Instead, evaluation will focus on the way in which retrospective generalizations relate findings to subsequent action and decision-making.

Three models of evaluation (cf. Lawton 1980) have come to the attention of ELT specialists of recent years. These are the illuminative, the professional and the case study models. The first relies on observational data gathered by the evaluator as participant–observer, using ethnographic techniques developed in social anthropological field-work. The dangers of subjectivity in such procedures are obvious, though less easily avoided. The teacher-as-researcher model derives from the work of Stenhouse, and is closely related to action research as proposed by Elliott (1981, 1985), and Cohen and Manion (1980). The case study model, as described by Adelman, Jenkins and Kemmis (1976) and Yin (1984), yields data that is 'strong in reality' and can be presented in such a way that readers can make judgements for themselves. The particular strength of case studies lies in their attention to the subtlety and complexity of the case in its own right (Lawton 1980).

Evaluation and Ethics

Evaluation is not without its problems, particularly ethical ones. These are discussed by Simons (1979), who lists five factors which the evaluator must take into account. It will take little imagination to see how these can apply to the evaluation of any aspect of the language curriculum.

1 Impartiality;
2 Confidentiality and control over the data participants;
3 Negotiation among all parties involved;
4 Collaboration by all concerned;
5 Accountability by *all* levels in the organizational hierarchy.

What seems to be clear is that evaluation can be regarded as threatening, can lead to misconceptions, and can be destabilizing because evaluations are, as Adelman and Alexander (1982) argue, political: by definition they entail value judgements, and there are a number of political danger-zones. Simons (1979) raises a number of difficult questions here. One concerns whose views will prevail in the reconciliation of irreconcilable judgements. Another concerns the redistribution of resources (including people) which may be indicated by evaluation. A third concerns confronting the consequences of appraising, both for individuals and the institution.

What is vital is that evaluation should focus on *issues* and not on individuals. Once individual teachers feel that they are being evaluated, problems are likely to occur. Openness, clarity of aims in evaluation and preparedness to collaborate are all, in Simons' view, fundamental.

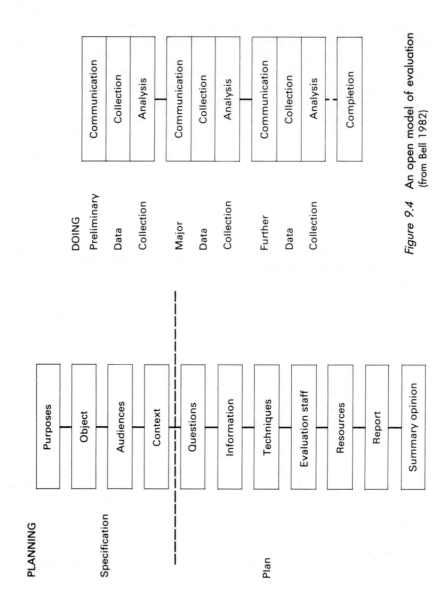

Figure 9.4 An open model of evaluation (from Bell 1982)

Evaluation: a Sequence

Harlen and Elliott (1982) and Bell (1982) have provided checklists for evaluation. Bell's model (see figure 9.4) can be reformulated as a series of questions, essentially the same as those provided by Harlen and Elliott, each of which gives rise to a further set of questions:

1 What are the purposes of the evaluation?
2 What programme, instructional material or issues are being evaluated?
3 Who are the potential audiences of the evaluation?
4 What particular characteristics of the context may be relevant?
5 What are the particular questions to be answered in order to achieve the purpose?
6 What types of information will be collected and from whom?
7 What techniques and instruments will be used for gathering the information?
8 Who is to be involved in conducting the evaluation and in what capacity?
9 How are time and funds to be allocated?
10 What is to be the form of reporting?
11 What difficulties, compromises, side effects do you anticipate?

In addition to these 11 questions, Bell outlines a series of principles of procedure in the Doing stage. These include:

keeping everyone informed

being open and sensitive

cross-checking information

keeping an open mind

trying to influence things as little as possible

maintaining promised confidentiality.

Methods of Data Collection

There is no one 'best' method of data collection, although some methods are better for some kinds of data than others. Some of these are summarized in figure 9.5.

It should be noted that problems can occur with observation, as it is a highly personalized form of evaluation and can affect the thing being observed. It is important to obtain several viewpoints of the same event or experience, and the use of triangulation is one means to this end.

Finally, Harlen and Elliott give a list of 16 questions for evaluating evaluations. They include:

1 Did the evaluation serve to inform the decisions or judgements for which it was originally intended?
2 What decisions have been taken as a consequence of the evaluation?
5 What steps were taken to allow for bias, unrepresentativeness, and low reliability in the information gathered?
9 Did those involved in supplying the information approve of the methods used for collecting it?
15 Was the evaluation reported in a way which communicated effectively with the intended audience?

They conclude that 'In most cases it is necessary to follow up initial answers with the further question, "If not, why not?"' (1982:303–4)

Conclusion

The stages and reasons for action which have been reviewed in this chapter are summarized below, followed by a summary of evaluation (LCD = Language curriculum development.)

Action/Stage	*Reason*
Clarify motivation for LCD	Initiative for LCD will influence or determine both process and product of LCD
	Defensive v. creative motivation will reflect the state of the organization
	Accountability may be involved
	Significance of initiative and LCD may be judged from motivation

Assessing soundness of proposed change

Clarify the purpose of LCD	Must know where you are going, why you are going there
Analyse the situation: (a) institutional	Know where you are at, and who is with you, what you hold sacred, what your resources are, what the organizational culture is and how all of this constrains or facilitates LCD

(b) wider environment	Know who calls the tune (or who would like to), what official policies are, what resources are likely to be available, who controls them, and how access to them is obtained, what the cultural background is and how this interacts with the institution and LCD changes

Reconnaissance, especially of the history and track record for innovation of the system, stake-holders' attitudes

Consult with all stakeholders, especially students and teachers	Find out what attitudes are to current practices, discover what works, what does not work and how current practices can be justified (or not); knowing above will set limits to what is possible or indicate where changes may be intended
Identify specific problems	These will be the points at which change is needed and about which care will be required

Describing the future

Define aims	Make sure everyone knows (and agrees on) where they are going and why
Evaluate	To be done at every stage as a way of ensuring a match between LCD and the situation and participants' requirements and capacities; an extension of needs analysis

Describing the present, environmental mapping

Establish appropriate structures, organization	Nothing is done without people to do it; must have a system to support initiatives
Ensure appropriate forms of support from top-down as well grass roots	Support from up top essential for most initiatives to flourish

Transition management

Refer to academic and professional authorities and theories	Reinventing the wheel is wasteful; LCD should be teacher developmental; new input important, but should be in response to an identified need

Developing a plan, gaining commitment

Choose appropriate syllabus type in consultation with all participants	Content and aims should be determined by aims, not vice versa; consultation important as a way of developing involvement, commitment, ownership, understanding
Choose appropriate methodology in consultation with all participants	Methodology choice should be informed by situational and means analysis and especially cultural and personal characteristics of students and teachers (plus other stakeholders); reasons for consultation as above
Design teaching–learning programme with maximum consultation and formative evaluation	Provides basis for concerted action
Interpret and implement the programme	Must be seen to get things done, however trivial the outcomes may seem
Evaluate	Keeping an eye on things; pre-empting problems, making sure that aims are being met and that adaptations to procedures are made according to feedback

Evaluation

Evaluation is concerned not with assessing individual achievement but with making judgements about the curriculum. Formative evaluation, using a variety of techniques similar to those of needs analysis, together with ethnographic techniques of participant observation, acts as feedback to curriculum developers. A wide variety of information sources is drawn upon in

Type of data	Method
Methods, classroom procedures	Observation, diaries, interviews, peer appraisal, questionnaires, ranking and rating scales
Content	Questionnaires, interviews, document analysis: text books, syllabuses, tests; ranking and rating scales
Learning achievement	Tests, assignments

Figure 9.5 Methods of data collection

such evaluation, including documentation and people from within and outside the institution concerned.

Because evaluation involves making judgements, ethical and political issues become associated with any evaluation process. Questions about ownership of information and the use of this information for decision-making become significant and must be acknowledged as important. Evaluation can be used for purposes other than feedback to teachers, and the purpose and use of evaluation are important considerations.

As with any procedure, evaluation can be carried out in a reasonably systematic way, following a sequence of stages. Openness, clarity and good communication assume importance in such an evaluation sequence, following essentially the same principles of good management practice reviewed elsewhere in this chapter.

Suggested Reading

Educational Management

Management has become a growth area in education, with the realization that managerial skills are needed in running schools and education systems. A very good, practical introduction to the field of educational management is provided by Everard and Morris in *Effective School Management* (1985), which can be supplemented by Bush, *Theories of Educational Management* (1986), and Paisey, *Organizational Management in Schools* (1981). A stimulating view of schools from an outsider is given by Handy in *Taken for Granted? Understanding Schools as Organizations* (1984).

A collection which assembles case studies of educational management is *Case Studies in Educational Management*, edited by Goulding, Bell, Bush, Fox and Goodey (1984). Another collection, focusing on the research aspect of educational management, is Bell, Bush, Fox, Goodey and Goulding, *Conducting Small-scale Investigations in Educational Management* (1984). This collection includes papers by Cohen and Manion and Elliot on action research, as well as a paper by Adelman, Jenkins and Kemmis on case study. A collection devoted entirely to action research has been edited by Hustler, Cassidy and Cuff (1986). There are also other papers on action research by Elliot (1981 and 1985).

Evaluation

A very good introduction to educational evaluation appears in chapter 6 of Rowntree's *Educational Technology in Curriculum Development* (1982). Collections of papers on educational evaluation are House (1986), McCormick et al. (1982), Hamilton et al. (1977) and Skilbeck (1984b).

Some of the evaluation literature from management training (e.g. Bramley 1986) has much of relevance to ELT specialists and course providers. Not surprisingly, in view of the significance of accountability in many ESP programmes, evaluation has occupied the attention of ESP specialists: witness Bachman (1981), 'Formative evaluation in specific purposes program development', Mackay (1981), 'Accountability in ESP Programs' and McGinley (1986), 'Coming to terms with evaluation'.

Other more general discussions of evaluation in ELT include Candlin and Breen (1979), and Alderson (1985). The 1981 Dunford House Seminar (British Council, 1981) addressed itself to design, evaluation and testing in English Language projects, while recent papers by Beretta (1986a and b) are another expression of this burgeoning interest. Richards and Rodgers (1986) put the case for comparing and evaluating methods. Meanwhile, some of the issues involved in ELT project management have been addressed by Kennedy (1988) in a paper on the evaluation of the management of change in ELT projects.

Appendix
Follow-up Activities

These activities are intended to be done by groups, and they should involve discussion. Some of the activities can also be done individually. They are linked to the content of the chapters concerned, and provide some 'hands on' development of the points covered in the chapters themselves. You may find it useful to skim the follow-up activities *before* reading each chapter.

Chapter 2

Activity 1

Review your own language teaching history.

In what tradition of language teaching were you initially trained?

How have your ideas of language teaching evolved as a result of experience as a teacher?

How have your ideas evolved under the influence of writers or lecturers in the field?

What is your current position on language teaching?

Discuss the answers to these questions with colleagues and compare and contrast your experiences. Then consider

What generalizations emerge from your collective language teaching histories?

Activity 2

This activity is probably best done collaboratively, with different members of the group being responsible for collecting different information.

Collect syllabuses, textbooks and examinations over a period of 20 or 30 years.

Compare the material you collect.

How does it vary in
    aims
    content
    methods
    form of assessment?

What do the differences suggest about the traditions and development of ideas in language teaching over the period concerned?

How rapidly have ideas changed?

Do some 'old' ideas linger on?

If they do, what does this suggest about the nature of change and development in language teaching?

Chapter 3

Activity 1

Either individually, or with a colleague, complete the questionnaire on teacher values. The questionnaire aims to reveal something of teachers' values; it is not to make judgements on whether some values are better than others. The questionnaire asks you to choose between two extremes, since a rating scale is not provided. This is because the questionnaire is not intended to be a survey instrument, but a stimulus for thinking and discussion, and extreme choices are more likely to provoke debate than bland statements upon which everyone will agree. A slogan to keep in mind here is

'When everyone thinks the same, nobody thinks.'

Even if you work with a colleague, your response to each item should be an individual one.

When you have completed the questionnaire, give a title to each section.

If you can, use the questionnaire as the basis for a general discussion among members of your department or group. Having completed the questionnaire individually, or in pairs, form syndicates of two or three pairs, and

discuss the titles which you have given to each section;

find six statements upon which you all agree;

report your consensus statements to the rest of the group;

from the discussion, clarify those statements upon which everyone agrees, and those upon which you agree to differ.

What does the range of agreement/disagreement tell you about possible

Figure A1   Questionnaire

The questionnaire is in 5 parts. Please complete all parts. Put a tick in the appropriate part of the column for each statement, depending on whether you agree or disagree with it.

Agree	*Disagree*	*Part A*
		1 Language is a system of grammatical rules.
		2 Vocabulary is the most important part of a language.
		3 Language is basically a means of spoken communication.
		4 Language is a means of establishing and maintaining social relationships.
		5 Each language provides a unique way of organizing experience.
		Part B 6 Learning grammatical rules is essential to learning a language.
		7 Languages can only be learned by the conscious application of grammatical rules.
		8 Language learning is best achieved by being exposed informally to authentic language in its native speech community.
		9 Language learning is best when a teacher provides a carefully controlled exposure to the language.
		10 Language learning is best promoted through using the language in authentic situations in the classroom.
		11 Meaning is best conveyed through translation between the target language and the mother tongue.

Agree	Disagree	Part B
		12 Language learning is best when the focus is on something other than the language itself.
		13 There is no transfer from one skill to another when learning a language.
		Part C 14 A carefully graded structural syllabus is the best way to organize a language course.
		15 Initial teaching should be based on a careful contrastive analysis of the grammatical differences between the mother tongue and the target language.
		16 A syllabus should be based on known areas of difficulty in grammar and pronunciation.
		17 A syllabus should be based on the students' communicative needs outside the classroom.
		18 A syllabus should take students' wants and interests into account even when these are different from their needs.
		19 Where there is a choice, communicative needs should take priority over grammatical grading in organizing a syllabus.
		20 The best syllabus is one which doesn't focus on language at all.
		Part D 21 It is the teacher's responsibility to keep things moving in the classroom.
		22 It is the teacher's job to provide a perfect language model for his/her students.

Agree	Disagree		Part D
		23	The teacher should not control or restrict his/her language in the classroom as exposure to rich and varied authentic language will help learning.
		24	The teacher must correct students' errors at all times.
		25	The teacher must encourage spontaneous student: student interaction in the classroom.
		26	The teacher must avoid deviating from either the syllabus, the lesson plan or the textbook.
		27	The teacher should promote an enjoyable, friendly and supportive atmosphere in the class.
		28	The teacher must remain in full control of the class at all times.
		29	The teacher should question his/her own teaching with a view to constant improvement.
		30	The teacher should view his/her work in the wider context of the school, community and society.
			Part E
		31	There are no important differences between students of different ages and backgrounds.
		32	Students need to be kept active and interested by the teacher.
		33	Students don't usually know what's good for them.

Agree	*Disagree*	*Part E*
		34 Students achieve best in a competitive atmosphere.
		35 Students should develop harmonious and supportive relationships with one another.
		36 Students pick up mistakes from one another, so all language in the class must be controlled and checked by the teacher.
		37 Students can help each other by pooling their collective knowledge.
		38 Spontaneous interaction helps students to learn to communicate.
		39 Students only learn things which are of interest or use to themselves.
		40 Students in a language class feel very vulnerable and sensitive.

Figure A1   Questionnaire

sources of strength and conflict within your department/institution?

How are values reflected in the choices people make over content and method of teaching?

Activity 2

Here is a list of language learning goals. Some of them are stated as behavioural objectives, some are not. Identify those which are stated in behavioural terms, and try to modify some of those which are not so that they are stated as behavioural objectives as defined by Steiner (1975).

1   Seeking information from a fellow student.
2   Exchanging information with a partner so as to gain a full picture of events reported in two different news broadcasts from which each student has taken notes.
3   Given a recorded news report from a BBC Radio 4 news broadcast,

played on a cassette player in the classroom, the student will summarize in writing the sequence of events in correct chronological order, state the identity of the people involved, and state the location and time of events within a period of 15 minutes.

4 Reading magazines for comprehension of details, meanings, inferences.
5 Indicating possession of an object.
6 Checking that the principal colours are known.
7 Asked by a stranger in the street for directions to one of a number of places, the student gives directions in spoken form, using nominated structures and vocabulary with 90 per cent accuracy.
8 Learning the first conditional pattern with the function of warning.
9 Writing narrative compositions in the past tense.
10 Given a picture sequence not exceeding 6 pictures in number, the student will write a narrative of 6 or more sentences, using correctly formed regular and irregular past tense forms to 90 per cent accuracy within 15 minutes.

Activity 3

Review the three curriculum models which have been described:

The Taba–Tyler Means–ends model

The Stenhouse Process model

The Skilbeck Situational model

Which model most closely matches the preferred way of operating within your own institution?

What benefits could you predict would arise from adopting each model? Be specific.

What difficulties could you predict would occur in trying to adopt the procedures outlined in each model? Be specific.

Which model most closely matches your own preferred way of working as regards language curriculum?

Chapter 4

Activity 1*

Below is a summary of the contents of the first 15 steps in a structural syllabus (Alexander et al. 1975). They are given here in random order. Try putting them in sequence, keeping in mind the various grading considerations

*Original Order of items in Activity 1   12, 10, 6, 11, 7, 4, 8, 13, 2, 15, 3, 1, 9, 5, 14.

that have to be taken into account. When you have ordered the items in sequence, compare your sequence with that of the original syllabus, which is given at the foot of page 163.

1 Do you know X?
Short answers with *do, does, don't, doesn't.*
Negative statements with *don't, doesn't.*

2 Please listen.
Object pronouns: *me, him, her, us.*
Verbs with two objects: *give, write, tell.*

3 Do you want + uncountable noun?
Yes/no questions with *do* and *does.*

4 Are you X?
Affirmative short answers with *be.*

5 Where's my + noun?
Possessive adjectives: *my, your, his.*
Possessive form of nouns: *John's* brother.

6 I'm a + noun.
Forms of *be*: *am, is, are.*

7 Are you and X brothers?
Forms of *be*: *you are, they are, we are.*
Personal pronouns with *am, are, is.*
Plural of nouns: *students, teachers, classes.*

8 Who is he?
Information questions with *be*: *who, what, where, how*

9 What's this?
Is this + noun?
Demonstratives *this, that, these, those.*
Numbers 1 to 20.
Irregular plurals: *men, women, children.*

10 Is X + preposition phrase?
Yes/no questions with *is.*

11 Are you X?
Negative statements and negative short answers with *be.*

12 This is + Proper Name (X).
Affirmative statements: X is a + noun.

13 Is X a + adjective + noun?
The articles *a,* and *the, a* and *an.*
Articles with singular and plural nouns
Position of adjectives

14 Subject questions with *who* and *what.*

15 X speaks English.
Third person singular -s of regular verbs.

Activity 2

Take a selection of three or four structure-based course books. Search through the books to find the unit or stage at which the following structural items are introduced. (For languages other than English, appropriate adaptation can be made so as to focus on analagous structures.)

Structure	*Unit of Course Book*			
	A	B	C	D
NP + have + NP, e.g. I have a book.				
NP + Transitive Verb + NP + to + NP e.g. I am giving these pens to Mary.				
Present simple tense for repeated or regular actions				
Past simple tense of 'be'				
Past simple tense of lexical verbs, e.g. live, stay				
Uncountable nouns with 'some' and 'any'				
Can = ability e.g. I can swim.				
Adjectives used attributively, e.g. It's a red car.				
Adverbs of manner				
Adverbs of frequency				
have got				

Chapter 5

Activity 1

Take a number of related situations (e.g. those involving public or occupational settings) and describe them in terms of

Where: location

Type: occupational, recreational, domestic, religious, etc.

Relevant objects: equipment, merchandise, money, etc.

When: time of day

Participants: Clerk/Customer; Stewardess/Passenger; Stranger/Local inhabitant, etc.

Activities: serving a meal, cashing a cheque, etc.

Then attempt to predict the language which would occur in each situation.

When you have done that, compare your predictions with the way one of the situations is realized in a language course book.

What do the similarities and differences suggest as to the stereotypic nature of some situations as compared with others?

Activity 2

Below is a list of topics taken from *Syllabus Guidelines 1: Communication* by Clark and Hamilton (1984). In this CILT publication, they outline a graded communicative approach for school foreign language learning, and among the communicative objectives they specify is the list of topics given here.

Study the list and discuss the entries with colleagues and students. Which topics are relevant to your students' interests and needs? Are there other topics which would be more relevant? Elaborate some of the topics, by adding sub-topics and different aspects. Finally, make up a topic list appropriate to your students' needs or interests.

Topics

Personal background

Hobbies and sports

Pop scene: records/music, pop stars, clothes

Fashion

Entertainment and Personalities

TV

Cinema

Clubs/societies

Holidays

Travel/school trips, etc.

Bikes/cars

Discos and dances

Relationships with parents

Relationships with others/other sex

Pets

Shopping/prices

Pocket-money

School world

Teenage reading

Personal experiences

Comparisons of own country/foreign country

Jobs and careers

Events in the media

Topics of general interest

Activity 3

Which skills (reading, writing, listening, speaking) are most relevant and important for your students?

What level of proficiency should they aim to reach in each skill?

How will you define proficiency levels in the skill concerned?

Take one of the four skills and specify those sub-skills which the students will need to develop in order to operate proficiently. Grade these sub-skills in increasing order of difficulty.

Discuss how you would match a graded skills syllabus with other elements, such as structures, topics and situations.

Chapter 6

Activity 1

Something which a syllabus designer has to consider is how best to present the syllabus so that it can provide a readily interpreted guide to the people who will use it. Some syllabuses follow a convention such that the vertical axis represents time, while the horizontal axis represents the main categories of components, with the leading component on the left and the subsidiary components to the right, thus:

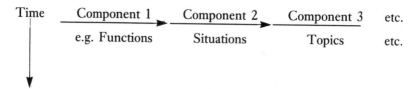

Time   Component 1   Component 2   Component 3   etc.

e.g. Functions   Situations   Topics   etc.

Make up separate lists of each component in a syllabus, and then attempt to match them horizontally and vertically in the way shown above. Do you find that you have a conflict between items, e.g. a given structure does not match a given function at any particular stage? What compromises do you have to make to produce a reasonably coherent ordering and matching of elements? What does this exercise tell you about the constraints which affect organizing a syllabus consisting of several major components?

Activity 2

Peter Shaw (1982) presents a procedure for ad hoc needs analysis which could be adapted for use before and during a course.

The students complete a form, arranged as follows:

In this course I want to:	1	2	3
1. understand English grammar better.............			
2. write English more fluently and correctly......			
3. write technical and scientific English fluently and correctly...			

etc., etc.

The form is completed individually (column 1), by small groups (column 2) and by the class as a whole (column 3).

Individually, the students rank the objectives in order from most to least important by writing 1 for the most important, and succeeding numbers in descending order to the least important.

In small groups of three or four, students then agree a rank order for their group, and individuals write the group rankings in column 2 of the grid.

The teacher, having drawn a grid on the blackboard, then asks each group to enter their rankings in the grid when they have reached consensus. At this point, students circle any objectives of their own which differ greatly from the group decision. The teacher draws attention to such differences.

When the grid is completed for the groups, a class ranking can be established by discussion and compromise by summing up the group totals and ranking the objectives accordingly, with the smaller totals receiving the higher rankings. Individual students then enter the group rankings in column 3 of their grid.

Individual students can then identify where their priorities differ from those of the group. The teacher can use this information for advising students or providing individual work. Meanwhile, those objectives which have common priority can form the basis of general work with the class as a whole.

Prepare a similar questionnaire for a group of your students and use it, following the procedures outlined above.

When you have completed the exercise with your class, plan ways in which you can use the information to plan your next phase of teaching or to give individual work to students.

Consider how you could use this technique to elicit feedback from your students during the progress of a course.

Chapter 7

Activity 1

The process syllabus depends on negotiation between the teacher and learners over content and activities and even, to some extent, as to aims. I have suggested that there are similarities with individualization of learning. Needs analysis also provides some procedures which can be adapted to negotiating a process syllabus with learners.

Step 1 Outline the ways in which you could enlist the learners' views on the content and method of learning for one week's work. To do so, adapt Peter Shaw's ad hoc needs analysis.

Step 2 When you have planned how you are going to do this, plan how you will administer the choices revealed in the survey.

You will have to consider how you will organize the class to ensure some sort of consensus among sub-groups (if not among the class as a whole), since accommodating the individual requirements of 20 or so students is not really feasible.

Step 3 After the planning and choosing stage, the actual operation of learning activities in the classroom should involve some discussion by learners and teachers of (1) why they chose the activities they did; (2) what they gained from the learning activities; (3) whether they would choose similar activities again, and if not, why not; and (4) what they plan to do next as a result of completing the activities in question.

If you can, try out the procedures you have planned with an actual class. Make sure that you explain to them why you are asking for their collaboration in planning the programme and activities, otherwise they may think you are simply trying to opt out of your role as teacher. You may find it useful to experiment with such a student-led period of work once a term or semester. It would also be a good idea to keep notes on the experience, including notes on observation of the students at work, what they did, and how involved they were. If possible, review the experiment with a colleague who can assume the role of 'friendly outsider' to help you clarify your thinking on what you have done.

Activity 2

The procedural syllabus is task-based, that is, students are given things to do from which there is an outcome or product of some sort. The tasks are conceptually graded.

The grading of tasks can be done on several bases:

how difficult it is to complete the task itself

the quantity and complexity of thinking required

the quantity and complexity of language needed

Plan several tasks, each one to consist of a teacher-led or teacher-modelled task and a parallel task which the students themselves perform. Grade the tasks in terms of the three criteria listed above.

Plan a lesson, using one of the tasks. You will need to consider how you will present and demonstrate the task, how you will guide the students, and how you will hand over the parallel task to the students. Consider, too, how you will evaluate the success of both the task and the lesson.

If you can, teach the lesson to a class. Explain why you are doing it and what you hope the students will get out of the lesson.

During the lesson, carefully observe student behaviour in terms of what they do and what they say.

In particular, take note of any 'critical incidents' – examples of behaviour (involving individuals or a number of people) which represent an important event in the learning activity. The animation and involvement of learners will be a good guide to such incidents – or the reverse, since the task may prove not to be engaging.

At the end of the lesson, discuss what has been done with the students. How did they feel about it? What did they learn? How did it promote language use? What improvements could they suggest?

If you can, discuss the lesson with a colleague, in the manner suggested in Activity 1. Better still, work together with a colleague and observe each other's lessons.

Chapter 8

Activity 1

Think of an example of innovation in a school or organization with which you are familiar.

What was the innovation? Was it an innovation in materials, hardware (e.g. video, computers), organization, assessment, syllabus or methodology?

Why was the innovation introduced?

Who first suggested the innovation?

How was it introduced?

What factors promoted or inhibited the implementation of the innovation?

What was the effect of the innovation on yourself and other people involved?

If you could run through the implementation of the innovation again, what changes or improvements would you make? Why?

From your answers to the above, list *three* points you would like to make to anyone concerned with introducing an innovation.

Activity 2

Each stage in an innovatory process raises a series of questions. Here, for example, are some such questions. They are in no particular order.

Can we justify dealing with the problem?

How can we find out what the reactions of stake-holders will be?

What effects will the innovation have on the people concerned?

How can the problem be dealt with?

What is the problem?

How has it arisen?

Who will be involved in dealing with it?

How did we first become aware of it?

Can we justify the resources required to solve the problem?

Who is affected by the problem?

What are their feelings about it?

Will the consequences of solving the problem be supported by other stake-holders?

Who is best qualified to deal with the problem?

Can we get outside advice?

Use these questions, those outlined by Skilbeck in his Situational Model (chapter 3), and, if you can obtain the article, the questions listed by Bowers (1983). Work out

1   sets of questions which should be asked at each stage in an innovatory process
2   who you would ask these questions of
3   what you would hope to do with the information so obtained

Chapter 9

Activity 1

Take Bell's questions and add sub-questions to which they would give rise.

Apply Bell's questions (and your sub-questions) to the evaluation of a curriculum innovation in a known situation.

Activity 2

Outline why and how you would go about evaluating one of the following:

a new technique suggested by a colleague

a new textbook

a new syllabus proposal

a new examination

a new language curriculum

Activity 3

Needs analysis and evaluation form a continuous sequence of information gathering. Needs analysis provides information as a basis for planning, while evaluation gives information needed for adaptation during implementation. Both needs analysis and evaluation use similar techniques, including questionnaire, observation and interview.

Consider how to adapt some of these techniques for both needs analysis and formative evaluation.

Activity 4

Evaluate what you have learnt from this book, and how it will affect your actions as a language curriculum developer and teacher.

Bibliography

Abbott, G. (1987) 'ELT as education'. *System*, 15/1:47–53.

Abbs, B., Ayton, J., and Freebairn, I. (1975) *Strategies*. London: Longman.

Adelman, C., and Alexander, R. (1982) *The Self-Evaluating Institution*. London: Methuen.

Adelman, C., Jenkins, D., and Kemmis, R. (1976) 'Rethinking case study' in Bell et al. (eds) (1984).

Alderson, C. (1984) 'Evaluating curricula and syllabus' in British Council (1984).

Alderson, C. (ed.) (1985) *Evaluation* Lancaster Occasional Papers. Oxford: Pergamon.

Alexander, L.G. (1967) *New Concept English*. London: Longman.

Alexander, L., Allen, W.S., Close, R.A., and O'Neill, R.J. (1975) *English Grammatical Structure*. London: Longman.

Allen, J.P.B. (1984) 'General-purpose language teaching: a variable focus approach' in Brumfit (ed.) (1984a).

Allen, J.P.B., and Corder, S.P. (eds) (1974) *The Edinburgh Course in Applied Linguistics*. Oxford: Oxford University Press.

Anthony, E.M. (1963) 'Approach, method and technique'. *English Language Teaching*, 17:63–7.

Ardener, E. (ed.) (1971) *Social Anthropology and Language*. London: Tavistock.

Aston, G. (1986) 'Trouble-shooting in interaction with learners: the more the merrier?' *Applied Linguistics*, 7/2:113–27.

Austin, J.L. (1962) *How to Do Things with Words*. Oxford: Oxford University Press.

Bachman, L. (1981) 'Formative evaluation in specific purpose program development' in Mackay and Palmer (eds) (1981).

Barrow, R. (1984) *Giving Teaching Back to Teachers*. Sussex: Wheatsheaf Books.

BBC (1981) *Get By in Italian*. London: British Broadcasting Corporation.

Bell, J., Bush, T., Fox, A., Goodey, J., and Goulding, S. (eds) (1984) *Conducting Small-scale Investigations in Educational Management*. London: Harper and Row and Open University.

Bell, M. (1982) *Guidelines for the Evaluation of TAFE Programmes*. Australia: Technical and Further Education.

Bell, R.T. (1981) *An Introduction to Applied Linguistics: Approaches, and Methods in Language Teaching*. London: Batsford.

Bennis, W.G., Benne, K.D., Chin, R. and Corey, K.D. (eds) (1976 edition) *The Planning of Change*. New York: Holt, Rinehart and Winston.

Beretta, A. (1986a) 'Toward a methodology of ESL program evaluation'. *TESOL Quarterly*, 20/1:144–56.

Beretta, A. (1986b) 'Program-fair language teaching evaluation'. *TESOL Quarterly*. 20/3:431–44.

Beretta, A., and Davis, A. (1985) 'Evaluation of the Bangalore Project'. *ELT Journal*, 39/2:121–7.

Berry, J. and Dasen, P.R. (eds) (1974) *Culture and Cognition: Readings in Cross-Cultural Psychology*. London: Methuen.

Bloom, B.S., Engelhart, M.D., Furst, Hill, W.H., and Krathwohl, D.R. (1956) *Taxonomy of Educational Objectives*. London: Longman, Green and Co.

Bloomfield, L. (1914) *An Introduction to the Study of Language*. New York: Holt.

Bloomfield, L. (1933) *Language*. New York: Holt.

Bloomfield, L. (1942) *Outline Guide for the Practical Study of Foreign Languages*. Baltimore: Linguistic Society of America.

Bobbitt, F. (1924) *How To Make a Curriculum*. Boston: Houghton Mifflin.

Bolam, R. (1975) 'The management of educational change: towards a conceptual framework' in Harris, Lawn and Prescott (eds) (1975).

Bowers, R. (1983) 'Project planning and performance' in British Council (1983).

Bowers, R. (1986) 'English in the world: Aims and Achievements in English Language Teaching'. *TESOL Quarterly*, 20/3:393–410.

Bramely, P. (1986) *Evaluation of Training: a Practical Guide*. London: British Association for Commercial and Industrial Education.

Breen, M. and Candlin, C. (1980) 'The essentials of a communicative curriculum in language teaching'. *Applied Linguistics*, 1/2.

Breen, M. (1984) 'Process in syllabus design and classroom language learning' in British Council (1984a).

Breen, M. (1987) 'Contemporary paradigms in syllabus design', parts 1 and 2, *Language Teaching*, 20, nos 2 and 3.

Bright, J.A. and McGregor, G.P. (1970) *Teaching English as a Second Language*. London: Longman.

British Council (1979) *Dunford House Seminar 1979: ELT Course Design*. London: The British Council.

British Council (1980) *National Syllabuses, ELT Documents 108*. Oxford: Pergamon Press and The British Council.

British Council (1981) *Dunford House Seminar 1981: Design, Evaluation and Testing in English Language Projects*. London: The British Council.

British Council (1982) *Dunford House Seminar 1982: Teacher Training and the Curriculum*. London: The British Council.

British Council (1983) *Language Teaching Projects for the Third World, ELT Documents 116*. Oxford: Pergamon Press and The British Council.

British Council (1984a) *General English Syllabus Design, ELT Documents 118*. Oxford: Pergamon Press and The British Council.

British Council (1984b) *Dunford House Seminar 1984: Curriculum and Syllabus Design in ELT*. London: The British Council.

British Council (1986) *Dunford House Seminar Report 1985: Communication Skills Training in Bilateral Aid Projects*. London: The British Council.

Brooks, N. (1960) *Language and Language Learning*. New York: Harcourt, Brace and World.

Broughton, G. (1968) *Success With English*. Harmondsworth, Middlesex: Penguin.

Brown, G., and Yule, G. (1983) *Discourse Analysis*. Cambridge: Cambridge University Press.

Brown, G., Anderson, A., Shillcock, R., and Yule, G. (1984) *Teaching Talk*. Cambridge: Cambridge University Press.

Brumfit, C.J. (ed.) (1983) *Teaching Literature Overseas: Language-based Approaches (ELT Documents 114)*. Oxford: Pergamon.

Brumfit, C.J. (1984a) 'Function and structure of a state school syllabus for learners of second or foreign languages with heterogeneous needs' in British Council (1984a).

Brumfit, C.J. (1984b) 'Key issues in Curriculum and Syllabus Design for ELT' in British Council (1984a).

Brumfit, C.J. (1984c) *Communicative Methodology in Language Teaching*. Cambridge: Cambridge University Press.

Brumfit, C.J. (1984d) 'The Bangalore Procedural Syllabus'. *ELT Journal*, 38/1:233–41.

Brumfit, C.J., and Carter, R.A. (eds) (1986) *Literature and Language Teaching*. Oxford: Oxford University Press.

Brumfit, C.J. and Johnson, K. (eds) (1979) *The Communicative Approach to Language Teaching*. Oxford: Oxford University Press.

Bruner, J.S. (1960) *The Process of Education*. Cambridge, Mass.: Harvard University Press.

Burt, M.K., and Dulay, H.C. (eds) (1975) *On TESOL '75: New Directions in Second Language Learning, Teaching and Bilingual Education*. Washington, D.C.: TESOL.

Bush, T. (1986) *Theories of Educational Management*. London: Harper and Row.

Butcher, F.J. & Pont, H.B. (eds) (1973) *National Research in Britain 2*. London: University of London Press.

Bygate, M. (1986) *Speaking* in *Language Teaching, A Scheme for Teacher Education* (C.N. Candlin and H.G. Widdowson (eds)). Oxford: Oxford University Press.

Canale, M. (1983) 'From communicative competence to communicative language pedagogy' in Richards and Schmidt (eds) (1983).

Canale, M. and Swain, M. (1980) 'Theoretical bases of communicative approaches to second language teaching and testing'. *Applied Linguistics*, 1:1–47.

Candlin, C. (1984) 'Syllabus design as a critical process' in Brumfit (ed.) (1984a).

Candlin, C. (1987) 'Towards task-based language learning' in Candlin and Murphy (eds) (1987).

Candlin, C., and Breen, M. (1979) 'Evaluating, adapting and innovating language teaching materials' in Yorio, Perkins and Schachter (eds) (1979).

Candlin, C., and Murphy, D. (eds) (1987) *Lancaster Practical papers in ELT*, Vol. 7. London: Prentice-Hall International.

Carrel, P. (1983) 'Some issues in studying the role of schemata'. *Reading in a Foreign Language*, 1/2:81–92.

Chin, R., and Benne, K.D. (1976) 'General strategies for affecting changes in human systems' in Bennis, Benne, Chin and Corey (eds) (1976).

Chiu, R.K. (1973) 'Measuring register characteristics'. *International Review of Applied Linguistics*. XI/1:51–68.

Chomsky, N. (1957) *Syntactic Structures*. The Hague: Mouton.

Chomsky, N. (1959) Review of B.F. Skinner 'Verbal Behaviour' *Language*, 35:26–58.

Chomsky, N. (1965) *Aspects of the Theory of Syntax*. Cambridge, Mass.: MIT Press.

Clark, J.L. (1979) 'The syllabus: What should the learner learn?' *Audio-visual Language Journal*, XVII/2, 99–108.

Clark, J.L. (1987) *Curriculum Renewal in School Foreign Language Learning*. Oxford: Oxford University Press.

Clark, J.L. and Hamilton, J. (1984) *Syllabus Guidelines 1: a graded communicative approach towards school foreign language learning*. London: CILT.

Clarke, M.A. and Handscome, J. (eds) (1983) *On TESOL 82 Pacific Perspectives on Language Learning and Teaching*. Washington, D.C.: TESOL.

Cohen, A. (1984) 'Studying second language learning strategies: How do we get the information?'. *Applied Linguistics*, 5/2:101–12.

Cohen, A. (1986) 'Mentalistic measures in reading strategy research: some recent findings'. *English for Specific Purposes*, 5/2:131–46.

Cohen, A., Aphek, E. (1981) 'Easifying second language learning'. *Studies in Second Language Acquisition*, 3/2:221–36.

Cohen, A., and Hosenfeld, C. (1981) 'Some uses of mentalistic data in second language research'. *Language Learning*, 31:285–313.

Cohen, L. and Manion, L. (1980) 'Action research', in Bell, et al. (eds) (1984).

Cook, V.J. (1983) 'What should language teaching be about?' *ELT Journal*, 37/3.

Corder, S.P. (1973) *Introducing Applied Linguistics*. Harmondsworth, Middlesex: Penguin.

Crawford-Lange, L.M. (1982) 'Curricular alternatives for second-language learning' in Higgs (ed.) (1982):81–112.

Crombie, W. (1985) *Discourse and Language Learning: A Relational Approach to Syllabus Design*. Oxford: Oxford University Press.

Cronbach, L.J. (1963) 'Course improvement through evaluation'. *Teachers College Record*, 64, 672–83. Also in Golby, Greenwald and West (eds) (1975).

Cronbach, L.J. (1975) 'Beyond the two disciplines of scientific psychology'. *American Psychologist*, 30/2:116–27.

Crystal, D. (1976) *Child Language, Learning and Linguistics*. London: Edward Arnold.

Crystal, D. (ed.) (1982) *Linguistic Controversies*. London: Arnold.

Crystal, D., and Davy, D. (1969) *Investigating English Style*. London: Longman.

Cunningsworth, A. (1983) 'Needs analysis – the state of the art'. *System*, 11/2:149–154.

Dakin, J., Tiffin, B., and Widdowson, H.G. (eds) (1968) *Language in Education*. Oxford: Oxford University Press.

Dam, L. (1985) 'Strategies for the correction of errors in different teaching situations and their implications for initial and in-service teacher training'. Greve Kommune, Copenhagen, Denmark (mimeo).

Davies, A. (1981) Review of J. L. Munby *Communicative Syllabus Design*. *TESOL Quarterly*, 15/3:332–6.

Davies, I.K. (1976) *Objectives in Curriculum Design*. London: McGraw Hill.

Doughty, C., and Pica, T. (1986) '"Information Gap" tasks: Do they facilitate second langauge acquisition?' *TESOL Quarterly*, 20/2:305–26.

Dubin, F., and Olshtain, E. (1986) *Course Design: Developing Programs and Materials for Language Learning*. Cambridge: Cambridge University Press.

Duskova, L., and Urbanova, V. (1976) 'A frequency count of English tenses with application to teaching English as a foreign language'. *Czechoslovak Academy of Sciences Prague Studies in Mathematical Linguistics, 2*. Munchen, Heuber: Prague Academia.

Early, P., and Bolitho, R. (1981) 'Reasons to be cheerful or helping teachers to get problems into perspective' in *ELT Documents 110*:71–84. London: The British Council.

Eastwood, J., Kay, V., Mackin, R., and Strevens, P. (1980) *Network*. Oxford: Oxford University Press.

Eicholz, G., and Rogers, E.T. (1964) 'Resistance to the adoption of audio-visual aids by elementary school teachers: contrasts and similarities to agricultural innovation' in Miles (ed.) (1964).

Eisner, E. (1972) 'Emerging models for educational evaluation'. *School Review*, 80, 573–90.

Elliot, J. (1981) 'Action-research: a framework for self-evaluation in schools', Schools Council Programme 2, 'Teacher pupil interaction and the quality of learning' project, *Working Paper No 1*, Cambridge: Cambridge Institute of Education (mimeo).

Elliot, J. (1985) 'Educational action-research' in Nisbet, J., Megarry, J., and Nisbet, S. (eds.) (1985) *World Yearbook of Education 1985, Research, Policy and Practice*. London: Kogan Page/Nicholas.

Ellis, R. (1984) *Classroom Second Language Development*. Oxford: Pergamon.

Ellis, R. (1985) *Understanding Second Language Acquisition*. Oxford: Oxford University Press.

Emmet, D. (1967) *Rules, Roles and Relations*. London: Macmillan.

Entwhistle, N. (1981) *Styles of Learning and Teaching*. Chichester: John Wiley.

Entwhistle, N. (1987) *Understanding Classroom Learning*. London: Hodder and Stoughton.

Everard, K.B., and Morris, G. (1985) *Effective School Management*. London: Harper Education Series.

Ewer, J. and Lattore, G. (1967) 'Preparing an English course for students of science'. *ELTJ, 21/3*.

Faerch, C. and Kasper, G. (1983) *Strategies in Interlanguage Communication*. London: Longman.

Fein, D., and Baldwin, R. (1986) 'Content-based curriculum design in advanced levels of an intensive ESL program'. *Newsletter, English for Foreign Students in English-speaking Countries Interest Section*, TESOL, 4/1:1–3.

Findley, C.A., and Nathan, L.A. (1980) 'Functional language objectives in a competency based ESL curriculum'. *TESOL Quarterly*, XIV/2:221–31.

Firth, J.R. (1957) *Papers in Linguistics, 1934–1951*, London: Oxford University Press.

Freedman, A., Pringle, I., and Yalden, J. (eds) (1983) *Learning To Write: First Language/Second Language*. London: Longman.

Freire, P. (1973) *Education for Critical Consciousness*. New York: The Seabury Press.

Freire, P. (1976) *Pedagogy of the Oppressed*. Harmondsworth, Middlesex: Penguin.

Freihoff, R., and Takala, S. (1974) *A Systematic Description of Language Teaching Objectives Based on the Specification of Language Use Situations* (abridged version). Report from the Language Centre, University of Jyvaskyla, Finland.

Fries, C.C. (1945) *Teaching and Learning English as a Foreign Language*. Ann Arbor, Mich.: University of Michigan Press.

Fries, C.C. (1952) *The Structure of English, an introduction to the construction of English sentences*. New York: Harcourt Brace.

Fries, C.C. (1959) 'Preparation of teaching materials, practical grammars and dictionaries, especially for foreign languages'. *Language Learning*, IX/1:43–50.

Fullan, M. (1982) *The Meaning of Educational Change*. New York: Teachers College Press, Columbia University.

Furey, P.A. (1984) 'Considerations in the assessment of language syllabuses', in Read (ed.) (1984).

Gagne, R.M. (1975) *Essentials of Learning for Instruction*. New York: Holt, Rinehart and Winston.

Galton, M. and Moon, B. (eds) (1983) *Changing Schools . . . Changing Curriculum*. London: Harper and Row.

Garton-Sprenger, J., Jupp, T.C., Milne, J., and Prowse, P. (1979) *Main Course English*. London: Heinemann.

Gass, S., and Varonis, E. (1985) 'Non-native/non-native conversations: a model for negotiation of meaning'. *Applied Linguistics*, 6/1.

George, H.V. (1963) *Report on a Verb-form Frequency Count*, Monograph of the Central Institute of English, No. 2. Hyderabad, India.

George, H.V. (1972) *Common Errors in Language Learning*. Rowley, Mass.: Newbury House.

Golby, M., Greenwald, J. and West, R. (eds) (1975) *Curriculum Design*. London: Croom Helm and Open University Press.

Goldsmith, W., and Clutterbuck, D. (1984) *The Winning Streak*. Harmondsworth, Middlesex: Penguin.

Goodman, K.S. (1967) 'Reading: a psycholinguistic guessing game'. *Journal of the Reading Specialist*, 6.

Goulding, S., Bell, J., Bush, T., Fox, A., and Goodey, J. (eds) (1984) *Case Studies in Educational Management*. London: Harper and Row.

Greens, D. (1973) 'A frequency list of sentence structures: preliminary considerations'. *ITL* (Belgium), No. 21: 39–55.

Greenwood, J. (1985) 'Bangalore revisited: a reluctant complaint'. *ELT Journal*, 39/4: 268–73.

Gregory, M., and Caroll, S. (1978) *Language and Situation: Varieties and Their Social Context*. London: Routledge and Kegan Paul.

Gross, N., Giacquinta, J.B. and Bernstein, M. (1971) *Implementing Organizational Innovations: A Sociological Analysis of Planned Educational Change*. New York: Harper and Row.

Gumperz, J. and Hymes, D. (eds) (1972) *Directions in Sociolinguistics: the Ethnography of Communication*. New York: Holt, Rinehart and Winston, reissued (1986) Oxford and New York: Basil Blackwell.

Halliday, M.A.K. (1975) *Learning How to Mean*. London: Edward Arnold.

Halliday, M.A.K., McIntosh, A. and Strevens, P. (1964) *The Linguistic Sciences and Language Teaching*. London: Longman.

Hamilton, D., Jenkins, D., King, C., MacDonald, C., and Parlett, M. (eds) (1977) *Beyond the Numbers Game*. Basingstoke: Macmillan.

Handscombe, J. Oren, R.A., and Taylor, B.P. (eds) (1984) *On TESOL '83: The Question of Control*. Washington, DC.: TESOL.

Handy, C.A. (1978) (2nd Edition) *Understanding Organizations*. Harmondsworth, Middlesex: Penguin.

Handy, C.A. (1984) *Taken for Granted? Understanding Schools as Organizations*. London: Longman and Schools Council.

Harlen, W. and Elliott, J. (1982) 'A checklist for planning or reviewing an evaluation' in McCormick et al. (eds) (1982).

Harris, A., Lawn, M., and Prescott, W. (eds) (1975) *Curriculum Innovation*. London: Croom Helm and Open University.

Hatch, E.M. (Ed.) (1978) *Second Language Acquisition: a Book of Readings*. Rowley, Mass.: Newbury House.

Havelock, R. (1971) 'The utilization of educational research and development'. *British Journal of Educational Technology*, 2/2:84–97. Also reprinted in Horton and Raggatt (eds) (1982).

Hawkey, R. (1979) 'Syllabus content specification', in British Council (1979).

Hawkins, E.W. (1981) *Modern Languages in the Curriculum*. Cambridge: Cambridge University Press.

Herriot, P. (1970) *An Introduction to the Psychology of Language*. London: Methuen.

Higgs, T.V. (ed.) (1982) *Curriculum, Competence and the Foreign Language Teacher*, Skokie, Ill.: National Textbook Company.

Hirst, P. (1969) 'The logic of the curriculum' in Hooper (ed.) (1971), 232–50.

Hirst, P. (1975) 'The curriculum and its objectives: a defense of piecemeal curriculum planning' in *The Curriculum*, Studies in Education 2. Windsor: National Foundation for Educational Research.

Holding, D.J. (1966) *Principles of Training*. Oxford: Pergamon.

Holliday, A.R. (1980) *Means Analysis and Communicative Curriculum Development*. MA Dissertation, University of Lancaster.

Holliday, A. (1983) 'Research into classroom culture as necessary input into syllabus design' in Swales and Mustafa (eds) (1983).

Holliday, A., and Cooke, T.M. (1982) 'An ecological approach to ESP' in Waters (ed.) (1982).

Hooper, R. (ed.) (1971) *The Curriculum: Context, Design and Development*. Edinburgh: Oliver and Boyd in association with the Open University

Hopkins, D., and Wideen, M. (eds) (1984) *Alternative Perspectives on School Improvement*. London: Falmers Press.

Hore, N., and Hore, M. (1982) *English Right from the Start*. Harmondsworth, Middlesex: Penguin.

Hornby, A.S. (1948) *The Advanced Learner's Dictionary of Current English*. London: Oxford University Press.

Hornby, A.S. (1959–66) *The Teaching of Structural Words and Sentence Patterns*, four volumes. London: Oxford University Press.

Horton, T., and Raggatt, P. (eds) (1982) *Challenge and Change in the Curriculum*. London: Hodder and Stoughton and Open University.

Hosenfeld, C. (1976) 'Learning about learning: discovering students' strategies'. *Foreign Language Annals*, 9:117–29.

House, E. (Ed.) (1986) *New Directions in Educational Evaluation*. Lewes: Falmer Press.

Howatt, A.P.R. (1974) 'The background to course design' in Allen and Corder (eds) (1974).

Howatt, A.P.R. (1984) *A History of English Language Teaching*. Oxford: Oxford University Press.

Hoyle, E. (1970) 'Planned organisational change in education'. *Research in Education*, 3.

Huberman, A.M. (1973) *Understanding Change in Education: An Introduction*. Paris: UNESCO.

Hughey, J.B., Wormuth, D.R., Hartfiel, V.F., Jacobs, H.L. (1983) *Teaching ESL Composition, Principles and Techniques*. Rowley, Mass.: Newbury House.

Hurst, P. (1983) *Implementing Educational Change: a critical review of the literature*. EDC Occasional Papers, No. 5. London: London University, Department of Education in Developing Countries, Institute of Education.

Hustler, D., Cassidy, T., and Cuff, T. (1986) *Action Research in Classrooms and Schools*. London: Allen and Unwin.

Hutchinson, T. and Klepac, M. (1982) 'The communicative approach: a question of materials or attitudes?' *System*, 10/2:135–43.

Hutchinson, T. and Waters, A. (1987) *English for Specific Purposes*. Cambridge: Cambridge University Press.

Hyltenstam, K., and Pienemann, M. (eds) (1985) *Modelling and Assessing Second Language Acquisition*. Clevedon, Avon: Multilingual Matters.

Hymes, D. (1966) 'On communicative competence'. Paper originally read at the Research Planning Conference on Language Development among Disadvantaged Children, Yeshiva University, June 1966. Reprinted, in part, in Brumfit and Johnson (eds) (1979).

James, C. (1980) *Contrastive Analysis*. London: Longman.

Jenkins, M. and Shipman, M.D. (1976) *Curriculum: an Introduction*. London: Open Books.

Johnson, K. (1982) *Communicative Syllabus Design and Methodology*, Oxford: Pergamon.

Johnson, K. (1986) 'Language teaching as skill training'. Reading: University of Reading, unpublished paper.

Johnson, K., and Porter, D. (eds) (1983) *Perspectives in Communicative Language Teaching*. London: Academic Press.

Judd, E.L. (1981) 'Language policy, curriculum development, and TESOL instruction: a search for compatibility'. *TESOL Quarterly*, 15/1:59–66.

Judd, E.L. (1984) 'TESOL as a political act: a moral question' in Handscombe, Oren and Taylor (eds) (1984).

Jupp, T.C., and Hodlin, S. (1975) *Industrial English*. London: Heinemann.

Kelly, L.G. (1969) *25 Centuries of Language Teaching*. Rowley, Mass.: Newbury House.

Kelly, A.V. (1977) *The Curriculum Theory and Practice*. London: Harper and Row.

Kennedy, C. (1987) 'Innovating for a change: teacher development and innovation'. *ELT Journal*, 41/3:163–71.

Kennedy, C. (1988) 'Evaluation of the management of change in ELT projects', *Applied Linguistics*, 9/4: 329–42.

Kerr, J.F. (ed.) (1968) *Changing the Curriculum*. London: University of London Press.

Kirwan, D., and Swales, A. (1981) 'Group work – an attempt to change teacher attitudes' in *ELT Documents* 110:64–70.

Kolb, D.A. (1984) *Experiential Learning*. Englewood Cliffs, N.J.: Prentice-Hall.

Kouraogo, P. (1987) 'EFL curriculum renewal and INSET in difficult circumstances'. *ELT Journal*, 41/3:171–8.

Kramsky, J. (1972) 'A contribution to the investigation of the frequency of occurrences of nominal and verbal elements in English'. *Czechoslovak Academy of Sciences Prague Studies in Mathematical Linguistics*, 4. Munchen: Heuber.

Krashen, S. (1982) *Principles and Practice in Second Language Aquisition*. Oxford: Pergamon.

Krashen, S., and Terrell, T. (1983) *The Natural Approach: Language Acquisition in the Classroom*. Oxford: Pergamon.

Lado, R. (1975) *Linguistics Across Cultures: Applied Linguistics for Teachers*. Ann Arbor, Mich.: University of Michigan Press.

Lavelle, M. (1984) 'The role of consultancy and OD in innovation in education'. *School Organisation*, 4/2:161.

Lawton, D. (1980) 'The politics of curriculum evaluation' in McCormick et al. (eds) (1982).

Leech, G.N. (1979) *A Linguistic Guide to English Poetry*. London: Longman.

Levelt, W.J.M. (1975) 'Skill theory and language teaching' in *Studies in Second Language Acquisition*, Indiana University Linguistics Club, 1/1.

Littlewood, W. (1981) *Communicative Language Teaching: an Introduction*. Cambridge: Cambridge University press.

Long, M. (1975) 'Group work and communicative competence in the ESOL classroom' in Burt and Dulay (eds) (1975).

Long, M. (1981) 'Input, interaction and second language acquisition' in Winitz (ed.) (1981).

Long, M. (1983) 'Does second language instruction make a difference? a review of research'. *TESOL Quarterly*, 17/3:359–82.

Long, M. and Porter, P.A. (1985) 'Group work, interlanguage talk and second language acquisition'. *TESOL Quarterly*, 19/2:207–27.

Lunzer, E.A., and Morris, J.F. (eds) (1968) *Development in Human Learning*. London: Staples Press.

McCallen, B. (1989) *English: A World Commodity*. The Economist Intelligence Unit, Special Report No. 1166. London: The Economist Intelligence Unit.

McCrae, J., and Boardman, R. (1984) *Reading Between the Lines*. Cambridge: Cambridge University Press.

McCormick, R., Byrner, J., Clift, P., James, M., and Brown, (eds) (1982) *Calling Education to Account*. London: Heinemann and Open University.

MacDonald-Ross, M. (1973) 'Behavioural objectives – a critical review', *Instructional Science*, 2/1:52–8.

McDonough, S. (1980) 'Psychological aspects of sequencing'. *International Review of Applied Linguistics*. xviii/4.

McDonough, S. (1981) *Psychology in Foreign Language Teaching*. London: Allen and Unwin. Second edn 1986.

McEldowney, P.L. (1976) 'Language functions and the English verb system'. *RELC Journal*, 7/1:31–9.

McGinley, K. (1986) 'Coming to terms with evaluation'. *System*, 14/3:335–41.

McGregor, D. *The Human Side of Enterprise*. New York: McGraw-Hill.

Mackay, R. (1981) 'Accountability in ESP Programs'. *ESP Journal*, 1/2.

Mackay, R., and Mountford, A. (eds) (1978) *English for Specific Purposes*. London: Longman.

Mackay, R., and Palmer, J. (eds) (1981) *Language for Specific Purposes: Program Design and Evaluation*. Rowley, Mass.: Newbury House.

Mackey, W.F. (1965) *Language Teaching Analysis*. London: Longman.

McLaughlin, B. (1987) *Theories of Second Language Learning*. London: Edward Arnold.

Maclure, S.J. (1968) *Curriculum Innovation in Practice: Canada, England and Wales, United States*. London: Schools Council.

Mager, F.F. (1962) *Preparing Instructional Objectives*. Belmont, California: Fearon.

Malinowski, B. (1949) 'The problem of meaning in primitive language', in Supplement 1 to C.K. Ogden and I.A. Richards (eds) (1949).

Markee, N. (1986a) 'The relevance of sociopolitical factors to communicative course design'. *English for Specific Purposes*, 5/1:3–16.

Markee, N. (1986b) 'Toward an appropriate technology model of communicative course design: issues and definitions'. *English for Specific Purposes*, 5/2:161–72.

Mead, R. (1982) 'Review of John Munby: *Communicative Syllabus Design*'. *Applied Linguistics*, 3/1:79–7.

Medgyes, P. (1983) 'The schizophrenic teacher'. *ELT Journal*, 37/1:2–6.

Medgyes, P. (1986) 'Queries from a communicative teacher'. *ELT Journal*, 40/2:107–112.

Merritt, J.E. (1971) 'Reading and the curriculum', in Hooper (ed.) (1971).

Nagle, S.J. and Sanders, S., (1986) 'Comprehension theory and second language pedagogy'. *TESOL Quarterly*, 20/1:9–26.

Naiman, N., Frohlich, M., Stern, H.H. and Todesco, A. (1978) *The Good Language Learner*. Toronto: Modern Language Centre, Ontario Institute for Studies in Education.

Nicholls, A. (1983) *Managing Educational Innovations*. London: Allen and Unwin.

Nicholls, A., Nicholls, H. (1978) *Developing a Curriculum: a Practical Guide*. London: Allen and Unwin.

Nisbet, J. (1974) 'Innovation – Bandwagon or Hearse?' in Harris et al. (eds) (1985).

Nisbet, J., Megarry, J., and Nisbet, S. (eds) (1985) *World Yearbook of Education 1985: Research, Policy and Practice*. London: Kogan Page/Nichols.

Nystrand, M. (ed.) (1982) *What Writers Know*. New York: Academic Press.

O'Donnell, W.R., and Todd, L. (1980) *Variety on Contemporary English*. London: Allen and Unwin.

Ogden, C.K., and Richards, I.A. (eds) (1949) *The Meaning of Meaning*. London: Routledge and Kegan Paul.

Olshavsky, J.E. (1977) 'Reading as problem solving: an investigation of strategies'. *Reading Research Quarterly*, XII/4.

Open University. *Making School-Centred INSET Work*. Code P536. Milton Keynes: Open University.

Page, B. (1983) 'Graded objectives in modern language learning'. *Language Teaching*, 16/4:292–308.

Paisey, A. (1981) *Organization and Management in Schools*. London: Longman.

Palmer, H.E. (1917/1968) *The Scientific Study and Teaching of Languages*. London: Harrap. Republished by Oxford University Press, 1968, D. Harper (ed.).

Palmer, H.E. (1921/1964) *The Principles of Language Study*. London: Harrap. Republished by Oxford University Press, 1964, R. Mackin (ed.).

Palmer, H.E. (1924) *A Grammar of Spoken English, on a strictly phonetic basis*. Cambridge: Heffer.

Parlett, M. (1970) 'Evaluating innovations in teaching', in Golby, Greenwald and West (eds) (1975).

Parlett, M. and Hamilton, D. (1972) 'Evaluation as illumination: a new approach to the study of innovatory programmes'. *Occasional Paper 9*, Centre for Research in the Educational Sciences, University of Edinburgh. Also in Hamilton, King, et al. (eds) (1977), 6–22.

Pelligrini, A., Yawkey, T. (eds) (1984) *The Development of Oral and Written Language in Social Contexts*, Vol. xiii, in the series *Advances in Discourse Processes*, Norwood, New Jersey: ABLEX.

Peters, A. (1983a) 'Language learning strategies: does the whole equal the sum of the parts?'. *Language*, 53:560–73.

Peters, A. (1983b) *The Units of Language Acquisition*. Cambridge: Cambridge University Press.

Piaget, J. (1967) *The Child's Conception of the World*. Tutowa, N.J.: Littlefield Adams.

Pica, T. (1983) 'Adult acquisition of English under different conditions of exposure'. *Language Learning*, 33/4:465–97.

Pica, T. (1984) 'L1 transfer and L2 complexity as factors in syllabus design'. *TESOL Quarterly*, 18/4:689–704.

Pica, T. (1987) 'Second language acquisition, social interaction, and the classroom'. *Applied Linguistics*, 8/1.

Pickett, G.D. (1978) *The Foreign Language Learning Process.* London: British Council English Teaching Information Centre.

Pienemann, M. (1985) 'Learnability and syllabus construction' in Hyltenstam and Pienemann (eds) (1985), 23–76.

Prabhu, N.S. (1987) *Second Language Pedagogy: a Perspective.* London: Oxford University Press.

Pugh, A.K. (1978) *Silent Reading.* London: Heinemann.

Quirk, R., Greenbaum, S., Leech, G., and Svartvik, J. (1972) *A Grammar of Contemporary English.* London: Longman.

Raths, J.D. (1971) 'Teaching without specific objectives'. *Educational Leadership*, (April 1971): 714–20.

Read, J.A.S. (ed.) (1984) *Trends in Language Syllabus Design*, Anthology Series No. 13. Singapore: SEAMEO, RELC.

Reasor, A.W. (1986) 'Dominant administrative styles of ESL administrators'. *TESOL Quarterly*, 20/2:338–43.

Reed, G.F. (1968) 'Skill' in Lunzer and Morris (eds) (1968).

Reynolds, M. (1981) 'Communicative syllabus design – the topic and task approach'. Paper given at BAAL Annual Meeting, September 1981.

Richards, J. (1984) 'The secret life of methods'. *TESOL Quarterly*, 18/1:7–23.

Richards, J. and Rodgers, T. (1982) 'Method: approach, design, procedure'. *TESOL Quarterly*, 16/2:153–68. Also in Richards and Rodgers (1986).

Richards, J. and Rodgers, T. (1986) *Approaches and Methods in Language Teaching.* Cambridge: Cambridge University Press.

Richards, J. and Schmidt, R. (eds) (1983) *Language and Communication.* London: Longman.

Richterich, R. (1972) *A model for the Definition of Language Needs of Adults Learning a Modern Language.* Strasbourg: Council of Europe.

Richterich, R. (1973) 'Definition of language needs and types of adults' in Trim et al., 1980:31–88.

Richterich, R., and Chancerel, J.L. (1977/80) *Identifying the Needs of Adults Learning a Foreign Language.* Strasbourg: Council of Europe. Also Oxford: Pergamon Press.

Richterich, R., and Wilkins, D.A. (1975/80) *Systems Development in Adult Second Language Learning.* Strasbourg: Council of Europe. Also Oxford: Pergamon Press.

Ritchie, W.L. (ed.) (1978) *Second Language Acquisition Research.* New York: Academic Press.

Rivers, W. (1964) *The Psychologist and the Foreign Language Teacher.* Chicago and London: Chicago University Press.

Roberts, J.T. (1982) 'Recent Developments in ELT'. *Language Teaching*, 15, nos 1 and 2, 94–110, 174–94.

Robins, R.H. (1971) 'Malinowski, Firth and the context of situation' in Ardener (ed.) (1971).

Robinson, P.C. (1980) *English for Specific Purposes.* Oxford: Pergamon.

Rogers, E.M. (1983) (3rd edition) *Diffusion of Innovations.* New York: Collier-Macmillan.

Rogers, E.M. and Schoemaker, F.F. (1971, 2nd edition) *Communication of Innovations: A Cross Cultural Approach.* New York: The Free Press.

Rowntree, D. (1982 2nd edition) *Educational Technology in Curriculum Development.* London: Harper and Row.

Rubin, J. (1975) 'What the "good language learner" can teach us'. *TESOL Quarterly*, 9/1:41–51.

Rubin, J. (1982) 'Study of cognitive processes in second language learning'. *Applied Linguistics*, 11/2:117–30.

Rudduck, J. (1973) 'Dissemination in practice'. *Cambridge Journal of Education*, 5/2:143.

Rudduck, J. (1980) 'Introducing innovation to pupils' in Hopkins and Wideen (eds) (1984).

Rudduck, J., and Hopkins, D. (eds) (1985) *Research as a Basis for Teaching: Readings from the Work of Lawrence Stenhouse*. London: Heinemann.

Saville-Troike, M. (1984) 'What *really* matters in second language learning for academic achievement?'. *TESOL Quarterly*, 18/2: 199–219.

Saylor, J., Galen, W.M.A., and Lewis, A.J. (eds) (1981, 4th Edition) *Curriculum Planning for Better Teaching*. New York: Holt, Rinehart and Winston.

Searle, J.R. (1969) *Speech Acts: an Essay in the Philosophy of Language*. Cambridge: Cambridge University Press.

Schumann, J. (1978) *The Pidginization Process: A Model for Second Language Acquisition*. Rowley, Mass.: Newbury House.

Selinker, L. (1972) 'Interlanguage'. *International Review of Applied Linguistics*, X:209–30.

Selinker, L., Swain, M., and Dumas, G. (1975) 'The Interlanguage hypothesis extended to children'. *Language Learning*, 25:39–52.

Selinker, L., Trimble, L., and Trimble, M.T. (1978) 'Rhetorical function shifts in EST discourse'. *TESOL Quarterly*, 12:311–20.

Shaw, A.M. (1975) *Approaches to a Communicative Syllabus in Foreign Language Curriculum Development*. Unpublished Ph.D. thesis, University of Essex.

Shaw, A.M. (1977) 'Foreign-language syllabus development: some recent approaches. *Language Teaching Abstracts*, 10/4.

Shaw, P.A. (1982) 'Ad hoc needs analysis'. *Modern English Teacher*, 10/1:10–15.

Shipman, M.D., Bolam, D., and Jenkins, D.R. (1974) *Inside a Curriculum Project: a Case Study in the Process of Curriculum Change*. London: Methuen.

Simon, S.B., Howe, L.W., and Kirschenbaum, H. (1978 revised edition) *Values Clarification: a handbook of practical strategies for teachers and students*. New York: A and W Visual Library and Hart Publishing Co. Inc.

Simons, H. (1979) 'Ethical principles in school self-evaluation' in Bell et al., (eds) (1984).

Sinclair, J.McH., and Coulthard, R.M. (1975) *Towards an Analysis of Discourse*. Oxford: Oxford University Press.

Skilbeck, M. (1976) 'Three educational ideologies' in Horton and Raggatt (eds) (1982).

Skilbeck, M. (1984a) *School-based Curriculum Development*. London: Harper and Row.

Skilbeck, M. (1984b) *Evaluating the Curriculum in the '80s*. London: Harper.

Skilbeck, M. (1985) 'Curriculum development – from RDD to RED: review, evaluate, develop' in Nisbet, J., Megarry, J. and Nisbet, S. (eds) (1985)

Skinner, B. (1957) *Verbal Behaviour*. New York: Appleton-Century-Crofts.

Skinner, B. (1968) *The Technology of Teaching*. New York: Appleton-Century Crofts.

Smit, G. (1979) 'Verzamelde reacties op een voorestel voor een leerplan voor de moderene vreemde talen op notionele functionele basis' ('Reactions to a proposal for a modern-languages curriculum based on a notional-functional approach'). *Levende Talen*, The Hague, 338/9:4–16.

Sockett, H. (1976) *Designing the Curriculum*. London: Open Books.

Steiner, Florence (1975) *Performing with Objectives*. Rowley, Mass.: Newbury House.

Stenhouse, M. (1970) 'The Humanities Curriculum Project'. *Journal of Curriculum Studies*, 1, 26–33.

Stenhouse, M. (1975) *An Introduction to Curriculum Research and Development*. London: Heinemann.

Stern, H. H. (1983) *Fundamental Concepts of Language Teaching*. Oxford: Oxford University Press.

Strain, J.E. (1986) 'Method: design-procedure versus method-technique'. *System*, 14/3:287–94.

Strevens, P. (1977) *New Orientations in the Teaching of English*. Oxford: Oxford University Press.

Strevens, P. (1982) 'Teacher training and the curriculum' in British Council (1982).

Stubbs, M. (1983) *Discourse Analysis*. Oxford: Blackwell.

Swales, J. (1980) 'The educational environment and its relevance to ESP programme design'. *ELT Documents Special, 'Projects in Materials Design'*. London: The British Council.

Swales, J. and Mustafa, H. (eds) (1983) *English for Specific Purposes in the Arab World*. Aston University: Language Studies Unit.

Swan, M. (1985) 'A critical look at the Communicative Approach'. *English Language Teaching Journal*, 39/1:2–12, 39/2:76–87.

Sweet, H. (1899/1964) *The Practical Study of Languages. A Guide for Teachers and Learners*. London: Dent. Republished by Oxford University Press in 1964, R. Mackin (ed.).

Taba, H. (1962) *Curriculum Development: Theory and Practice*. New York: Harcourt, Brace and World.

Taylor, P.H. (1970) *How Teachers Plan Their Courses*. Slough: National Foundation for Educational Research in England and Wales

Taylor, P.H. and Richards, C. (1979) *An Introduction to Curriculum Studies*. Windsor: NFER Publishing Co.

Tongue, R., and Gibbons, J. (1983), 'Structural syllabuses and the young beginner'. *Applied Linguistics*, III/1:60–9.

Trim, J.L., Richterich, R., Van Ek, J.A. and Eilkins, D.A. (1980), *Systems Development in Adult Languge Learning: A European Unit/Credit System for Modern Language Learning by Adults*, Oxford: Pergamon. First published 1973 by Council of Europe, Strasbourg.

Trudgill, P. (1974) *Sociolinguistics*. Harmondsworth, Middlesex: Penguin.

Trump, J.L. (1967) 'Influencing change at the secondary level' in Miller (ed.) (1967).

Tumposky, N.R. (1984) 'Behavioral objectives, the cult of efficiency and foreign language learning: are they compatible?'. *TESOL Quarterly*, 18/2:295–310.

Turano-Perkins, J. (1979) 'Frequency: a criterion for syllabus development' in Yorio, Perkins and Schachter (Eds. (1979).

Tyler, R.W. (1949/1973) *Basic Principles of Curriculum and Instruction*. Chicago and London: University of Chicago Press.

Ullman, R. (1982) 'A broadened curriculum framework for second languages'. *ELT Journal*, 36/4:255–262.

Turano-Perkins, J. (1979) 'Frequency: a criterion for syllabus development' in Yorio, Perkins and Schachter (Eds. (1979).

Tyler, R.W. (1949/1973) *Basic Principles of Curriculum and Instruction*. Chicago and London: University of Chicago Press.

Ullman, R. (1982) 'A broadened curriculum framework for second languages'. *ELT Journal*, 36/4:255–262.

Valdman, A. (1974) 'Error analysis and pedagogical ordering'. Paper produced by L.A.U.T. (Linguistic Agency University at Trier).

Van Ek, J.A. (1975) *The Threshold Level in a European Unit/Credit System for Modern Language Learning by Adults*. Systems Development in Adult Language Learning. Strasbourg: Council of Europe.

Van Ek, J.A., and Alexander, L.G. (1977) *Waystage*. Strasbourg: Council of Europe.

Waters, A. (ed.) (1982) *Issues in ESP, Lancaster Practical Papers in English Language Education*, Vol. 5. Oxford: Pergamon.

Welford, A.T. (1968) *Fundamentals of Skill*, London: Methuen.

Wells, G. (1981) *Learning through Interaction*. Cambridge: Cambridge University Press.

Wells, G. (1985) *Language Development in the Pre-school Years*. Cambridge: Cambridge University Press.

Wenden, A.L. (1986) 'What do second-language learners know about their language learning? A second look at retrospective accounts'. *Applied Linguistics*, 7/2:186–201.

Wenden. A.L. and Rubin, J. (eds) (1987) *Learner Strategies*. Oxford: Pergamon.

West, M. (1926) *Bilingualism (with special reference to Bengal)*. Calcutta: Bureau of Education, India.

West, M. (1933) *On Learning to Speak a Foreign Language*. London: Longmans, Green.

West, M. (1935 onwards) *New Method Readers (Alternative Edition)*. London: Longmans, Green.

West, M. (ed.) (1953) *A General Service List of English Words, with semantic frequencies and a supplementary word-list for the writing of popular science and technology*. London: Longmans, Green.

West, M. (1960) 'Vocabulary selection and the minimum adequate vocabulary'. *ELTJ*, VIII/4:121–6.

Weston, P.B. (1979) *Negotiating the Curriculum*. Windsor: NFER.

White, R.V. (1974a) 'Communicative competence, registers and second language teaching'. *IRAL*, XII/2:127–41.

White, R.V. (1974b) 'The concept of register and TESL'. *TESOL Quarterly*, 8/4:401–16.

White, R.V. (1983) 'Curriculum development and English language syllabus design' in Johnson and Porter (eds) (1983).

White, R.V. (1987a) 'Managing innovation'. *ELT Journal*, 41/3:211–18.

White, R.V. (1987b) *Writing Four* in *Oxford Supplementary Skills Series*. A. Maley (ed.) Oxford: Oxford University Press.

Widdowson, H.G. (1969) 'The teaching of English through science' in Dakin, Tiffin and Widdowson (eds) (1979).

Widdowson, H.G. (1975) *Stylistics and the Teaching of Literature*. London: Longman.

Widdowson, H.G. (1978) *Teaching Language as Communication*. Oxford: Oxford University Press.

Widdowson, H.G. (1979) *Explorations in Applied Linguistics*. Oxford: Oxford University Press.

Wilkins, D.A. (1976) *Notional Syllabuses*. Oxford: Oxford University Press

Wilkins, D.A. (1982) 'Dangerous dichotomies in Applied Lingusitics and Language Teaching' in Crystal (ed.) (1984), 221–30.

Wilson, G.H. (ed.) (1976) *Curriculum Development and Syllabus Design for English Teaching*, Anthology Series No. 3. Singapore: SEAMEO, RELC.

Winitz, H. (ed.) (1981) *Native language and Foreign Language Aquisition*. Annals of the New York Academy of Science.

Wiseman, S., and Pidgeon, D. (1970) *Curriculum Evaluation*. Slough: The National Foundation for Education Research in England and Wales.

Witkin, H.A., Dyk, R.B., Faterson, H.F., Goodenough, D.R., and Karp, S.A. (1962) *Psychological Differentiation*. New York: Wiley.

Witkin, H.A. (1967) 'Cognitive styles across cultures' in Berry and Dasen (eds) (1974).

Wong Fillmore, L. (1982) 'The language learner as an individual: implications of research on individual differences for the ESL teacher' in Clarke and Handscome (eds) (1983).

Wrigley, J. (1973) 'The Schools Council' in Butcher, H.J. and Pont, H.B. (eds) (1973).

Yalden, J. (1983) *The Communicative Syllabus: Evolution, Design and Implementation*. Oxford: Pergamon.

Yalden, J. (1987) *Principles of Course Design for Language Teaching*. Cambridge: Cambridge University press.

Yin, R.K. (1984) *Case Study Research: Design and Methods, Applied Social Research Methods Series, Vol. 5*. London: Sage Publications.

Yorio, C.A., Perkins, K., and Schachter, J. (Eds) (1989) *On TESOL '79 The Learner in Focus*. Washington, D.C.: TESOL.

Index

Index by Justyn Balinski